HOW TO CUT THE COST OF EDUCATION

Also by Shelley Umans
NEW TRENDS IN READING
DESIGNS FOR READING PROGRAMS
THE MANAGEMENT OF EDUCATION

With Joseph O. Loretan:
TEACHING THE DISADVANTAGED

HOW TO CUT THE COST OF EDUCATION

by Shelley Umans

McGraw-Hill Book Company

New York   St. Louis   San Francisco   Düsseldorf

London   Mexico   Sydney   Toronto

123456789BPBP79876543

Library of Congress Cataloging in Publication
Data

Umans, Shelley.
    How to cut the cost of education.
    1. Education—United States—Costs. I. Title.
LB2825.U43   371.2'07   72-10038
ISBN 0-07-065753-X

To my sons Robert and Peter

Acknowledgments

Obviously, writing a book means more than gathering materials. A book such as this calls upon the author to take a point of view, adhere to a philosophy, if you wish, and then to document it. When, as here, the topic is current, that is, in a state of formulation, research into the literature is not sufficient, for very often not too much has as yet been recorded. It, therefore, requires meeting with people who are in the process of inventing, observing programs in action, and sifting the wheat from the chaff. Much of this book required this kind of searching. I would like in particular to thank Evans Clinchy, an outstanding innovator, for his invaluable assistance; Carole Rosenfield for her insightful suggestions; and the members of the National Consortium on Educational Alternatives, who generously shared with me their plans and problems.

I would also like to acknowledge the help given me by my husband, Henry, who would read my rough copy and often say, "I don't understand that; what exactly do you mean?" After much interchange and many a flared temper, he would finally say, "Great—if that's what you mean, why don't you say it that way?" For smoking me out of a maze of "pedaguese," I want to thank him with all my heart.

Shelley Umans

Contents

Foreword

The cost of education is high. The price tag to build and operate schools has made education a luxury item. Yet it must be paid for by the ordinary taxpayer, one who can hardly afford luxuries. Just as with anything else you buy and cannot afford, the problems are many. How will you be able to meet your bills? Where can you borrow money? Where can you cut corners?

The cost of education is high for still another reason. Forty percent of all high school students drop out before graduation. Forty-five percent of those who enter college do not graduate. In October 1969, there were 25.5 million young people from 16 to 24 years of age in our civilian population, of whom 10 million were enrolled in school. Among those young people no longer enrolled in school, 5.1 million were elementary or high school dropouts. This results in the entry into the labor force each year of hundreds of thousands of young people who lack the basic knowledge which employers require for most jobs. Moreover, because of the uneven quality of education in different localities, many high school graduates are ill prepared for today's jobs or for constructive roles as citizens.

More and more, economists are beginning to look upon education as a capital resource, yielding income increments to individuals and society in much the same way as does investment in nonhuman capital. Therefore, public education, as an institution, must start to view itself realistically as the largest single producer of "resources" in our country. Can we afford to "lose" almost half of our population to unproductive living? Can we calculate in dollars and cents how much it costs the country to function with only half of the human resources it could have.

This book, then, will address itself to these two aspects of the cost of education—the dollar cost and the human resource cost, and to how we can reduce the expense in each category. It would be illogical as well as "bad business" to examine one without the other. Simply to cut the cost of education by voting less money to the existing system would be to yield less of that which is not adequate in the first place. On the other hand, to come up with new forms of education which, while exciting or appropriate, are prohibitively expensive would be equally self-defeating.

The problem, therefore, remains one of achieving a workable balance between the need to provide functioning, well-adjusted youngsters and the cost of meeting that need. Can this be done? Perhaps the question should be, can we afford the future. If the future comes to us at no cost, there is no problem and no question. But, if the future in education bears a price tag, we have decisions to make. And since money is not the only price of the future, we can no longer afford to operate with an institution that was designed for other times and other conditions.

Can we afford the future? That he who wishes to save his life must lose it, is a statement of hard fact and not a pious epigram.

I

The Cost of Education Today

THE DOLLAR COST

In the state of Ohio, on the November 1970 ballot, only 68 out of 243 school budgets were passed; out of 61 school-construction budgets only 14 passed. In New York State, which is known for its dedication to education and which has always had one of the most liberal education budgets in the nation, one-third of its school budgets was rejected in May 1971. In some counties in New York State, as many as 20 out of 36 budgets were defeated. In California, 30 school districts went bankrupt, and 60 percent of proposed increases in school taxes and new bond issues for education were rejected by voters. The number of teachers employed dropped by 9,000 while enrollment climbed by 100,000.

Throughout the nation, less than half the dollars requested for school construction in 1970 was approved by the voters. Fewer new schools and additions were built last year than at any time since 1962. Local newspapers, nationwide, carried headlines of school budget defeats. According to the Investment Bankers' Association, voters in 1960 rejected 11 percent of the school bond issues put before them; in 1965 the rejection rate was 33 percent; in 1970 the rate was 52 percent.

In 1971, George Gallup made his third annual survey of the public's attitude toward the public schools. In 1969 and 1970, the major problem facing the public schools had been discipline. In 1971, finance—how to pay for the schools—was cited most often as the biggest problem with which the local public schools had to deal.

What has happened in the years between 1960 and 1970 to account for this rejection of school budgets and for this absorbtion with the problem of finance? A first conclusion might be that money is tight and people are resisting the escalating burden of taxation. However, that contention would appear to be only partially true, since in all of the 50 states, bond issues for recreation, highways, and pollution control generally passed. Moreover, education budgets are steadily being turned down with full knowledge that in many cases we are not talking simply about curtailing school expansion or cutting back on auxiliary programs: we are talking about closing schools early because they cannot meet payrolls; we are talking about a 4-day school-week; we are talking about bankrupt school systems. What has brought us from wide acceptance in the early 60's to such drastic rejection in the 70's?

Admittedly, one reason is the money drain. The extraordinary rise in the cost of education, together with other inflationary increases, is hurting and the local taxpayer is re-evaluating his priorities. What, he asks, is he getting for his money? More parks, healthier air, clearer waters—these are tangible, practical benefits that have great appeal ecologically. Besides, father, mother, and all the family can enjoy these facilities. Education, on the other hand, offers relatively long-term goals, impalpable and somewhat obscure. It may call for sacrifices to provide children with a diploma they deride or disdain. To many parents, it offers a long-delayed reward of doubtful value for the trouble and expense involved.

There are, of course, other factors that contribute to the reluctance of the taxpayer to assume the educational burden. The problem of school integration is a major one, and it is typical of the social and psychological issues that are equally a part of the problem.

In general, however, issues of this nature tend to fall within the realm of legal adjudication or social adjustments. The cost of education, on the other hand, or the quality and nature of the educational process, are more logically the province of those who deal in administration and the theories and principles of instruction. Unquestionably, all these issues, social, economic, and educational, are inextricably intertwined so that the limitation of this book to financial and instructional remedies should not be deemed an indifference to or unawareness of the other problems involved.

A consideration of the immediate background of this changing attitude toward education might not be amiss at this time. Perhaps the most important year in education in the 60's was 1964. It was the year of discovery, of dedication, of promise, of Johnson's opening gun in the war against poverty. First came the realization that education was not reaching the poor of our nation, and that its quality was in direct ratio to the financial level of the children. Second came the discovery that poverty has no race. In the United States, three quarters of the 11 million illiterates, or nearly 8 million, were white. Both of these "discoveries" were hardly new. Since the black people comprise only 10 percent of the population of our country, it should be no cause for suprise that there are more white illiterates than black. Perhaps the discovery really was that the public was ready to acknowledge the correlation between poverty and education. In the face of angry criticism and protest by minority groups, the facts could not be avoided.

For example, 35 percent of all high school students dropped out of school before graduation; 40 percent of those who entered college did not graduate. Almost 1½ million young people were not in school and not working. This resulted in the entry into the labor force each year of thousands of young people basically too uneducated to be employable.

Then again, there was an awakening to some hard economic facts—that it costs as much to keep one delinquent youth in a state or county reform school as it does to keep two youths in an expensive college; that it costs approximately $9,600 a year to keep one youth in a Federal detention home and the same amount to keep 8 youths in state institutions of higher learning.

As a result of minority group prodding, public pressure, and governmental interest, the 60's was a decade in which the American public appeared to have dedicated itself to uplifting and equalizing educational opportunities for all people from every stratum of society.

And so a new coalition grew of the poor white, the poor black, the liberals, the politicians, the educators, the industrialists, and, of course, the public, better known as the taxpayer. They all saw the need for enlightenment, social welfare, and productivity.

In fact, from 1961 to 1968 more legislation affecting education was passed by the Federal and state governments than was passed in our entire previous history. This was accompanied by the expenditure of larger sums of money for education than ever before. The new education programs provided employment for literally millions of people: teachers, paraprofessionals, book salesmen, printers, school bus operators, machine-makers, the building trades, and many others. Industry for the first time saw education as a fertile market. Xerox, IBM, RCA, among others, opened education divisions. Book publishers doubled their sales staffs, the construction industry burgeoned, and the furnishing of educational materials became a prime industry. Teacher organizations pressed for a place in this new course of events. They charged that their conditions and salaries were those of sweatshop laborers when compared to those in other comparable areas of education. And so the National Education Association moved from a mild, professionally oriented group to an aggressive, somewhat militant organization, introducing for the first time in its history the exercise of sanctions against school boards. The growing and militant American Federation of Teachers set off a series of teachers' strikes for more money and better working conditions. The cost of education skyrocketed.

Helpless to meet this unprecedented burden, the state and local governments turned to the Federal government for assistance. The Federal government was already carrying about 8 percent of the national educational budget, but it was enmeshed in an expensive struggle in Vietnam and was facing an expanding social welfare budget. To add to the problem, we were in the midst of a general business decline, with a resultant drop in tax revenue.

The reluctance of the Federal government to pick up a larger share of the cost of education meant that local communities had to absorb the problem. It meant, too, that many of the larger cities, particularly in the North, were facing a disproportionate share of the burden because of an influx from southern rural areas of large numbers of the impoverished and illiterate. Attracted by the lure of better jobs, higher wages, and superior living conditions, they all too often met with disillusion and added to the burden of cities already overwhelmed with inflationary welfare and education costs.

But any mention in 1968 of curtailing expenses, of evaluating the cost effectiveness of programs, of applying any kind of even crude cost benefit analysis to education was anathema. At stake was a host of new or expanding vested interests—builders, publishers, construction unions, teachers, paraprofessionals, and many others. In addition, parents who never before had thought to measure the merits of their children's education became aware, for the first time, of what the other half had and they too wanted it. For the first time young people realized that a higher education was not beyond their reach—and so "quality education" and "education for excellence" became a banner and a goal.

Unfortunately, however, expenditures for education were beginning to outpace the growth of our economy as a whole. During the last decade, education averaged a 9.7 percent annual growth in expenditures while the Gross National Product was averaging an annual increase of 6.8 percent. When measured against the growth rate in per capita personal income, the expenditures per pupil for education were nearly three times greater. "Education for excellence" indeed! With money running short, it has become apparent that it is a far cry from the slogan to the goal. The nation's public elementary and secondary schools spent more than $40 billion in 1970-71 excluding monies borrowed for new buildings. Next to national defense, education is the government's most expensive operational budget item. The cost of public education in the United States since World War II has been rising at an annual rate of 12½ percent, far out of proportion to national income. In fact, from the equivalent of 2 percent at the end of the war, the proportion of GNP spent for education has risen to between 6½ and 7 percent today.

Today the median school district is spending $409 more per elementary school pupil than in 1957–59. In 1959, the average spent per pupil was $306.10. In 1971 it is $776.19—an increase of more than 100 percent. Of this figure, between 70 and 85 percent goes for instruction, and in almost every case teachers and administrative salaries are the largest single item in the instruction budget.

However, salary increases alone do not tell the whole story. District retirement funds have risen sharply. For example, last year they jumped 41 percent over the previous year. This year they are expected to rise above 50 percent. It is the practice of the teachers' organizations, when salary increases are stalled, to shift the bargaining emphasis to retirement funds. In some places, the state itself has taken over payment of retirement contributions as well as health and welfare payments. Since the need for funds in the categories of retirement, welfare, and health have almost doubled in the past 2 years, it is understandable how the school dollar bypasses children.

Another factor in the money drain is the union demand that teachers be given smaller classes. As the class size per teacher constantly decreases, more teachers are needed. This practice continues in spite of the lack of evidence that there is a correlation between class size and pupil achievement.

To this can be added increased expenditures for clerks, secretaries, and aides, and the enormous increase in the costs of school maintenance and custodians' salaries. While all of this accounts for the $407 billion spent on education for 1970–71, it does not include funds for new buildings. Since 1947, school building costs have increased 133 percent. In the past decade alone, they have increased more than 40 percent. In 1969 alone building costs rose an average of 7 percent over 1968. The following graph shows the growth in the cost of school buildings from 1960 to 1970.

In the light of this extraordinary rise in expenditures, what

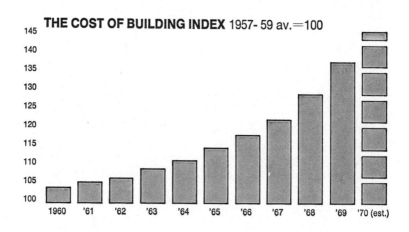

THE COST OF BUILDING INDEX 1957- 59 av.=100

has been accomplished toward attaining the goal of equal education for all segments of our society? Federal funds, since 1964, have, to a great extent, been allocated to the poor communities. Title I funds are designated primarily for the children of the poor. Most other Federal funds, if not so allocated originally, do nevertheless find their way eventually into poverty programs. But these funds alone cannot possibly "equalize" education. Most school districts still depend upon real property taxes for their revenue so that there is a tremendous disparity between the funds available to the poor and the wealthy communities. Education, therefore, prospers in some districts and falters in others, regardless of need or enthusiasm. Today, in some states, the taxable wealth per pupil in the richest districts is 100 times the wealth in the poorest. This does not mean, however, that these wealthy districts spend sizable sums for education. It merely means that the unit expenditure per child is greater.

Let us take an example of how much wealthy communities typically spend for education as opposed to poor communities. Table I, below, is divided into eight groups on the basis of income:

1. below $10,000
2. $10,000 to $16,000
3. $16,000 to $22,000
4. $22,000 to $28,000
5. $28,000 to $34,000
6. $34,000 to $40,000
7. $40,000 to $46,000
8. $46,000 and above
(see Table 1, page 8)

As would be expected, group 8, the wealthiest group, spends more for a pupil's education than any other group. However, both extremes—the lowest income group and the highest—spend only a little more than $100 below or above the national median. The figures tell us a great deal about the values within each group. The wealthiest group, 8, spends proportionally more money on administration than the poorest group and less money on transportation. Both spend about the same for textbooks but the wealthier district puts 8 percent more into teacher materials. Generally speaking, the wealthier district spends more money on noninstructional items such as capital outlay, teachers' materials, administration, etc.

	Group 1 Median District	Group 8 Median District	National Median
Net Expenditure per pupil	$558.68	$776.34	$667.00
Expenditures for instruction per pupil	413.42	564.57	506.35
Expenditures for textbooks per pupil	6.16	7.62	7.19
Expenditures for other teaching materials per pupil	14.06	22.15	18.84
Expenditures for administration per pupil	21.59	32.42	25.30
Expenditures for transportation per pupil	29.12	27.94	28.68
Expenditures for debt service per pupil	36.34	68.54	64.50
Expenditures for capital outlay per pupil	14.15	20.87	16.01
Amount raised locally per pupil	199.78	598.68	413.34
Amount received from state per pupil	297.33	231.55	288.78
Amount received from Federal government per pupil	27.11	11.18	11.89
Local Effort	2.90%	0.78%	1.4%

Table I

It is also interesting to note the extent of state and Federal support in these two financially opposite districts. Generally, state and Federal support of poor districts is about five times that of wealthy districts. However, this is not true in all states. In California, Wisconsin, and Illinois, for example, millions in "state aid" have been identified which, under existing legislation, actually benefit only the wealthy districts. This kind of aid has become, in many states, highly political. The consequence of the system is a disparity in spending, which, in California districts, ranges from well *below $500* to *$3,000* per pupil. Recently, several suggestions have been offered in an effort to equalize distribution of the education dollar. One is simply to require a state-wide basis for fixing the amount allotted for each pupil. Another is to prohibit any differences, by virtue of place of residence, in the number of dollars spent on any one child.

Basically, the line of battle is drawn between the centralists and those favoring local incentive. The former are outraged that the quality of education should be determined by the disparity in the funds available from district to district. The latter, on the other hand, see in local allocations a source of healthy variety and citizen involvement plus an insurance against the statewide mediocrity suggested by centralization.

The California State Supreme Court took a giant step forward in August 1971 in the long legal battle to provide equal educational opportunity regardless of whether the schools were located in city slums or wealthy suburbs. By a 6 to 1 ruling, it struck down the state's system of financing public schools—based largely on local property taxes—on the ground that it violated the "equal protection clause" of the United States Constitution. The case involved a claim that the Baldwin Park school district, located in a lower middle-class area, paid twice as much in school taxes per assessed valuation as the affluent Beverly Hills district, and yet, despite this lower tax rate, the Beverly Hills district was able to spend 50 percent more per pupil. Baldwin Park spent $840 per student in 1968–69 while Beverly Hills spent $1231 per student.

Similar examples can be found throughout the nation. In New York State, Manhasset and East Meadow, communities in suburban Nassau County, are only 20 miles apart, but from the disparity in their educational allotments, they might well be on opposite coasts. In Manhasset, the per pupil expenditure is $1721; in East Meadow it is $968. East Meadow is a two-bedroom community with no special tax base. Manhasset, on the other hand, has taxable properties consisting of luxury department stores and expensive residences. The result is an expenditure of almost twice the amount per pupil.

In California, until the recent decision of its Supreme Court, 56 percent of school costs had been paid through local property taxes, 35 percent by the state, and 9 percent through Federal grants. Under this decision, the court, while leaving open the question of how public schools shall be financed, has ruled out heavy reliance on local property taxes in California, which, the court said, "makes the quality of a child's education a function of the wealth of his parents and neighbors." It appears to leave no doubt that the court considers the present system a violation of the equal protection clause of the United States Constitution.

This case will eventually reach the United States Supreme Court. Virtually all states follow substantially the same pattern

California does in financing public education. Thus, of the $41.9 billion spent nationally on public elementary and secondary education last year, $21.8 billion, more than half, came from local property tax revenues. If the decision is upheld it will revolutionize the method used by the states to finance their educational budgets.

Once we have achieved a more equitable distribution of the education dollar, we will have to face up to another issue of equal importance. That is the restoration of public confidence in the quality of our schools, and a resultant willingness to contribute the funds necessary for them to function at their best.

THE HUMAN COST

While the dollar cost of education is skyrocketing and taxpayers are rejecting its burden, the human cost is accelerating and cannot even be estimated in dollars. The Gross National Product could not accommodate the loss we are suffering in human resources. Young people today, in large numbers, are just not going to school. Recently, in a report by New York City Comptroller, Abraham Beame, it was noted that, in a normal day, high schools in New York City are attended by 62 percent of the students registered—a frightening statistic; 38 percent of the young people just do not bother to go to school. On some days, attendance in schools in inner cities is below the 50 percent mark. In suburban communities, a higher percentage attends school because of greater visibility, but the spirit of rebellion is no less rampant. Whether apathetic or hostile, such students are virtually truants if measured by their interest in their studies.

What happens to these youngsters when they do not go to school? In poor neighborhoods, the dropout may be found sitting on a broken stoop surrounded by litter, playing cards, listening to a radio, or just staring into space. Many have become drug addicts. In the more affluent neighborhoods, parents will tell you that their son or daughter has taken a backpack, a pair of bluejeans, perhaps picked up a girl, and "hit the road"—hoping to panhandle enough money for a meal and to be allowed to sleep in a public park. In many instances, this young person is also on drugs. Are these things the measure of their aspirations? Is it for this that they leave school? Is the world of the hallway, the stoop, the public park, and the cheap hash joint the fruition of their

desires? Of course not. Most truants leave in order to "get out."
It is what they are escaping from—not what they are escaping to.

The rich and the poor, of whatever color, are rebelling
against a system they regard as irrelevant to the realities of life
and as a dictatorial imposition by a hypocritical and bureaucratic society. Dropouts know no economic or social classes. The
"families" of Charles Manson, the gypsy colonies, the communes, the pads, draw their members from all types of homes
including the rich, the cultured, the advantaged.

Perhaps one of the greater tragedies of all this is not the
comparatively few children for whom school is a total disaster
and destroying force, but the large bulk of our young people who
spend up to one-fourth of their lives in school and who gain little
or nothing from their education. In their own way, they, too, are
truants or dropouts; they sit in class with little or no interest in
what is going on. Several senior high school principals, at a
recent meeting of the National Association of Secondary School
Principals, observed that at certain times during the day (other
than change of periods) there were more students in the corridors and on the stairwells than in classrooms. Some make
it through school because they know how to be selective in what
they need and are able to reject everything else. Others, less able,
just pick up information at random and wait for the day that
they can legally leave school.

Recently, a young man was interviewed on a television
program entitled "The Thoughts of a June Graduate." He had
just graduated from Yale Law School and seemed to be an example of the successful graduate. He was asked whether he found
his years in school satisfactory, and if they had helped him to
become what he was. He answered, "I had to go through successive levels of schooling in order to get into college and law
school, but I always felt that the many years at school should
have been different. It just didn't do anything for me as a person.
I felt as if what went on in school had practically no connection
with my life. It was, for me, a totally external experience. This,
I think, was what bothered me more than anything else, the fact
that school was so impersonal. I had no role but that of a "taker"
—a "sponger"—school was my master. It controlled everything
that I was to learn, how I was to behave. It completely ignored me
as an individual, and set me in a 30-seat classroom mold. No one

in all my years in schools ever asked me what I *wanted* to learn, how I *felt* about myself, my classmates, about school. I had absolutely no say, no control, over so many years of my life." This young man's point of view is all too widely representative.

This sense of powerlessness seems to be the paramount grievance of students. Regardless of their social or economic backgrounds, most students are searching for greater control over their lives, for the power to make choices, to create, whenever possible, part of the environment in which they live, and to be free of the constraints of the adults controlling them. In a speech given at a superintendents' workshop at Teachers College, Columbia University, in July 1970, Ewald B. Nyquist, Commissioner of Education of the State of New York, said: "Our present system of education is monolithic with largely homogeneous institutions, coercive, frequently repressive, and authoritarian in nature. It is a closed teaching system as against an open system of *learning*. As a recent author stated, it ignores the requirements of normal growth, subordinates everything to remote, centralized impersonal administration, and 'undermines the very best of our democratic ideals.' The school is still too much an institution closed off or set apart from its surrounding community."

What are some of the other grievances of those who have not totally rejected school but who are prepared to tolerate it, if certain conditions can be changed? Important among student grievances is the imposition upon them of rules and regulations they regard as arbitrary and unjust. They are required to "do as you are told," to dress in a certain manner, to make a public declaration in class if they wish to go to the bathroom. The rules and control mechanisms may appear even more unrealistic in the case of the minority youth, sensitive to any real or fancied slight to his color or race.

Add to this the related grievances of practically all students: the lack of an educationally relevant curriculum and the low quality of classroom teaching. What is the incentive to attend class when a student must listen to a teacher discussing the leading wheat-producing states? What relevance does this have to the average city school student? Is it any wonder that they seek a voice in selecting their curriculum or their teachers?

Thomas A. Billings, onetime director of Upward Bound, a United States Office of Economic Opportunity program for high school youth, speaks to this disenchantment with established education. He says that in education our curricular innovations lag dangerously behind the realities they are supposed to engage and meliorate; our mode of school governance is archaic and inefficient; our method of school finance has been chronically inadequate, and what was chronic has now become acute. He finds that schools today are analagous to plantations, a sharecropper system in a world of corporate farms. He calls our schools small, feudal acreages, tenants crippled by harvests at the subsistence level and bewildered by the complexity of the great world around them. Probably millions of casualties pour from these sharecropper operations each year to wind up on the welfare rolls, a woe to themselves and an escalating burden on the rest of the nation.

It would be interesting if we really did list our casualties and in a parallel column costed out our losses. How much does it cost our nation for every student who is 10 percent educated, who is half educated, every student who does not reach his potential? Perhaps it is this type of shock approach that is necessary to incite society to do something about its educational investment. Until we begin to probe and find some answers to this question, we will resolve neither our dollar cost problem nor our resource cost problem. It is obvious that it is costing us more to do less. No business can operate on this basis.

It was once said that there was a 20-year lag between education and the world around it. Is it only 20 years? A young child today gets very much the same education as his father did, with some minor additions. Yet they are worlds apart—as far apart as the horse and buggy from the rockets, the moon landings, the computers, and the laser beams. While everything else in the nation has grown and changed, we have been singularly unimaginative about our nation's educational effort. Almost since the inception of public education in the middle of the 18th century, the schoolhouse has been the great common denominator of our democratic citizenry. As such, it has been operating on two basic assumptions: (1) that there is an identifiable common heritage or basic body of knowledge that all should experience, and (2) that this heritage or body of knowledge tends to be somewhat static or permanent (or, at best, slowly evolutionary) rather than dynamic and fluid.

The "identifiable common heritage" is today being questioned. Whereas we hold some of our heritage in common, can we say that it is truly homogeneous and that we can base our educational system on the assumption that it is? For example, the years of struggle of the Polish and Irish immigrants, in their effort to find their place in the industrial age of the 1890's and early 1900's, were not the same experience as the years of bondage of the black man or the years of hardship of the western settlers. Most of these are distinct experiences, with very little in common. For the immigrants and the western settlers, each in his way, it was the land of opportunity; for the black man, it was a country of oppression. The concept of the melting pot, then, is questionable.

The second assumption requires only cursory reflection to demonstrate its invalidity. In this century that knew the advent of the nuclear age, the landing on the moon, and the orbiting of Mars, the idea that knowledge is static needs no further refutation.

Together with Chancellor Harvey Scribner, head of the New York City school system, we would do well to repudiate the notions that "school is the exclusive place of education, that youth is the exclusive age of learning, that knowledge flows exclusively from the teacher, and that education is properly and accurately measured by the accumulation of credits." To this can be added another notion, that the flame of knowledge can be frozen and packaged and passed on from generation to generation.

Inherent in these two basic assumptions of a common heritage and of its static or permanent quality, is the human aversion to change. We hand our concepts on from one generation to another with "adjustments" along the way, but major revisions we regard as revolutionary.

Yet change is very much the American way of life. Bennis and Slater in their book, *The Temporary Society*, classify Americans as nomads. They note that the average period of residence in one place in 70 of America's major cities is less than 4 years. Of the 885,000 listings in the 1969 Washington, D.C. telephone book, over half had not been listed the year before (p. 76). In 1955, apartments accounted for only 8 percent of the new starts in housing. In 1969, for the first time in history, more per-

mits were issued for the building of apartments than were issued
for residential homes. The trend toward apartments is particularly evident among the younger population, who, according to Professor Burnham Kelly of M.I.T., want "minimal involvement"
housing characterized by short time obligations (p. 58). Americans change their cars the way they change their houses. In
European countries, cars are purchased on the average of once
every 8 years. The average American car ownership is 3½ years.
A car is sold or traded long before its utility span has expired.
And to educators the syndrome of change is expressed most
significantly, perhaps, in the fact that the Board of Education
of Los Angeles has decided that 25 percent of its classrooms
in the future shall be temporary structures so as to facilitate
movement to different locations when necessary (p. 53).

Margaret Mead, 20 years ago, said that members of the
"next" generation, which is the "now" generation, will change
their jobs up to 8 times in a lifetime. Toffler, in *Future Shock*,
identifies our society as tentative, temporary, fluid, and ever
changing.

A *Fortune* survey of 1,003 young executives in the mid-60's
revealed that one out of three held a job that simply did not
exist until that person was appointed to the position. Obsoles-
cence is the creeping malady of our times. Something is no
sooner discovered than it is replaced by a more effective product.
Change is accelerating so rapidly that it constantly takes new
skills to learn how to cope with it.

If change is so much part of the things we do, why, then, do
we resist change so adamantly in education? The year 2000 is
approaching faster than we think, and to be realistic we should
prepare for it now. Otherwise, we may soon find ourselves far off
course and in treacherous waters. The portents are apparent in
the turbulence about us, the crises in the classrooms, campus revolts, arson, and vandalism in the schools. The inertia of the
educational establishment in meeting the needs of an archaic
system has generated a climate of resentment against its authority, resentment by taxpayers who must foot the bills, students
who feel that the schools are only a bypass to life, and the educators themselves, who, in the face of inadequate funds and student rebellion, turn defensively against both as the cause of all
their problems.

Admittedly, the critics of education, something like the Greek chorus, are always present to tell us our ills, but rarely do they come up with solutions. Howard Becker, a not unsympathetic critic of the public schools, in a paper entitled "A School Is A Lousy Place to Learn Anything In" (Autumn 1969, Unpublished Paper, prepared at the Center for Advanced Study in Behavioral Sciences, Stanford, California), wonders whether the frozen, structured, hierarchical organization of the school is the villain. John Holt says school is a place where children learn to be stupid. Paul Goodman "would not give a penny and would largely dismantle the present school machinery." Jonathan Kozol, in his description of the Boston schools, demonstrates how schools destroy the minds and hearts of black children. George Leonard, Peter Marin, and Edgar Friedenberg see schools stifling the finest and most passionate impulses of young people.

On the other hand, Brzezinski, the scholar, decries this mood of self-criticism as excessive, as self-flagellating. Perhaps we should answer the voices of doom and despair in the words of Saul Bellow:

> Maybe civilization is coming to an end, but it still exists, and meanwhile we have our choice: We can either rain more blows on it, or try to redeem it.

Indeed, if redemption be called for, we have gone far to recognize the position of youth in the modern scheme of things. This is a generation in which youth has more going for it than in any time past. The young man or woman of today is not Tuesday's child, full of woe. The love beads, long hair and beard, and blue jeans represent an emancipation of the spirit, indicative of this new way of life. Those young people travel everywhere by thumb; economic status, age, color, religion are declining hindrances. They have a voice in the world they help to shape. They can vote. They have more sexual freedom today than probably at any other time in history. Never before has youth been so able to "do his own thing." This is not the youth to give up on.

Indeed, it is a generation with whom we must join in a partnership of self-renewal and self-preservation. As John Gardner has said:

*The tasks of renewal are endless. Society is being continual-
ly recreated, for good or ill, by its members. This will strike some
as a burdensome responsibility, but it will summon others to
greatness.*

We cannot afford the waste of human resources that now exists.
It is for us, therefore, to find ways of renewing, as John Gardner says. It is our task to recreate a society that is productive because it fosters values that are sound, not only spiritually and
intellectually, but operationally as well.

If this is to be done, if our mission is to find a viable way of
building an educational system that we can afford both in dollars and human resources, then our first task is to be clear about
the implicit purposes and goals of education. It is these goals
that lend direction to whatever organizational structure we may
come up with. Once these goals have been established and accepted, we can adjust the approaches and the programs necessary
to their attainment.

In setting objectives in education, the primary assumptions
must be that students and not teachers shall be the focus of
schooling; that success is indicated by the degree to which
schools are responding to the *differing* needs of students; that
school experiences shall be centered around real concerns rather
than artificial disciplines, bureaucratic requirements, and adult
ideas of what children should learn. To that purpose, the educational policy decisions of a school should be determined after
joint consultation between students and teachers, and the success of those policies should be predicated on the extent to which
the students feel they are learning and gaining a sense of their
ability to contribute to the control of the environment in which
they share.

If we can accept these broad general goals, how, then, do we
design ways of attaining them? One way is to remodel our house
while living in it—a sort of redesign of our existing educational
environment. Another and more radical way is to discard what
we now have and start anew by creating alternatives to schools
as we know them today. Still another way of realizing these goals
is to combine both approaches by creating a system of education
that allows for options whereby each youngster with the aid of
his parents and other suitable guidance selects that kind of
schooling that best fits his style of learning.

MEETING THE PROBLEM

Redesign

As of 1972, there are 113,323 educational institutions—elementary and secondary schools, universities, and colleges. Almost every institution is housed in a building generally termed a school. More than 63 million Americans are engaged full time as students, teachers, or administrators. The estimate of the cost of education made by the United States Office of Education and the National Education Association for the year 1971–72 is $85 billion.

One cannot ignore these figures when we talk about restructuring education in this country. As attractive and important as "new" educational systems may be, we must give serious consideration to what we can do with the existing one. You cannot say abracadabra and have it go away. It is here—it is monumental—it represents a tremendous dollar investment. What can we do with this edifice to remodel, to refurbish, to reconstruct it, so that it can become a more effective establishment?

There are three main ingredients in any school system: space, people, materials. These make up the operational budget of any school. What if we first looked at our present structures to see how we can use them to better advantage. Can we remove some walls and create more flexible learning areas, and, at the same time, accommodate more youngsters? Can we extend the utilization time? Where is it said that a building shall be used only from the hours of 8 to 4 for 10 months a year? Can we not accommodate at least a third more students if we extend the school day and the school year? If new space is needed, are there not less expensive, perhaps mass-produced, types of buildings that can be constructed? What, for example, if instead of building more schools we were to look elsewhere for space? After all, the initial cost for construction of a school may vary from $15 to $40 million. Once it is built, attendance officers, guidance counselors, and "Big Brothers" are hired to keep them tenanted. Yet the students say, "We don't want schools run by middlemen feeding us information secondhand. We want to learn by living our experiences." Therefore, schooling and learning experiences might better take place in industry, in government, on farms, in storefronts, rather than in school buildings.

Adding on "wings" for education or learning space to existing businesses or agencies is far less expensive than building new schools. Why, indeed, do we need more school buildings? The large organizations and bureaucracy that they require make ever more questionable the assertion of a functional relationship between large school buildings and bureaucratic organizations on the one hand, and learning to read, write, and do math on the other. It is hard to see why the business of learning cannot be managed more economically and efficiently by the use of skilled people working simply, directly, professionally with small groups wherever they can find adequate space. If we study the daily activities of children and ask ourselves how these might best be channeled to create a happy climate for learning, we must certainly conclude that it is best to avoid large institutions, over-organization, and any unnecessary kind of complexity.

What about the "people of education" or the professional teacher as we now know him? The cost for professional teachers, in many parts of the nation, has doubled from 1960 to 1970, this at a time when dissatisfaction with the quality of teaching is steadily increasing. Therefore, a rethinking of the role of the professional teacher and a consideration of possible alternative types of staffing may well be in order. Students are calling for "real" experiences with "real" instructors, as opposed to teachers who are interpreters of knowledge—brokers or middlemen. Why not call upon specialists from industry, cultural and public service agencies, from the community, parents, retired professionals, etc., *and* students within the school? Why cannot these become the new "people of education?"

Professional educators obviously have much to offer to the education process, but the day of their handing down blueprints should be ended. They alone do not hold the secret of education. Education is served by many people in many vocations, in addition to teaching. In many of the new programs now being tried, local townspeople are part of the instructional staff, and students are taking on responsibilities once held only by paid professionals. A whole new way of thinking about education is taking place. The approach is not to throw out everything we have but to be selective in what we retain and to add new dimensions—to make education more experiential, to bring it closer to reality, and to orient it more to the individual than the mass. At the same time, expensive structural and administrative setups can be minimized.

Serious consideration should also be given to the management of school systems. Should educators who have not been trained in educational administration be selected to manage large systems? In today's complicated world this role calls for the special skills of people who are trained in management techniques. Very often, using a management team is more economical than paying educators to do things they are not trained to do. What is more, administrative tasks done by principals, supervisors, and myriads of clerks and assistants can often be done by computer more quickly and accurately and for a small portion of the cost of professionals. The computer is currently being tapped for only 1 percent of its potential for school administration.

Educators, perhaps more than others, are notorious for duplication of activities. Travel through a single school system and you will find duplication of equipment, much of which is idle a good part of the time; duplication of teacher specialists; and duplication of building facilities. Cooperative educational services can be provided by concentrating human resources and equipment and making them available to units of large numbers of students from a variety of schools and school districts. In New York State, Boards of Cooperative Educational Services have been set up to do just this. The procedure has been fairly successful since it has cut down on costs and offered superior facilities to larger numbers of children.

Materials can also be shared through computer-assisted instruction. A team of "experts" can develop curriculums that will not only reach innumerable students by means of computers, but will also individualize instruction to a far greater extent than was ever possible in a traditional classroom. Furthermore, many of the current technologies are more appealing and, therefore, offer students more opportunities for success than the traditional teacher–pupil interaction (especially among disadvantaged youth).

In other words, then, there are ways of redesigning education while, hopefully, producing a more effective product at a reduced cost. There is much literature on this subject but little has been done; or what has been done is piecemeal with little regard for education as a total process. Besides, there is a caution that should be mentioned: the school that installs an information management system but "manages" dull, irrelevant information has made little change except to "modernize" obsolete information. A school that brings in personnel other than teachers but does not revise *what* they are teaching is simply going through motions but making no real changes in education. Redesign, in order to be meaningful, demands a thorough knowledge of educational goals and of the means to attain them.

Redesign or remodeling, no matter how well thought out it might otherwise be, will not succeed if it does not meet the major criteria for survival. First, it should cost less than the existing school budget, and, secondly, it should have an educational payoff by recapturing the students in a meaningful, fulfilling experience. Unless we can afford it and unless we can develop young people to the fullest potential, we have gone through an exercise—we have rebuilt our house but still not made it livable.

Alternatives

Some prominent educators feel that any attempt to use the present framework as a basis for change can only be a makeshift device and that we will never discard the impedimenta of an obsolete system unless education is completely restructured. Perhaps the most radical of all such "changers" is Ivan Illich, who works out of the Center for Intellectual Documentation in Cuernavaca, Mexico. He is an abolitionist who calls for the total elimination of schools. As an alternative, Illich's theory of radical reform is as much political as it is educational. He says:

> *Deschooling the cultural and social structure requires the use of technology to make participatory politics possible. Only on the basis of a majority coalition can limits to secrecy and growing power be determined without dictatorship. We need a new environment in which growing up can be classless, or we will get a brave new world in which Big Brother educates us all.*

Illich claims that as a person grows up he needs access to things, to places, to processes, to events, to records. He claims the structure of our society as it is reflected in our schools does not allow this. To quote him further:

When knowledge became a commodity, it acquired the protections of private property, and thus a principle designed to guard personal intimacy became a rationale for declaring facts off limits for people without the proper credentials. In schools teachers keep knowledge to themselves unless it fits into the day's program. The media inform, but exclude those things they regard as unfit to print. Information is locked into special languages, and specialized teachers live off its translation. Patents are protected by corporations, secrets are guarded by bureaucracies, and the power to keep others out of private preserves—be they cockpits, law offices, junkyards, or clinics—is jealously guarded by professions, institutions, and nations.

He suggests two major steps to combat control by political institutions and their spokesmen—in this case, teachers.

First, that students be given direct access to knowledge through technology—computers, programed instruction, television, and other teaching/learning machines. This would circumvent the teacher and the institution he represents. This technology, properly controlled, would provide each man with the ability to understand his environment better, to shape it peacefully with his own hands, and to permit him full intercommunication to a degree never before possible.

The second major step is to offer students direct access to skills. He claims that the entire structure of schooling is irrelevant for gaining competence on the vast majority of American jobs. People with skills should be the teachers. The student, or apprentice, would learn directly from the artisan, the teacher, the physician. School, Illich claims, is the unnecessary middleman. It misinterprets, exercises the wrong controls, and generally impedes learning.

His theory, revolutionary as it is, has many supporters. For example, it has been found that few people today credit schools with contributing to their success, their cultural enrichment, or, for that matter, their functioning in their field of endeavor. Astin (1968) cast considerable doubt on the effect of college on students' intellectual development and learning. Bright students, he found, did just as well irrespective of the college they went to; the same is true for "dull" ones. Simon, Gagnon, and Carnes (1969) indicate that college experience has almost no influence on political attitudes of students, either while they are in college or after they leave.

Michael Crichton, the physician and writer, claims that the training for a physician as provided by most medical schools has little application to medical practice. Osler Peterson (1957) examined the quality of medical practice among general practitioners in North Carolina and discovered that there was no relation between the medical school that doctors graduated from and the quality of their practice, nor was there a relationship between the quality of practice and the rank in the medical school graduating class. Hoffman, studying actors, discovered that almost none of the actors regarded as "good" by their peers ever attended a drama school. Philip Jacob (1957) reviewed hundreds of studies of the influence of college on student values and found little evidence of a liberalizing change. Supreme Court Justices Hugo Black and Robert Jackson had little, if any, legal schooling. Justice Story, the father of American legal schooling, had none at all. Caryl Chessman became a lawyer, not in law school, but in prison.

How important, then, are our schools? This is a fighting question, and we should be cautious about simplistic answers. Illich claims that American education is in the business of teaching and perpetuating the values of the small elite minority. He agrees with Dreeben, who, in *On What Is Learned in School,*[1] says that the school structure communicates particular norms; the learning of those norms has priority over the learning of skills. Those norms that are crystallized into contemporary educational forms reflect the purposes of education that have dominated American schools. As Ivan Illich puts it: "All over the world schools are organized enterprises designed to reproduce the established order, whether this order is called revolutionary, conservative, or evolutionary."

The concept of state control and domination over what is taught and, therefore, what is passed on was a concern of John Stuart Mill over 100 years ago:

> A general state education is a mere contrivance for molding people to be exactly like one another; and as the mold in which it casts them is that which pleases the predominant power in the government—whether this be a monarch, a priesthood, an aristocracy, or the majority of the existing generation—in proportion as it is

---

[1] Robert Dreeban, *On What Is Learned in School,* Reading, Mass.: Addison-Wesley Publishing Company, 1968.

*efficient and successful, it establishes a despotism over the mind,
leading by natural tendency to one over the body.*

If, then, one wants to throw off the cloak of reproducing the established order, one must radically restructure educational reform.

Illich, therefore, is really suggesting a system of education that emphasizes skills, that allows and invites people to share their skills with those entering the world of work in a setting devoid of governmental and ideological controls; it provides a setting for learning from one another.

Everett Reimer, in his latest book, *School Is Dead* (Doubleday, 1971), suggests a technological process he calls a network system, not unlike the one suggested by Illich, in which schools would be replaced by informational records, skills models, peer matching, and educators. It is difficult to picture the process because no clear blueprints or working models exist. Apparently, the records in the form of data stored in cassettes and computers would contain information of all kinds to be made quickly and cheaply available to any person who wanted them. The skill models refer to people who could demonstrate desired skills, such as vocational, linguistic, and mathematical competence. A peer group would emerge through a computerized matching of fellow learners with whom the learning could be shared. Last on his scale of priorities are educators whose experience might facilitate these learning resources.

Reimer is convinced that this network system will increase the demand for education and place the greatest importance on the architects and administrators of the educational resource networks. Next in popularity, he thinks, would be the designers of individualized programs and those who could diagnose educational difficulties while prescribing effective remedies. Third would come the leaders in every branch of learning. In this system, which Reimer acknowledges as a utopia, the assignment he sets for the designers of the new networks is "to understand knowledge, people, and the societies they live in." As for teachers who were greatly honored before there were schools, they will be honored again when they are freed to practice their profession without the constraints of forced attendance, mandatory curriculums, and classroom walls. "While the task of this new competent pedagogue is not for the fainthearted," he tells us, "the practitioner will nevertheless find in it the rewards of the old family doctor."

James Herndon, who wrote the book *The Way It Spozed To Be*, goes a step further than Reimer and even Illich by resting his hopes not on the possibility of changing education, but on just getting it "off people's backs." "There is no law any more that people must go to church or pay attention to the church," Herndon writes, "and so many people don't, while others do. That is the best you can expect, and good enough. . . . The public school is the closest thing we have in America to a national established church, Getting-an-Education the closest thing to God, and it should be possible to treat it and deal with it as the church has been treated and dealt with."

To meet the criticisms of Ivan Illich, James Herndon, and Reimer, one would either abolish the schools altogether or create a society that not only learns from one another but that uses technology for self-education. It would remove completely the "control" of education by the government and its agencies. Although radical to an extreme, this "reform" presents a point of view shared by many young people today, and to some small degree is an alternative already in practice. In an antic way, this approach has a special fascination for the pennywise, since the abolition of schools would remove the second largest item of the national budget and of most state budgets.

Reimer suggests, as one form of financing, giving the task of developing and administering the skill models to a public utility whose responsibility it would also be to finance the models. Another form of funding, he suggests, could be through personal education accounts and a system of public education utilities that would have to be self-supporting, as our postal system is supposed to be.

Illich suggests that a portion of the money spent on schools could be spent for technological services and equipment and for paying those who share their skills with others. To some extent it would be a redistribution of educational funds. Nevertheless, the cost could be vastly reduced as school buildings, professional staffs, and bureaucratic systems would be completely eliminated. The vital question, however, is whether people would be getting a better education. If not, then the money saved would have to be used for other kinds of rehabilitation services.

Less radical in their approach than Illich, Herndon, and Reimer is a small but vocal group of reformers who believe in the political decentralization of the school system. They maintain that a symbiotic relationship between institutions and the communities they serve is absolutely necessary to inspire any degree of meaningful activity. Their claim is that if education is controlled by local communities, as opposed to central bureaucracies, it will be less impersonal, more humane, and, consequently, more effective. They say, further, that finances will not be a problem since the parents who pay the bills will have a feeling of control and ownership over what happens to the money. They will be better informed, and paying for education will be little different from paying rent. The school budget will be theirs and not one drawn up by outsiders.

The most able of these reformers are experienced, deeply committed teachers who sensitively distill the history of their involvement with the schools. Representative of this group are such leading educators as Sylvia Ashton-Warner, George Dennison, and A. S. Neill.[2] They have an almost romantic dedication to the potentialities of mass education. These reformers, unlike Illich, do not believe in the abolition of the institution of schools, but they do believe in alternatives to the current structure of schooling. They talk about small, democratic, communally controlled, humanistic education, as opposed to large "inhumane" bureaucracies. Their premise is that until the schools treat the student as a highly individualistic human being, he will be destroyed by the structure and become incapable of responding to the educational function. School, as they see it, destroys education as well as children; schools are cold, impersonal prisons. Whereas Goethe with his dying words asked for "Light, light, more light," G. Stanley Hall, a psychologist at the turn of the century, observed that intellect was a speck on the sea of emo-

[2] See Sylvia Ashton-Warner, *Teacher*, New York: Simon and Schuster, 1963; George Dennison, *The Lives of Children: The First Street School*, New York: Random House, 1969; Alexander S. Neill, *Summerhill: A Radical Approach to Child Rearing*, New York: Hart Publishing Company, 1960.

High School, a film produced and directed by Frederick Wiseman. Available from Zipporah Films, 54 Lewis Wharf, Boston, Massachusetts 02110.

Jonathan Kozol, *Death at an Early Age: The Destruction of the Hearts and Minds of Negro Children in the Boston Public Schools*, Boston: Houghton Mifflin, 1967.

tion and called for warmth, warmth, and more warmth. Harold Gores, in commenting on the two remarks, said, "Wouldn't it be nice if our symbol, the lamp of knowledge, were located on the mantle of a fireplace?"

Those in favor of these community-controlled "free" type schools claim that they are humane environments in which real learning can take place and where children can grow because they are loved, cared about, and allowed to realize their intrinsic value as human beings. They believe that only in this environment can a child's potential be developed to its fullest.

These reformers place their emphasis on the development of attitudes rather than a fixed curriculum. If skills are mastered, it is only by indirection, as an offshoot of the primary focus. Critics of this approach question whether the development of attitudes should take precedence over all other purposes of education. Are we seeking to produce beautiful people, nobly motivated, who cannot function in or for society? Another question is whether or not, even if one accepts the development of attitudes as the primary function of education, it is achievable? After all, in 125 years of compulsory public education, with tremendous amounts of money spent, and the student as a captive consumer, the schools have been able to do little toward developing an attitude favorable to learning. Perhaps the power of the schools has been vastly overrated. Perhaps the attitudes one speaks of belong more properly in the area of social, rather than educational, reform.

Nevertheless, there are large numbers of alternatives currently in operation which incorporate the views of these reformers. They are locally controlled educational "experiences," sometimes run by a group of parents, at other times by whole communities. They attempt to make learning a more personalized, humanistic experience. They rarely employ professional teachers; instructors are educational aides or parents or older children. Learning usually takes place in a home, a storefront, a series of rooms, a remodeled building. Materials are inclined to be more "natural" than manufactured. All of this immediately adds up to greatly reduced costs for education. Storefronts, nonprofessional teachers, homemade materials are vastly less expensive to build and support than large school structures, manned by expensive professionals, and using publisher-produced materials.

Schools based on the tenets of these reformers can be found in small numbers throughout the country: Herbert Kohl's Other Ways School in Berkeley; the CAM Academy in Chicago; Shule Ye Uhura, a freedom school in Washington, D.C.; a middle class free school in suburban Montgomery County, Maryland; Harlem Prep in New York City; George Dennison's First Street School; the super-free public school called Fernwood in rural Oregon; and others.

New alternative schools are appearing all the time; older ones are closing down for lack of money or because of defects. It is time we took a hard look at these schools. To adopt them wholesale as a remedy to our current ills is irresponsible; to reject them totally is equally irresponsible. If our objective is to find viable means of education that will best develop our human resources, and, at the same time, will carry with it a price tag that we can live with, we must consider those parts of alternative schools that work and that we can afford.

In education, we usually designate programs as being totally effective or totally ineffective. This is a mistake, since many a program declared ineffective has elements that are important, that work, and that should be saved. And the same is true about these programs; they are not *all* good or *all* bad. Jerome Bruner has said that children very rarely give a "wrong" answer to a mathematics problem. If you follow the sequence, you will find, he says, that up to a certain point the thinking and the calculations are correct; an error is then made and, based on that error, the youngster continues on, possibly being "right" as to all the following steps. But because of the error, the answer the student gives for the whole example is "wrong." In reality, however, why isn't the answer right? Only one step or calculation was wrong. Why penalize the student for the whole example? School programs should be viewed in that way. What are the elements or parts of the experience that are good and should be used?

An example of how we can learn from alternative schools is that of the mini-schools now being created in a small experimental way in larger cities like New York and Chicago for the purpose of trying to find some antidote to the large, impersonal, overpowering atmosphere of high schools. In New York City, for example, in some high schools as many as 6,000 students attend school on double sessions in a single building, where often a student can enter only after identifying himself by showing a program card to an anonymous security guard, where he can go from year to year without meeting his guidance counselor, where he is told in countless ways, each day, that he is only one of 1.1 million students and will be accommodated only as long as he fits the system.

The mini-school is small, with no more than 100 students. It is planned to provide an intimate environment and allows for personal contact between the teacher and the student, his family, his way of life. Instructional programs are planned for the individual youngster based on the teacher's knowledge of the child and his family, thus making education a more humane experience for him. A mini-school can be housed in a storefront, in an apartment, in any space that is available and inexpensive. In some instances, the existing high school situation has been turned into a series of mini or alternative schools, each with its own headmaster. Haaren High School in New York City is an example of a 5,000-student high school that has been converted into a series of small mini-schools.

The mini-alternative schools in these respects are very similar to community-alternative schools—small, personalized educational environments. However, there are two major differences. The mini-school has, among its objectives, the mastery of skills. The development of attitudes, although important, is not the program objective. Students in mini-schools have the same literacy goals as those in the traditional schools. Another difference is the cost. Since mini-schools are part of the system rather than outside of it, they are required to hire professional teachers and administrators, usually pursuant to a union contract. If they want to employ parents, paraprofessionals, streetworkers, etc., they must add them to their payroll of professionals. The cost of alternative or mini-schools within the system is large, almost twice as much, in fact, as the cost of educating a student in the conventional high school. The value of small groups in relation to their cost, therefore, must be carefully evaluated by a school system before it embarks on such a program.

Where, then, are we going? That the traditional schools—

public, private, and parochial—have not been responsive to the needs of many in our society cannot be denied. In spite of a decade of dedicated professional effort to improve public education, the situation in 1970 was not significantly better than in 1960. Professional criticism of the schools continues unabated; public disenchantment, as demonstrated by the defeat of so many school budgets, is at an all-time high. Reform through decentralized community boards, or by way of humanistic experimental schools, has had little effect on education as a whole. After about 10 years of experimentation with the reform movement's community schools, only a smattering of cities are picking up the concept. Few, if any, suburban or rural schools are looking seriously at alternatives to their present systems.

The ultra radicals, like Illich and Herndon, are unlikely to find a receptive audience in a nation still recuperating from the effect of campus revolts. Theodore Sizer, retiring Dean of Education at Harvard, says that education now needs a "healer," that the wounds of revolt are still open, that little has been done to remedy the recently diagnosed maladies.

We are indeed a tired nation. Even the reformer faction, although less extreme than the radicals, seeks change of revolutionary dimensions. The transfer of power to the community is a concept the value of which has not yet been proved. Like that of Illich, it is unstructured, personalized, community directed, but with objectives stated only in the loosest terms, and with outcomes that cannot be measured.

At this point in American Education, we are caught between the orthodoxy of the conformists and the orthodoxy of the nonconformists. Michael Katz[3] of the Ontario Institute for the Study of Education says that education as represented by radicals and reformers reflects an attempt at cultural imposition fully as much as the traditional educational emphasis on competition, restraint, and orderliness, whose bourgeois bias radicals are quick to excoriate. Educational radicalism and reform offer more an ideology than a solution. Katz claims that educational realism has passed from a sect to a church; in that process it has lost much of its inspiration.

The monolithic structure that has characterized American

[3] *Harvard Educational Review*, August 1971, p. 354.

education is cracking, but to date the mainstream of the profession has failed to recognize and engage the problem. It may well be that the generation currently in school represents the last generation that will go from kindergarten to college in lock-step. What then will the education of the future look like? Where will concerned educators focus their efforts in the 70's?

Options of the 70's

Local control has always been a bulwark of American education. We elect local school boards who, in turn, make decisions for us. The majority rules, and parents, educators, and taxpayers must go along with their decisions. Public schools, then, become social institutions which foster uniformity rather than diversity. Parents who want something different must turn elsewhere, usually to private schools that are accredited by the state. That option, however, is not usually open to those with low incomes.

The problem of freedom of choice versus acceptance and compliance does not strike only at the poor. At the time this book is being written, the Amish, a religious sect, are before the United States Supreme Court for the purpose of determining whether or not the State of Wisconsin may constitutionally limit the free exercise of religion by means of a compulsory school law aimed, in effect, at inculcating majority-approved "secular" values in the minds of dissenters. By their act of conscience, the Amish defendents raise another major issue in the conflict between state power and individual freedom.

This issues brings with it far-reaching implications for public policy. The case does, in fact, call into question the entire rationale for compulsory schooling. *Wisconsin vs. Yoder* confronts us with the fact that state establishment of educational or ethical values, like the establishment of religion, may be a threat to the principles set down by the Bill of Rights. Is it a violation of the Bill of Rights if we must send our children to the "school down the street" regardless of what it offers or represents, or if we must bus our children to a distant school no matter what it offers or stands for?

The issue of the state versus the individual is a philosophical as well as a legal one and, as we know, it has been debated through the ages. Basically, however, our concern in this instance is to provide a supportive, humanistic, and self-actualizing climate for learning. Yet, one has only to talk to the children on the street or in the schools to realize that they are not finding it in the conventional public school.

What, then, is the solution? It has been suggested that we should consider a system of options, a sort of internal voucher system under which the student and his family are offered a variety of types of schooling, *all within the public school system.* In this way, public schools will have to rearrange themselves and accommodate themselves to both the dissenter and the conformist. Let us see what this means in practice.

The concept of differentiating learning experiences for the student is based on the premises that people and their needs should be matched up with the education they require to attain their purposes or goals; that this education can take place at any time in one's life, at any place that is appropriate (yes, even a schoolhouse); that it can be provided by anyone possessing the appropriate skills. This process for education can take many forms and it is the students and their parents who will control the form they choose. Education is not decreed—courses of study are not "developed" on a mass basis—teachers are not automatically assigned from some elusive list made up by people who know little about the needs of a particular school or a particular group of students. The student's goals, his style of learning, his personality are all taken into consideration in finding the right educational program for him. He is given a choice, a series of options. He and his parents may select the kind of education or schooling that they believe will best fit the youngster. Paul Goodman calls it permitting alternative ways for people to grow and live. Ronald Gross refers to it as free learning, where it is impossible to tell where school begins and life stops.

Optional schools can range from the most traditional types of education, centered around the teaching of the classics, to the "openness" of the British system or their Leicestershire system, to schools emphasizing vocations and built in industrial centers run by industrialists, to schools built in homes and run by parents and people in the neighborhood, to automated schools that are completely independent of people, to schools that are "owned" by students and schools that are "rented" by students. The key to optional schools is their variety. There is no one way. The student who functions best in a free school should be matched up with one; the one who does best in a disciplined environment should be able to attend that kind of school; he who does well in our existing schools should be able to continue in them. The older student who wants to learn a vocation should be matched up with workers at a plant or other location where he can receive the most realistic training. In other words, the clientele, the students and parents, should have a choice, from the most traditional to the most unique.

Educational options can take place within a whole community or within a single school. In fact, in a single school there may exist a wide variety of approaches. For example, in early childhood a single school might offer as options: 1) a Montessori program, 2) an established kindergarten program, 3) a British infant school program, and 4) a reward-for-learning system such as proposed by Bereiter-Engleman. Again, parents, teachers, and students will have to understand fully the significance of each program and be free to choose from among them.

There are many possibilities. Options may be developed in a school district, in a single high school, or in a group of comprehensive high schools. Options may combine public facilities with private facilities and personnel. The choices are limitless. The essence of it all is flexibility. Providing choice in education can be the most powerful change agent in education available to us today. Choice legitimizes new programs. Parents may select an option or form of schooling and, therefore, they are disposed to support it. This is unlike our current system where a "new kind of education" is installed by "the powers that be." Parents do not understand it, do not know why their children have to be made guinea pigs. This tends to maximize conflict.

On the other hand, more choices must also be given to teachers. Professionals who are attracted to a Summerhill-like school are different from those who prefer a classical school environment. If teachers are allowed to match their style to an educational program, if they can choose the environment in which they function best, we thereby legitimitize both old and new approaches and make them operational by general consent. Moreover, by enhancing the teacher's sense of professional satisfaction, we minimize the traditional resistance to change.

The cost factor in schools of choice need not be any higher

than our present costs, and, in most cases, if carefully planned, should be lower. One of our great errors in educational budget making is the emphasis on *building* the institution rather than on the *product* of that institution. We must never forget that larger capital costs mean increased operational costs.

If we plan options or a variety of educational modes, let's start looking at budget making differently. Let's start with the product and let us build the learning experience into the process of production. What learning experiences does a student need to become an automobile mechanic, a physician, a housewife, a lawyer, a carpenter, or a teacher? Where is the best place to prepare him for these vocations? Who are the best people to impart this knowledge? What should the product look like; what should it cost to produce? This calls for a totally different way of viewing the education budget. Costs will no longer be the same for all students. Costs and experiences will vary depending upon a student's goals. It may cost $10,000 to teach one student as opposed to $25,000 for another, *but* we would eliminate the waste of time and money spent on "common," standardized experiences. To meet an individual's needs, it is far more realistic if we relate cost to acceptance value, if we measure success in terms of the ratio between our efforts and our productivity.

This concept of education is established practice in industry. It should be developed intelligently in the field of public education. If it is not allowed to get out of hand, it offers great promise to society and to the individual.

In a 1970 Gallup Poll, the question was asked, "Do you feel that the public schools are not interested enough in trying new ways and new methods or are they too ready to try new ideas?" The highest percentage of public-school parents thought that the public schools were just about right. However, the highest percentage of students said that the public schools were not interested in trying new ways and new methods.

This highlights the gap between those who pay for education and those who are being educated. Unless the taxpayer, the general public, sees the need for change, little will happen. Students are without franchise. They have no power, either financial or political, to make things happen. Granted, they have "other ways," but experience has shown us that in the final analysis it is those who pay the bills who make the decisions.

If the public is unwilling to pay for the type of education it now receives, will it pay for a radically different and unfamiliar pattern? Perhaps it will, but reluctantly.

It is quite possible that the budget crunch may yet turn out to be our most potent motivating force for change, a sort of blessing in disguise. It compels us to twist and turn to fit into our financial straitjacket. These are days of nonconformance. The mood and the need may be the joint incentives that we need to provide a new, yet viable, educational system.

II
Redesign within our Present Structure

In recent years, the voices of young people have been raised against the established order in general and against the educational system in particular. The counterculture they proclaim has been joined by the poor and the blacks. The cry for relevance has echoed through our compartmentalized schools with their lockstep programs, standardized schedules, and prescribed curriculums. Instead of being man-centered, problem-oriented, and interdisciplinary, present education is too frequently an exercise of the memory, rewarded by grades, interrupted by bells, and arbitrarily partitioned both as to space and subject matter.

Increasingly, critics of the system have called to our attention the detrimental effects of many of the sacred cows of our instructional system. Professionals, nonprofessionals, and students are asking for a different kind of education; one in which the classroom is learner-centered rather than teacher-dominated; where, indeed, technology may become, in many instances, the new "teacher" and the new strategy for an individualized approach to education.

There is little doubt but that schools must substantially modify their approaches in response to the basic changes in our society. The educational system in a dynamic society cannot remain stagnant. The question is whether or not our present structure can adapt to innovation. Are educationists and school board members ready for change? How much will they concede to the inroads of new interests and values?

It is said that times of crisis create the best climate for change. Fiscal crisis is upon the schools; the options are narrowing. Either a school system is independently rich enough to ignore the demand for innovation, or it must adjust its expense budget to meet escalating costs and tightening purse strings and, presumably, pare down the educational product. Whichever the case, the fact remains that students in droves are manifesting their dissatisfaction with the educational system as it now exists. Perhaps these two forces, fiscal deterioration and rejection, will combine as a massive motivating force to transform our system of education.

This chapter will concern itself with renewal or redesign of the schools as they now exist, as opposed to a consideration of alternative ways of schooling. There are approximately 113,000 school buildings in this country representing an investment of several billion dollars. There are 5 million teachers and administrators, a majority of them represented by two of the largest unions in the country, the NEA and the AFT, and we cannot expect them to preside over their own dissolution. In any event, these resources are obviously not expendable.

There are all kinds of publishers' materials in our schools, as well as millions of dollars' worth of educational media: television, radio, films, cassettes, etc. They exist and school systems are not about to put them in cold storage. Furthermore, our system of compulsory public education is overseen by elected or appointed public officials and presided over by licensed administrators and teachers, most of them tenured. Aside from other considerations, therefore, it would not be practical to seek their removal. There is good reason, then, for striving to change education within the present structure, for better utilizing existing school space, for being imaginative in finding new space, for assigning new roles to administrators and teachers, and for employing the new technologies to the advantage of both the professional staff and the students.

School systems divide the monies they spend into two parts: (1) the operational or instructional budget, which includes two major items—salaries for administrators and teachers and the technologies for learning (more often referred to as instructional materials)—and (2) the noninstructional budget, which includes capital expenditures such as school space, both land and buildings, and such services as pupil transportation; purchasing, storage, and distribution; and operation and maintenance.

The first part of this chapter is concerned with the noninstructional items, space and services. The second part will talk to the "innards," the pedagogical guts of the school: teachers and the technologies for learning. Each component will be viewed from the points of view of the dollar cost and the human resource cost.

NONINSTRUCTIONAL ACTIVITIES

The Use of Space

A large part of the noninstructional budget goes for school construction. School buildings are expensive no matter where they are built. It is estimated that a school can cost anywhere from 2 million to 40 million dollars, depending upon the price of land and the size of the school. Construction budgets are highly inflammable topics at any school board meeting. Although need, location, and design are important, the problems arise when the cost is estimated and presented to the board.

Less than half the dollars requested for school construction in 1970 was approved by the voters. Fewer new schools and additions were built last year than at any time since 1962. Partly, of course, the reason is inflation. In 1969, construction costs rose a record nine points on *School Management's* Cost of Building Index. This reflects at least a 7 percent increase over 1968. In many parts of the country, building costs rose 10 percent or more. Paraphrasing one social commentator: "Schoolmen have met the enemy—inflation—and they are his."

Need this be? Are we really chained to a deficit operation? Certainly, it is difficult to see how we can continue to build new schools at current costs. A new school costing from 2 to 40 million dollars takes from 2 to 4 years to build. By the time the school is built, the population for which it was designed has already graduated or diminished and the "forecasting" of the new population is very often way off base. To remodel an old school costs less, of course, but it still takes a long time, and very often runs into all kinds of problems such as the need for additional sewerage, fire exits, toilet facilities, student exits, and a long list of "surprise" headaches. Yet education must take place somewhere and that "somewhere" must cost money. What then can a conscientious school board or administrator do? How can they provide space for new and innovative programs and still be able to pay for it?

This national dilemma has encouraged many school systems to explore a growing range of alternative economical solutions to the problem. "Economical" in this context can have one of several meanings: providing new space at a reduced cost, usually ·by getting more space or better space for the same amount of money; getting greater use out of space a system already has; finding less expensive alternatives to conventional school space.

However, basic to exploring such alternative solutions is the need for a rethinking on our parts of what schools should look like. After all, concepts of schooling are changing. There was a time when concepts like "teacher," "class," "curriculum," "class period," "textbook," "classroom," and "school" each had an accepted definition. Everyone knew—or thought he knew—what a teacher did, what the "ideal" class size was, what a curriculum consisted of, and what a schoolhouse was like. And these definitions saved a lot of troublesome thinking, because in combination they served to answer a great many questions about how to provide education. Schools, almost by rote, built a program out of these basic blocks, bringing teachers together with uniform numbers of children of a given age, supplying them with syllabus and textbook, chopping up the day into standardized units of time, and deploying people and resources throughout the boxlike classrooms.

As in other fields, these unitary educational concepts helped people to see similarities but prevented them from seeing differences. Now these traditional building blocks or compartments are being broken down. The words usually applied to education—monolithic, collective, rigid, uniform—are giving way to such words as flexible, individual, varied. In order to move with the changing concepts of education, we must envisage a schoolhouse different in structure and climate. The conventional classroom with a fixed number of seats is making way for the open classroom and flexible spacing.

This does not mean that the idea of the schoolhouse is being abandoned. It does mean that instead of thinking of it as the usual 2- or 3-story structure, we think of it as any space that is safe, pleasant, and accessible, and is a specialized facility for the purpose of its intended function. This definition, which applies to both old and new space, loosens up some traditional assumptions.

William Caudill, the architect, uses the terms *expansible space* to mean that it can allow for ordered growth, *convertible space* to indicate that it can be economically adapted to program changes, *versatile space* where it may serve many functions, and *malleable space* if it can be changed "at once and at will." If we use these four terms as general definitions, we can start to examine some modern ideas for the use of school space.

In quoting the cost of space in different school systems, we must, of course, be aware that prices for land and equipment vary drastically, depending upon the real estate values in the community. A basic figure for space in a rural county would be much less than in a large urban area.

BUILDING NEW SCHOOLS

Schools On Land When we think of building schools, let us extend our perimeter and think of utilizing our total environment for school space. Keeping in mind that space should be expansible, convertible, versatile, and malleable, can we still build schools and reduce the cost of construction? (*see p. 167.)

One method now being applied in the construction of school buildings is the systems approach. In its broadest terms, it attempts to make the entire process of planning, designing, bidding, and on-site construction as rational, efficient, economical, and technologically modern as possible. Although the systems approach is still in a rudimentary stage of development, it is already producing significant reductions by cutting the time required to plan and construct a schoolhouse, by improving the quality of the space, and by diminishing the cost of labor and materials.

It brings the industrial techniques of prefabrication, mass production, and standardization to an essentially nonindustrialized construction business. It also makes use of basic dimensional units, so that the same components may be repeated again and again, with every component designed to fit with all other components. This minimizes the cost of creating new blueprints each time a unit is designed. The various components and subsystems are designed to fit together precisely, easily, and quickly, thus radically reducing the time required to construct a building on the site.

A system is composed of integrated subsystems which, together, form the component parts of a building. Typically, in construction, the most common subsystems are the structural subsystem, the heating-ventilating-air conditioning subsystem, the lighting-ceiling subsystem, and the interior partitions. The parts of a subsystem are generally known as components; for example, the components of an air conditioning system include chillers, fans, pumps, ducts, etc. A system may be put together in any one of a variety of ways, depending upon its particular purpose. These quickly assembled industrialized subsystems are substituted for the myriad smaller pieces that have traditionally been put together on the site. Using these subsystems still allows for variations in size or shape of an individual schoolhouse, since a system can be put together in varying ways. The subsystems arrive at the site preassembled so that they can be fitted together quickly (like a jigsaw puzzle) on site, avoiding traditional painstaking piecemeal assembly. By the time materials arrive at the site, the building is more than half finished. Installation of various components can occur simultaneously, again saving time, and interior items may be prefinished so that, for instance, no on-site painting is necessary, again saving time and labor costs.

There are several ways one can use this predesigned and prefabricated approach to building schools. One is what is referred to as a closed or total package approach; that is, a single company provides all the major subsystems designed to integrate exclusively with each other. The other is an open approach or one in which the school system buys the same building components from different manufacturers, which can be used interchangeably. Different subsystems manufactured by different suppliers must, of course, be compatible. This means, for example, that several ceiling-lighting systems can integrate with the structural system and yet satisfy performance requirements. This latter method encourages more competitive bidding.

The first approach or closed system has been used quite successfully by a group of school systems that combined to form the California School Construction Systems Development (SCSD). Begun in 1962 as the first school systems building project in the country, it is an example of a total package or closed system. SCSD started with 13 schools, for which producers developed an integrated package of 6 subsystems based on a 5 foot x 5 foot module: steel structural components, lighting-ceiling, heating-ventilating-air conditioning, interior partitioning, cabinets and casework, and lockers. These were designed as a package to work together according to performance specifications which were developed in four stages: (1) study of user requirements; (2) establishment of performance standards; (3) testing of subsystems for satisfaction of performance standards; (4) integration of individual subsystems into a *coordinated building system*.[1]

The success of the California School Construction Systems Development, which was the first systems-built school program in North America, encouraged other states and cities to explore their own paths to systems building. The systems approach to building schools and other public buildings had been used in other countries but never in the United States. SCSD gave everyone a chance to see that a systems construction program could work in the United States economy.

The initial success was scored under public bidding both for the components themselves and for contracts to build individual schools using such components. Furthermore, the completed schools successfully demonstrated that they possessed all the predicted virtues of flexibility of space areas so that their areas could be made smaller or larger when needed and interestingly enough, could be converted to other type facilities. And, since these virtues stemmed from the construction of a building with systems components, owners of commercial and industrial buildings likewise are beginning to adopt systems construction. Thus SCSD sired a family of systems buildings that is still growing.

Today, more than 1,300 schools, with a construction volume valued at $1 billion-plus, contain one or more subsystems developed through the SCSD program. In ever-growing numbers, building product manufacturers are competing for the burgeoning systems-building market. For each of the four major subsystems introduced by SCSD—structure, air conditioning, lighting-ceiling, and relocatable partitions—from 6 to 12 manufacturers are presently qualified to compete. Most of these subsystems are available on a nationwide basis. Local school boards all over the

[1]Educational Facilities Laboratories, *Systems*, 1971.

United States have adapted SCSD performance criteria to their own local requirements. While conventional building costs have been skyrocketing over the past several years, systems-building costs have remained relatively stable.

The spatial flexibility provided by these new subsystems has already proved its feasibility and economy. In several SCSD high schools, the staffs have made extensive changes required to adapt their schools to modern instructional techniques. From a practical viewpoint, these changes would have been impossible in conventionally built schools with fixed partitions.

Nonetheless, despite their achievements, many SCSD schools fell short of the potential created by the new designs. Successful use of the SCSD building system requires a skill, imagination, and sensitivity still lacking among many American architects. For example, despite the availability of excellent sound-damping components, the architects failed in varying degrees to create a suitably quiet learning environment. Often there was little communication among architects; thus success often depended chiefly on the skill of each project architect rather than on combined thinking.

Another way of utilizing a systems approach is to purchase individual subsystems rather than whole systems from a single manufacturer. As we said before, this often nets a lower price because of competitive bidding. A pioneer in this somewhat brave new approach was the Toronto School System and its Study of Educational Facilities (SEF). They began developing user requirements for schools at all grade levels. What must go into a school? How many conventional-sized classrooms, how many large convertible areas, how many small study rooms? Is there to be a science laboratory, an environmental laboratory, a multimedia library? Will each teacher need an office? Will the school want a recreation room? Whatever the requirements for the school, there had to be performance specifications for the subsystems.

The Metro Toronto School Board was then ready to solicit industry's help in organizing existing skills, technology, and capital resources for modern, efficient production. Bids were taken on subsystems representing about 80 percent of total construction cost. A detailed analysis was made of the cost structure, performance, and interfacing of each subsystem, and selection was made of those offering the best over-all value, with a balanced emphasis on quality and cost.

Toronto's major goal was to upgrade the general quality of education and to provide new school facilities of improved quality and greater responsiveness to user needs. In terms of physical facilities, SEF's objectives were manifold: to increase building flexibility, to improve value, to shorten construction time, to reduce initial costs, and to reduce operating costs.

Toronto feels it has received extra value for its money. The school board estimates that it would have cost about 30 percent more to build traditional schools with the facilities, services, and amenities equal to those in SEF schools.

The first SEF school, the Roden Elementary School, was constructed in 7 months, instead of the usual 14–18 months for conventional construction. Thus, a time saving of at least 50 percent was achieved. The SEF staff has found no trouble maintaining the time schedule they set, systems being the main reason for this. The average construction time for the most recent 10 schools has been 7–7½ months. The scheduling has also been improving with time. This year Toronto gained one month over the previous year's projects. As to costs, they set a target figure of $19.10 per square foot, allowing one-half percent for inflation each month.

The first 11 SEF schools were constructed as a group last year and are now occupied. Of the 10 which underwent construction this year, one is completed and occupied, 3 have been completed and are not yet occupied, and 6 are still under construction. The Roden School, for which SEF was its own architect, came in at $18.71 per square foot, 2 percent below the $19.10 target; the inflation factor brought costs up to $20.31, still under the anticipated inflation cost. The remainder of the first group, except one, came in above $19.10, while the second group has been held at or under $19.10. The second group was able to meet the target because of experience gained with the first group. Architects knew what to look for and could make more efficient choices. General cost control at the local level was improved. Also, catalogues which had been sketchy for the first project, were in finished form for the second.

Thus, despite snags, SEF has been able to demonstrate that

savings from systems are possible; it has ironed out its inflation problem, and has been bringing the base cost down and an-
ticipates its going even lower. Toronto has been able to cut construction time dramatically and, most importantly, has achieved
a much better quality of space for its money.

The state of Florida has been developing its Schoolhouse
Systems Project (SSP) since 1966. It is a bulk-purchase type of system, using performance specifications for available components
and subsystems. Its objectives are to provide higher quality
schools at reduced costs, to introduce the systems building concept to Florida, and to attempt to build a large, statewide market.

The SSP has produced progressively impressive savings.
Over the past 2 years, while conventional construction costs have
been rising rapidly, SSP has achieved an 18 percent reduction in
bid prices for 3 basic building subsystems. A recent group of 8
high schools was constructed with a 40 percent reduction in construction time. Another group of 14 elementary schools came in
with a 12 percent reduction.

How the size of a school system's market affects—or can affect—costs is also demonstrated by the Florida project. SSP estimates that if a systems building program is as low as 100,000
square feet or about $2 million, the cost of systems building is
about the same as for conventional techniques. If the program
rises to 500,000 square feet or about $10 million, the cost of sub-
systems drops to around 20 percent below conventional costs.

In addition, through experimentation with the inclusion
of more and more subsystems, Florida has found that the higher
the percentage of a building that is in systems construction, the
lower the cost per square foot.

The development of the systems approach, whether it be
with a single contractor or a multiple contractor, has progressed
to the point where any school district in the country should be
able to avail itself of the benefits of systems construction, assuming that there are local architects who are knowledgeable about
systems. In the United States alone, as of June 1970, there were
218 systems projects completed, under construction, or in design.

Attempts have been made to systematize not only construction but other aspects of the school-building process. One is
bulk-purchase of existing prefabricated and standard items off
the manufacturer's shelf, when possible, in large quantities.

Because items specified are fairly standard, local manufacturers can bid, and specialized or distant suppliers do not have to be relied on. The Florida SSP uses bulk-purchase in their systems approach.

Another method is "fast-tracking." In conventional building development, the programming, design, and bidding stages follow each other in a linear, sequential order. Each tends to take a given amount of time, and each successive step cannot be taken until the preceding one is finished. A management technique known as "fast-tracking" attempts to telescope these preconstruction steps so that they can overlap. It is conceivable with fast-tracking to be doing simultaneously preliminary design for one portion of the job, subsystem building for another, and working drawings on a third. As soon as rough design requirements are blocked out, subsystems may be bid. This means that contracts may be let simultaneously, at earlier dates, for different portions of the work. It requires commitment to build long before the final contract is let. It means, too, that the entire sequence is speeded up.

Because the architect must be able to anticipate what will be happening at any given point in time, careful control must be kept of all phases. This requires careful coordination and decision-making, rather than step-by-step scheduling. Every portion of every job must be initially scheduled from the first through the final day. Decisions at each stage become irrevocable. If all goes well, all the steps are completed according to schedule, materials arrive on-site at the proper time, and construction can proceed without intervening delays. Heery & Heery Associates of Atlanta find what they term the Critical Path method of scheduling helpful. It consists of diagramming the time-control sequence of operations. This method may either be fed into a computer or done by hand.

In this field, the first major success with fast-tracking occurred in Athens, Georgia, in 1966. A 2-elementary school project took only 188 days to design, bid, and construct. The architects, Heery & Heery, believe that even a 200,000 square foot high school should take not more than 15 months to design and build. The Hillsboro School, a high school for 1,600 students near Portland, Oregon, was designed and constructed in only 8 months using systems components. Compare this to New York

City where it takes up to 4 years to build a high school. By that time, the costs have escalated far beyond the original allocation and, equally disastrous, the pupil population has enlarged to an extent where often the "new" building is obsolete. In Oregon, in order to get the fast-tracking in motion and to use saved time to save money, architects DeKanter and Holgate took prebids on ceiling and lighting and structural room components thereby accomplishing a savings of over $5 per square foot on 193,000 square feet of high school space. The Hillsboro School came in at $18 per square foot. The architects estimate that the school system saved approximately $1 million over-all on the project compared to the cost of conventional construction in the Portland area.

Merrick, a small school district on Long Island, wanted to put up additions to 3 elementary schools (about 25,600 square feet total), within 10 months. By using fast-tracking and bulk-purchase building systems, the architects Caudill, Rowlett, and Scott estimate that the schools will be occupied 10–15 months earlier than if conventional methods were used. Assuming cost escalation of one percent per month, this is a savings of at least 10 percent.

Four subsystems contracts (structure, lighting-ceiling, air conditioning, roofing) were prebid 6 weeks after the design contract was let. Nonsystems contracts (general construction, electrical, plumbing) were bid 8 weeks later. Actual bids for the total contracted cost came in about 7.3 percent below the architects' estimate.

The Merrick project has shown that the combination of fast-tracking scheduling and building-systems techniques developed for large-scale projects can be successfully applied to a small project as well.

Broward County, Florida, has combined building systems with fast-tracking. The subsystems were prebid for six schools: 2 high schools (220,000 square feet each), 2 middle schools (105,000 square feet), and 2 elementary schools (42,000 square feet). The architects were commissioned in August 1970, and pre-bidding began 21 days later. The entire project was expected to be completed and ready for occupancy in September 1971. However, there have been delays in site selection for one middle school and a delay on one elementary school due to a high general contract bid. Four schools, however, were still on schedule for completion in September; total time for the four—just about one year. School builders no longer need to start systems building from first principles. There is now sufficient knowledge, experience, and technology to enable any district to build a single school through the systems approach. The processes and products have been carefully tried out, and more than 50 companies manufacture structural, lighting-ceiling, mechanical, demountable, and portable partition subsystems. The development projects in Florida and Georgia illustrate that school districts can build upon the systems work pioneered by others. And these 2 states are not alone; at the end of 1970, over 200 systems schools were in use or in development in 33 states.

Evans Clinchy, in a publication prepared for Educational Facilities Laboratories on New Directions in Schoolhouse Economy, says that the most significant savings resulting from both building systems and fast-tracking is *time*, and this is achieved by speeding up the entire building development process. A systems building, he says, can be put together more quickly on site than one that is handcrafted. Fast-tracking speeds up the entire process of decision-making and design. With prebidding, the manufacturer can get a head start on delivery; time will not be wasted waiting for materials to arrive on site. The fast-tracking management techniques are applied to construction too, making this phase more tightly organized and simplifying and streamlining an enormously ponderous and complicated construction process. There are also other indirect time savings, because the school buildings are finished more quickly and are, therefore, ready for occupany much sooner. This may lead to savings in busing costs (busing students to distant neighborhoods until school is ready) or to eliminating the need for leasing of temporary space to house students during construction.

Major economies of mass production are also to be gained from use of a good building system. Of course, as the industry grows, components will be produced in greater quantity by more manufacturers, introducing further economies of competition. Components will then be even easier to obtain and still cheaper.

Labor costs can also be considerably reduced. On-site labor is generally more expensive than factory labor—so that the more assembling that is done in the factory the less expensive the subsystems and the lower the labor costs. Labor construction costs have been escalating at the rate of one-half to one percent per month. Time savings gained from a systems approach can reduce these costs substantially.

Indirect economies can also accrue from the greater reliability yielded by fast-tracking. By eliminating the degree of chance usually present in construction planning, the owner can have a pretty good idea of when his building will be ready and when to plan for occupancy. The manufacturer will know when to schedule delivery, and the subcontractor will know how to schedule his availability. In addition, prebidding helps all concerned to know ahead of time what the project will cost.

Under the systems approach, one can acquire space of much higher quality, for the same amount of money, than is possible in a nonsystem building. Systems often include special features not found elsewhere. Or they may include various amenities, such as climate control, carpeting, and movable partitioning, as part of the package. A construction systems approach can assure the high quality of materials by demanding performance standards of strength, fire resistance, durability, and insulation. Another important benefit to be achieved with a systems approach is flexibility. Because the various components are designed to be compatible and to be put together in a planned variety of ways, they are rearrangeable.

Schools on Water When one thinks of buildings or other places where pupils live and work and go to school, one thinks automatically about land-based buildings. Except for the relatively few people who live on houseboats, most people live on solid ground. Why, however, should we ignore water as a site for educational structures? This is an area until now largely overlooked.

In places where land is expensive or difficult to find or where school space is needed immediately, floating schools may provide a solution. A recent study suggests that barges or floating platforms built as schools can be more economical and can be constructed in much less time than conventional land-based schools.

It has been found that the total development cost for a single prototype Floating Classroom Complex is about $42.69 per square foot. This can be compared to from $47.17 to $54.66 per square foot for land acquisition, site development, design, and construction of the most recent land-based Boston schools. This is an average of about a 15 percent direct saving on construction.

Although no established figure is available, it is assumed that maintenance costs would be higher for a Floating Classroom Complex, because of the need for frequent painting. The saving in docking fees, on the other hand, would probably more than compensate for the revenue lost to the city by maintaining land-based schools on tax-free land.

There are generally no special problems associated with towing a vessel of the size of a Floating Classroom Complex. For this reason, additional savings may be achieved even if it would be necessary to build the complex at a shipyard in another area and tow it to its final location. Due to competitive bidding, shipbuilding costs are somewhat lower on the Gulf Coast and Great Lakes than on the Atlantic Coast. A floating complex built in the Great Lakes is estimated to cost $1.39 per square foot less than one built in Boston. A prototype design based on conditions in Boston, Massachusetts, was estimated to cost 15 percent less to acquire and to take 43 percent less time to construct than the most recent conventional schools, land costs included.

The prototype design would house learning space for 500 students on three decks, 19,500 square feet each, of gross floor area. The top deck would be a walled outdoor play area. Space below the lowest deck is allocated to machinery, tankage, and storage. The overall dimensions of the barge structure are 265 feet by 78 feet, with a depth of 43 feet.

The design meets the requirements of the American Bureau of Shipping and the National Electrical Code and the safety code of the United States Coast Guard. The cost is based on actual shipbuilding cost experience in the Boston area, assuming no mass production economies. Included in the cost are labor, materials, overhead, and wastage.

Costs can be substantially reduced by procuring more than one floating school at a time. Once production begins on a large scale, costs will begin to decrease even more rapidly. This is due to usual mass production economies: using one set of templates for a large order, ordering equipment and materials in large lots, and applying assembly line methods. Thus, when the estimated cost of one prototype unit would be $42.69 per square foot, it has been estimated that the cost for three units would be $38.56 per square foot, and for 10 units, as low as $32.99 per square foot.

Perhaps the greatest economy of the floating school idea is that it reserves valuable city land for other than school uses. Land not used for a school could be used, for example, for commercial development that would help pay in tax revenues for the cost of the floating school.

But what about the educational potential of schools on water? What an exciting experience—new sounds, new smells, new voices, new people in the surrounding area. What an opportunity to change the whole image of school for many students. Just imagine the conversation: "What school do you go to?" "I go to the Ellenville Junior High School on High Street. And you?" "I go to the SS Perry on the lake at Front Street."

Schools In Space Up to this point we have spoken about creating new structures or redesigning old ones along fairly traditional lines. Whether the structure was bought as a package, whether built on a barge, whether partitioned in one way or another, it emerged looking very much like the school most of us are familiar with. Now, architects are beginning to use new technologies to produce totally different types of school structures. These are sometimes referred to as "space" schools. Of course, they are not built in space, but they utilize space in such a way that large areas can be converted more cheaply and quickly into structures that can house children.

Back in the 1920's, Buckminster Fuller began developing geodesic domes. These domes enclose large areas of space unsupported by columns, thereby providing completely open, unobstructed expanses readily adaptable to many types of activities. Roof, walls, and structural support are all integrated into one unit. The structure consists of three basic elements: the struts which form the frame, the skin which covers them, and the joints in between. Struts can be made of metal or wood; skins can be made of plywood, vinyl, fiberglass, or metal sheets. It is exceedingly strong and lightweight. Geodesic domes have been used at World Fairs, at Expo 67 in Montreal, and Expo 70 in Osaka, Japan.

Although encapsulated space, or "bubbles," have been around for close to 50 years, much experimentation has had to go into them in order to make them practical. This includes the problems of creating inexpensive coverings that last for 20 to 40 years, the prevention of the buildup of solar heat, and vandal resistance, as well as that of providing regulated temperatures inside such large open spaces. All these problems are presently being solved.

Inflated bubbles were used for schools and colleges almost a decade ago as coverings for physical education space. One of the pioneers was the Forman School in Litchfield, Connecticut, which, in 1961, erected two bubbles, one enclosing a swimming pool, and the other enclosing tennis courts.

Antioch College is now planning to enclose one acre of land with a 44,000-square-foot, 30-feet-high, bubble, for a satellite campus in Columbia, Maryland. The bubble is a response to the need for inexpensive space and for "nomadic" space—space that can be easily moved to another location after several years. It will house classrooms, studios, information resources, living accommodations, a college green, and administration space for 300 students. The architect is Rurik Ekstrom.

The structure will consist of two clear vinyl membranes reinforced by cable, with an air layer between them for insulation. The outer skin will be reflective to reduce solar heat gain. Conventional heating equipment will be used, and a pipe grid inside the bubble will support lighting equipment.

One of the devices being considered at Antioch College for separating interior spaces is a small dome suitable for specialized purposes. One, the O'Dome, is a pod which snaps closed and can be erected in three hours. Another is a 20-foot-wide styrofoam dome that can be carried from place to place. Where various levels are desired, scaffolding can be constructed.

It was anticipated that the campus would be ready by fall, 1971. Total construction time, including earthwork and mechanical, was estimated at one month, the structure itself to take only a few days to construct. Total cost (including site, mechanical, plumbing, and major interior equipment) was estimated at a phenomenally low $4 per square foot maximum. Current costs of Maryland schools range from $17 to $25 per square foot.

The college has now put up a prototype structure covering 1,000 square feet, made up of exactly the same materials as the proposed campus structure.

Buckminster Fuller's much improved version of the 1920 geodesic dome is being used in the East Windsor, New Jersey, Regional School District, which needed 300 elementary school seats in a hurry. Planning started in January 1970 for a hoped-for opening date of September 1970. The decision to use a geodesic dome helped cut design and construction time for the school from New Jersey's average 2½ years to less than one year.

The pentagon-shaped dome was assembled on-site out of anodized aluminum, diamond-shaped panels and tubular aluminum hexagonal struts. Each ring of panels was built out from the center and was cable-suspended from the center.

Site preparation and pouring of the foundation occurred on site while the geodesic components were being prefabricated at the factory. The structure was completed (including floor and buttresssing) one month from the date the panels arrived at the site.

The area of the dome is 16,000 square feet and its height is about 30 feet; the entire school is 23,000 square feet, including the mezzanine. The interior space consists of an open learning area equivalent to 12 classrooms, a multipurpose room, a kitchen, a science materials center, and an art materials center, plus a large library, administration, and health suites on the mezzanine.

Except for a few leaks, the dome school, in its first year, appears to be quite comfortable. Leakage can be a problem with a dome because each panel must be carefully caulked and sealed and all holes must be plugged.

The total development cost, including all site work and landscaping, was $520,000. This is a cost of $22.61 per square foot of floor space, and is at least a $5 per square foot savings over conventional schools in New Jersey with the same facilities (about $27 to $29 per square foot).

There are three distinct advantages to encapsulated space of this nature:

1. You can enclose large amounts of space—as much as 4 or 5 acres—without resorting to columns for support, thus providing completely open, unobstructed, but protected, areas for activities requiring large spaces or even for entire schools.

2. You can erect such structures quickly, and just as quickly

take them down and move them elsewhere. Using such a structure, a school can, in a matter of days, convert a stadium into a fieldhouse for day and night all-season use.

3. All of this can be done at greatly reduced cost.

Another device that incorporates the modern trend toward large interior areas is what is termed the open-plan school. It is, in a way, a cross between a geodesic 'dome and a traditonal school. It captures the concept of wide open space, but applies the principle to a conventional school building. A minimum number of partitions is used, most corridors are eliminated, and, where there are partitions, they are movable and flexible.

The major aim of this type of open-space school is to provide an environment which encourages greater interaction between teacher and pupil, and between teacher and teacher. There are no partitions to fragment learning by dividing teachers, children, and subject matter into tight standardized compartments. And there are no halls to funnel children from compartment to compartment at the arbitrary dictate of a bell. Each child is encouraged to find his own place, create his own path.

Not only do such open-space schools provide a new environment for learning but, by using open-plan design, they are able to achieve financial economics by:

> Building the same gross floor area but getting more usable space, thus increasing the operating capacity of a building and lowering the per-pupil cost. Conventional schools use 66 percent of the gross floor space for educational purposes; open space schools use 80 percent or more.

> Building less gross floor area than normally needed to get a predetermined amount of usable space, thus reducing the actual cost of the building (in addition to increasing its operating capacity) and continuing to realize a lower per-pupil cost.

> Simplifying the design and leaving out expensive partitioning, thus lowering the square-foot cost of construction. Heating, ventilating, and electrical work thereby become less complicated. A simpler system also means faster construction.

In addition to these savings, teachers and administrators claim, open-plan space affords both greater flexibility and more efficient use by allowing a variety of group sizes to meet in one space, thus eliminating poorly utilized or half-occupied classrooms.

An open-plan school requires an approach to furnishings and equipment very different from that of the traditional school. Visual space dividers are usually in the form of shelf-storage and blackboard units. Furniture should be movable, and preferably have multiple uses (such as a storage unit used as a space divider or a desk that converts to a chair).

New kinds of furniture are already being designed for these new spaces. Cameron McIndoo, Inc. and similar companies developed a system of molded polyurethane foam containers and panels in modular sizes for the Toronto school system. These can be used as shelves, desks, and storage units. Cherry Creek, Colorado, has adopted the "lego," a plywood box in various sizes, that can be used as a chair, table, or desk.

Carpeting is the rule in an open-plan school, and other acoustical controls such as ceiling sound insulation are usually required. Both of these items have been included in the quotations of open-plan construction costs which follow, yet the total costs are still lower than those of conventional schools.

Open-plan schools are springing up throughout the country. One example is the above-mentioned Cherry Creek school system in metropolitan Denver. The Walnut Hills school there, an open-plan school, opened in September. It consists of four large learning modules built around an open, book-lined educational mall. William C. Haldeman, the architect, says that almost 85 percent of Walnut Hills is instructional space compared to 65 percent in an adjoining conventional elementary school.

The total construction cost for this facility was about $155,000 including carpeting, acoustical ceilings, and built-in cabinetwork, but excluding fees, site work, and movable equipment. According to Haldeman, the cost per square foot was $19.25, which compares favorably with the estimated cost in 1970 of a conventional school of the same capacity—$22 per square foot—or a savings of $2.75 per square foot. Cost per student was about $1,200 including furnishings, which is at least $500 less than the comparable figure for a conventional school.

In addition to elementary schools, several open-plan secondary schools have been built. One of these is the new senior high school in East Aurora, New York. This school, serving grades 9–12, with a 1,200 student capacity, has a gross floor area of 168,500 square feet. It includes 6 general learning areas, a large science center, specialized learning facilities, a swimming pool, 2 large group instruction rooms, and an 800-seat auditorium. It is extensively carpeted and is air conditioned throughout.

The total construction cost was $20.68 per square foot. Carpeting cost $.49 per square foot. The total, $21.17, is at least $2 per square foot less than the New York State average for high school construction during the same period ($23.20), even with additional cost for carpeting. Warren Ashley, architect for the East Aurora school, has achieved similar economies in Union High School, Rockingham, Vermont; Kearsage Regional High School, Sutton, New Hampshire; and Lisbon Falls, Maine, Senior High School.

Several junior high schools in the San Francisco area have added open-classroom clusters to house teacher teams responsible for such subjects as science and social studies. How well these open-plan secondary schools will function remains to be seen. But at the lower levels, at any rate, the success of schools without walls ultimately depends on people. As Superintendent Charles Knight of the Cupertino Union School District in California (which includes the Faria and DeVargas Schools and an open junior high addition as well as Dilworth) puts it, "Making open-space work takes constant work in training faculty and students."

Most teachers are used to self-contained classrooms. They close the door and "shut out the outside world." Any action or sound in the classroom is generated by that teacher and his students. In an open-space school, there are no walls to "shut out the outside." Action and sound are generated by all and this may mean several hundred students and a dozen or so teachers. Therefore, teachers must be prepared to raise their tolerance for sound and free movement. But above all, they must be able to adapt to the use of open spaces. The aim is flexibility, mobility, people-flow. When a teacher is working with some children, the others should be programed to join other children in independent or group activities or other teachers in the open space. In visiting a dozen open-space schools, I have seen instances where, within 2 months of moving into an open-space situation, teachers have moved bookcases, lockers, and chalkboards into positions where they served for walls, and thereby created their own compartmentalized classrooms—hardly the objective of open spaces. In other situations, I have seen utter chaos with students running around, joining groups at will without being programed into them. Teachers knew little of where the child was or what he should be learning. The sound level was intolerable and no one was either learning or happy in the situation. This is, perhaps, an extreme, but it points up the misuse of open space. It points up, as Superintendent Knight said, that the success of open space depends on a well prepared teaching staff. Teachers should be asked to volunteer to teach in open-space schools and then should be given training and strong support.

Schools In Partnership Another means of cutting the cost of educational space is by working in combination with an income-producing private enterprise and sharing the occupancy of the land and the building. Under conventional methods of planning and building schools, the entire cost of a school plus interest on bonds must be carried by local and state taxes. In addition, the land used for schools is, in most cases, removed permanently from the tax rolls, thus decreasing the local tax base. To avoid this burden, land and airspace can be occupied jointly by a school and income-producing private enterprises such as housing, retail stores, or offices. In most cases, the structure or complex is jointly designed, constructed, and operated. The ideal arrangement is to include enough taxpaying commercial space to carry the cost of the debt service on the school. The school, in this sense, "pays for itself" from the expanded tax base.

The most dramatic example of the economies of joint occupancy is perhaps the New York City Educational Construction Fund, a state authority created in 1966 expressly for the purpose of planning and constructing joint occupancy projects in New York City. At the moment, the Fund is building $140 million worth of new schools for the city in combination with $300 million worth of new housing and other commercial space. Because of the tax income from the commercial space, the city will not have to invest capital funds in the construction of these schools.

The Fund is empowered to issue its own bonds to cover the cost of the schools, to plan the project and select the private developer, and to pay back the debt service on bonds out of the income from the private space. After the Fund's bonds have been paid off, the income from the commercial space will revert to the city as normal revenue and as a permanent addition to the city tax base.

Indeed, New York City considers joint occupancy so relevant to its problems that the city is considering a law that would require future commercial buildings (and public housing) to include school space. This space would then be leased or sold to the city for educational purposes.

A desperate need to modernize its facilities convinced the Friends Select School in Philadelphia to become a landlord and lease one of its three acres of inner city land for commercial office space. Friends Select is an independent school founded by William Penn in 1689. Since 1885, it has been located on 3 acres of land across from Philadelphia City Hall. When pressed by the need to make major changes in its facilities, Friends Select was reluctant to fly to the suburbs to find new space. Instead, it decided to develop a joint-building project with a private company.

The arrangement has allowed Friends Select to build a new facility to replace its antiquated plant. The old building had about 65,000 square feet of space. In the new climate-controlled facility, the school has about 120,000 square feet, including a large auditorium, swimming pool, and gymnasium. Friends Select has been able to finance its new school plant from the income it receives from a 20-story, 525,000-square-foot office building built on its land.

The office building, constructed by the Pennwalt Chemical Company, yields enough rental to provide Friends Select with a working endowment and economic security for the future. The rents cover the $175,000 per year debt service on the $3.2 million school facilities. The two buildings were jointly planned, but there is no physical or programmatic relationship between them. They are, in fact, 18 inches apart.

The concept of joint occupancy is being successfully implemented in cities all around the country—in New York, Philadelphia, Boston, Chicago, and Pontiac, Michigan, to name a few. The concept applies to private as well as public schools. It is clearly an important way of reducing the financial impact of new school construction. Joint occupancy does not necessarily reduce the actual cost of construction although there appear to be economies if the total complex is built by the private developer under a single construction contract. But it can, under ideal circumstances, provide a way of creating new schools without raising the tax rate.

Another form of joint occupancy is a partnership of several municipal or governmental institutions with schools. This is a public–public partnership as opposed to the public–private partnership previously described. For example, day care centers, public libraries, community colleges, health and welfare services, cultural and recreational facilities, all make likely sites for schools. They often have their peak periods at times of the day other than when children come to school, or they can easily and without danger of overcrowding, share facilities while the children are at school. In fact, a combination of a day care center or a geriatric center and a school makes an extremely compatible partnership, since small children, school-age children, and old people can interact and be of service to each other. Although this combination is not currently in existence, a similar one, inasmuch as it combines a community resources center and an elementary school, is under construction in Pontiac, Michigan.

There, the Human Resource Center is situated on the edge of the predominantly black area. The aim of the HRC is to revitalize not only the black ghetto, but the downtown section of the city as well. Integration, elimination of overcrowding, and better community services are its basic goals.

Community space, including a public library, restaurant, medical suite, lounge, and gymnasium, is being built over elementary school space for 1,800–2,000 students. The classrooms will be placed around specialized facilities such as music rooms and a mini-theater.

Money to build the HRC has been jointly provided by a $4.5-million school bond issue and the Federal government. The Department of Housing and Urban Development granted $1.5 million under the Neighborhood Facilities Act to underwrite the community facilities. Nonprofit community groups, including a health and day care center, will share space with the school when the project is complete.

It is evident that in land and planning costs the HRC is economical, considering the type and quality of space being provided. Moreover, shared planning and programming have removed the need to duplicate facilities. Bert Van Koughnett, the school system's project director, is convinced that the city has saved money ("at least 50 percent of the cost of the gym alone") by over-all community planning.

As an investment for the future, the HRC is expected to reap increasingly valuable dividends over the years. By revitalizing human resources in the area, it should be able to stimulate sufficient interest in the city to reverse the trend toward downtown deterioration.

The School and Recreation Departments of Arlington, Virginia, have pooled $6.5 million of earmarked bond money to build a combined new junior high school and municipal recreation center on a 26-acre prime site. The idea of cooperative construction emerged from a controversy over the land. Both groups had laid claim to the 26-acre site, which would probably have had to be divided.

Preliminary planning revealed, however, that both groups needed more facilities than either could pay for alone. They, therefore, decided to plan and build a combined facility. The aim was to avoid unnecessary duplication, and to demonstrate the results of good community planning.

The school people wanted to provide art, industrial arts, a theater and auditorium, music rooms, cafeteria space, a gym, and outdoor recreation areas. The recreation people wanted to provide these same facilities after school and on weekends, and during summer vacations. By putting the two facilities together and planning for shared use, they have been able to get *more* and *better* space for the combined $6.5 million than either group would have been able to obtain separately.

This center, named the Junior High School and Community Center will be a regular junior high for 1,400 students. It will also provide programs for dropouts and for the elderly, games, art and project rooms, an auditorium and theater, a snack bar, music-practice rooms, and large outdoor playing fields and tennis courts. The money saved by not duplicating facilities has been used to improve the specialized space. In addition, the community has been able to acquire more space than would have been possible if two separate facilities had been built.

The school and community will share a 68,000-square-foot enclosed multiuse space, called the Controlled Environment Facility, that could not have been built without cooperative planning and the pooling of funds.

Shared space and facilities, whether they be a partnership with the private sector or the public sector, have many advantages. They usually mean much more efficient and, therefore, more economical use of space than is possible in the case of traditional buildings. But, like any other partnership, unless everyone knows the ground rules and agrees to joint goals and planning, these can easily be ill-conceived unions. Such a case exists in Portsmouth, Virginia, in which a joint school library and public library are to be built, with only a coil grille which can be loosened, to separate them.

Students are expected to have primary use of the facilities during the day. High school students and the public will share them at night. The entire school is to be used as a community center for all age groups, and is to include a planetarium, field house, and little theater.

As interesting as this may sound from the point of view of community sharing of facilities and from the fact that if it had not been done this way the community could not have afforded to build a library at all, the project is meeting with stiff opposition.

The library facilities had been planned with an eye on the economies of joint use. While the public library space will be only 3,300 square feet as compared with about 6,000 square feet for a normal branch library, students and the community will share the same reference room and books. Furnishings, bookshelves, carpeting, etc., for both libraries will be jointly purchased.

The project's architects emphasize increased service to the community as a far more important factor than dollar savings in the project. Yet the money savings will probably amount to

$60,000 on the library, and joint use has enabled Hodges Manor to build a library that the community could not have afforded otherwise.

The problem at Hodges Manor, however, is that although school and community are nominally cooperating to build a joint facility, the library people are far from satisfied with their role. They say that no real joint planning was attempted before the Hodges Manor plans were drawn, and as a result their needs have not been properly met. Although they do not object to the idea of a school–library cooperative, they would have preferred a location near a shopping center for better accessibility. Also, they feel that the library is being included for one reason only— obtaining a cheaper facility through shared financing.

This type of "partnership," economical though it may be, is likely to produce only limited benefits. It underscores the crucial importance of adequate and thorough preplanning before a binding partners project is undertaken. Regardless of cost benefits, real economies can only be achieved if both partners are happy with the results. Joint occupancy requires the willingness of two parties to sit down and work out a long series of details, even if these two parties are not in the habit of collaborating with others. This is particularly true during the participants' first joint occupancy project; further projects become much easier.

Very often legal mechanisms must exist or be created to make joint occupancy possible. In Massachusetts and New York, the laws had to be changed to accomplish this. In Pontiac and Chicago, governmental regulations had to be altered. In the cases of Trinity and Friends Select Schools, new legal entities had to be formed.

The concept of joint occupancy offers great benefits to those alert enough to take advantage of it. Indeed, schools that pay for themselves may, in the near future, be the only kind of schools that many cities will be able to afford.

UTILIZING EXISTING SCHOOLS

Open Them Up It is all well and good to talk about building more efficient and attractive new schools, but that is something like building a new house when you already have a fairly comfortable old one. It is exhilarating to build creatively, but, more often than not, we do not have sufficient funds and we have no assurance that we can sell our old house at a reasonable price. Building a new house, therefore, becomes both a risk and a luxury. This holds true with schools. The first part of this chapter speaks of new and less expensive ways of building new schools, but what can we do with our old ones? New York City has 986 school buildings; Chicago over 600. We can not replace them all. It would take a good part of the national budget to launch such a building program.

Many of our existing school buildings have long corridors, thick walls, classrooms which look like egg crates, large and often inadequately employed auditoriums and cafeterias. In order to find space in these old buildings, walls have had to be knocked down and other changes made in line with revised teaching concepts. Various school systems have begun to rearrange their interior space to meet the need for additional working areas.

The Cherry Creek school system in Colorado needed at least 100 new seats in its Eastridge Elementary School. Originally the district planned to add a 6-classroom wing to the school's existing plant, thus increasing capacity by 150 students. The cost of this project was estimated at $240,100. Instead, for almost the same amount of money, Cherry Creek has doubled the 300-student capacity of Eastridge by modernizing, opening up the interior of the existing building, and adding 7,100 square feet of space.

The renovation not only increases capacity but is compatible with the new educational program that evolved within the district during 1966–67. This program is mainly directed toward individualized instruction, multiage groupings, and team teaching.

The renovation program concentrated on opening up space. Walls between classrooms and hallways were removed. The 12 original classrooms were converted into 4 learning areas. Learning space from these classrooms was increased by 4,000 square feet. A 7,100-square-foot building, including a kitchen, administrative offices, and a multipurpose room was added; and the old multipurpose room was converted to an instructional materials center and two more learning areas.

The Rios School in the Cajon Valley Union School District, California, part of the San Diego County Department of Education, is another example of a school that was able to increase its existing space by opening up the interior of the building. Cajon Valley was able to add new space in such a way that both existing and new space could operate as open plan. The district wished to increase capacity, and to modernize the learning environment to permit team teaching, flexible programming, and large- and small-group meetings.

Built in 1958, Rios is a finger-plan school, typical of many in the southwest. Four buildings are connected by a covered walkway. The school had a capacity of 430 in 14 standard classrooms. Rather than build new wings as called for in the master plan, the school district roofed over and enclosed the two end spaces between the fingers. In addition, nonbearing walls between classrooms were removed, and air conditioning and carpeting were installed throughout. This created 2 open-learning centers, one serving K-3, one serving grades 4–6.

The new building added 13,600 square feet of gross and 10,600 square feet of net instructional space, increasing the capacity to 660 students. According to Dr. M. Ted Dixon, Area Superintendent, the net gain was probably even greater than 10,600 square feet since service space was converted to instructional space and walls were eliminated in the existing building.

The principal of the Rios School has reported that the "open space facility has enhanced the educational program considerably; it allows for individualizing instruction and makes freedom of movement of the children and flexible scheduling a reality." Construction time took only 7 months, less time than it would have taken to build new wings.

The Cajon Valley School District found it less expensive to construct open space than to build a conventional school addition. The California school construction allowance for the space built was $406,000 (about $30 per square foot), but the Rios project cost considerably less and achieved a saving of at least $40,000. The total cost of the addition and renovation including carpeting, furnishings, and equipment came to $25 per square foot.

A recent Portland Public Schools study concluded that "old buildings can be reused and considerable money saved by extensive remodeling and addition when compared to the cost of a new school." The city had found that its school plant was not as serviceable as it could be for modern educational programs and practices. In an attempt to reorganize the educational structure (converting from K–8, 9–12 to 4–4–4), and to update educational facilities, they were faced with the choice of building new schools to accommodate the revised program or of doing something about the existing schools. Since the Portland school population is fairly stable, it was difficult to justify building new schools. After intensive study, the school department found it could accomplish its aims by maintaining almost all of the existing schools through renovation and modernization. Only about a dozen pre-World War I buildings would be demolished. This approach to up-dating the school plant required total planning, a process which in some cases included the application of systems techniques.

Just as a systems approach can be used for new buildings, so in a limited way it can be used in remodeling or modernization. It is a much more difficult problem than building new buildings, since older buildings tend to vary so greatly in size and shape. Many older buildings were not designed on a uniform grid or module, thus making it difficult to use uniform subsystems.

There are instances, especially in large cities, where many schools were designed and built during the same period and where a single design was repeated, perhaps only with variations in size. In these situations, it makes a great deal of sense to think of modernization in terms of a large number of schools, all having basically the same general requirements. If this is followed by careful planning and designing of the intended individual modernizations, the economies of the bulk-purchase type of system can be realized.

The city of Portland, Oregon, for instance, is undertaking the first phase of a $150 million project to remodel 20 elementary schools into middle schools, renovate 13 high schools, create 5 early childhood centers, and renovate and maintain all lower schools. Many of these schools are similar to each other in period and design. What Portland has done is to create a Systems Building Program Office to supervise the planning, design, and construction of this large modernization enterprise. Although the staffs of the individual schools will have a wide range of options about what their space will look like, the basic modernization will be done on the bulk-purchase systems model.

For all of the schools in the project, a 5-foot module was selected. All modernization designs have been performed within the module. This allows the use of subsystems, especially ceiling and lighting, HVAC, partitions, doors, wall coverings, and casework subsystems. These subsystems will be bid in bulk, thus permitting component manufacturers to base their bids on large, continuous runs, and reducing the unit or subsystem cost. Bulk-purchasing will also permit the manufacturers to put a larger amount of time and effort into tailoring the subsystems to Portland's specifications and, in some instances such as on casework, actually to design new and better products.

Portland, according to Systems Building Program Director Edward C. Wundram, expects to realize a direct cost reduction of 10–15 percent on the total project as a result of their systems approach. This saving is in addition to indirect savings in time (more rapid occupancy and less inflation of construction costs), on higher quality components, and lower maintenance costs for modernized as opposed to unmodernized space.

However, Portland is also moving in other directions in the area of redesigning old buildings, since few old buildings lend themselves to uniform modules or grids. Therefore, new space had to be found in other ways. Since a major emphasis of the Portland program was the creation of middle schools for grades 5–8, some of the existing elementary schools had to be converted. The buildings were generally sound and well maintained. The school department developed prototype designs for 1,200-student middle schools.

In order to expand capacity and provide increased resource and support facilities for the middle school program, the elementary schools now housing about 600 had to be increased in size. However, in the prototypical cases, the addition of space is far from extravagant. Rather it brings the gross floor area up to approximately 120 square feet per student, which is about average for newly constructed middle school space throughout the country.

The prototype design for the Beaumont School, a school of about 50,000 square feet gross, calls for an addition of 95,000 square feet gross, conversion of the old gym into a learning resource center, and conversion of the old auditorium into a large group instruction space. The George School design demolishes three classroom wings, leaving the gyms, cafeteria, auditorium, and administrative spaces—a total of 26,000 square feet. To this will be added a 2-story structure of 119,000 square feet. The converted building will not necessarily be open plan but Edward C. Wundram, Systems Building Program Director, does feel that opening up the buildings will provide more usable space than otherwise. The reorganization plan will eventually convert all the lower schools to allow for open-plan teaching.

The construction cost for providing a 1,200 student middle school was estimated for both new construction and conversions, using a building-systems approach. This figure includes gutting and remodeling, demolishing portions of the existing structure where necessary, site work, and fixed equipment. It appears that the school department could save about $775,000 per building by renovation and addition to existing buildings instead of new construction. The estimated savings per student would be about $650. Costs were based on estimates of $15.75 per square foot for gutting and remodeling; $21.70 per square foot for building additions; and $23.50 per square foot for new school construction.

When schoolmen in Elkhart, Indiana, began planning an addition to the Brookdale Junior High School, they were expecting an increase in student enrollment due to redistricting. But many staff members hoped the addition would provide more than just space to handle the overload.

Some teachers wanted to implement team teaching, but the old building was not suitable for the different sized groups it would require. The staff was also anxious to take advantage of more of the multimedia techniques available to them, but the school's traditional design—which necessitated rolling equipment through the halls from room to room—hampered most innovation. Other physical problems included severe congestion and confusion in the corridors, caused by the school's L shape (there was only one route between any two points in the building), and a woefully inadequate cafeteria–kitchen.

When the architects commissioned by the board took all of these factors into account, along with others that came to light

in an outside consultant's study of available and needed resources, their addition to Brookdale created a very different
school.

The addition, located between the wings of the original
building, is largely open space. Fully carpeted, it is designed for
large- or small-group instruction. A section of the large-group
area is used as a cafeteria for part of the day, but the entire area
can be opened up for concerts and assemblies. There is also a
library–media center, equipped with dial-access retrieval, and
teacher prep areas. Arranged around the perimeter are enclosed
rooms for metal, graphics, and wood shops, "wet" and "dry"
science labs and recitation areas, classrooms for home economics,
two language labs, audiovisual and electronics workshops, a
new kitchen and a boys' locker room, which relieves pressure
on gymnasium facilities in the old wing.

The design of the addition made a number of changes
possible in the original building. The new cafeteria–kitchen
allowed the architect to remodel the space devoted to cafeteria
and kitchen in the old building into a suite of administrative
and guidance offices. At the same time, extensive mechanical
and electrical improvements were made. Closed circuit television was installed, and traffic congestion in the old structure
was greatly eased. The addition absorbed part of the student
population and now offers alternate routes between different
points in the building.

The entire cost of the project was $1,020,421, with the addi-
tion running $969,533 and the remodeling $50,888. The cost per
square foot was approximately $20.03, which is about $2.50 less
than the cost of totally new buildings.

Most old schools do waste space; cafeterias used *only* for
eating, auditoriums *only* for large audiences, corridors *only*
as passageways, and walls, walls, walls, only to keep the children in and the outside world out. Yet often the buildings are
structurally sound and should not be abandoned as useless. As
was illustrated above, they can be modernized and redesigned
to accommodate modern, contemporary education, some by re-
arranging interior space, some by adding new space that enables
more effective use of existing space.

USE THEM FULLY

The Extended Day Besides building new schools more cheaply
or remodeling old schools there is another approach that may

be the least expensive of all. It entails no construction, no land bids, no partnerships. It merely calls for fuller use of what one has—our existing school buildings—but using them for an extended day and extended year. This concept is new only to educators. Office buildings, industrial plants, governmental agencies, utilize both their staffs and their buildings over a 12-month period and for at least a 10-hour day. Shifts that carry through 24 hours are not unusual in many industries. When the need for more work or more workers occurs, rarely do you see new buildings constructed. Existing facilities are put to fuller use, and that is what is suggested here.

If a school district's enrollment has burgeoned suddenly and there are not enough classrooms available (unless, of course, you want to increase class size), one way of solving the problem is to extend the school day by several periods. In this way everyone is fitted in and class size is not increased. For instance, a classroom in continuous use during a 6-period day will accommodate $6 \times 25 = 150$ students. The same classroom operating on an 8-period day will accommodate $8 \times 25 = 200$ students. This represents a one-third increase in scheduling capacity.

However, this rather simple approach brings difficulties with it. You may have solved your scheduling difficulties but created new difficulties. If the day has been extended from six to eight periods, students have several "free" periods. This is a situation which can invite boredom and tension if students are not given alternatives to the traditional study hall, and if administrators try to impose tight controls on their behavior. To avert this problem, many school administrators have resorted to a "staggered" schedule, permitting students who would otherwise be assigned to study halls to report to school late and leave early. In this way, overcrowding is relieved, but only at the beginning and the end of the school day.

Another approach to overcrowding while using existing facilities is to use the schools for different purposes at different hours of the day, for a high school program, for example, in the daytime and an evening school program in the evening. In Las Vegas, "Four O'Clock High" gets under way at 4 PM. Some students may have chosen to enroll at the high school because they want to work and earn money and still have a chance to finish high school. Others find themselves unable to adjust to the regimen of the normal school. A few want to attend school because their parents work at night, and, in this way, the family can be together during the day. In any case, all of the students are volunteers.

Las Vegas is an expanding community in need of additional school space. Four O'Clock High or Urban High, as it is called officially, was undertaken only in part as an answer to overcrowding. It was also created to provide a more convenient school for a small number of students. However, the success and the popularity of Urban High have started the school administration thinking about expanding the program to two other schools. In this way Las Vegas will have added 1,800 seats to its high school capacity without spending a penny for new facilities. The Las Vegas Superintendent, Kenny Guinn, hopes and expects to avoid building a new school with equivalent capacity, thus saving about $10 million.

Adams High School in Portland, Oregon, in addition to its regular daytime schedule has a similar program. It begins at 4 PM and runs on into the evening, and was created in response to the needs of students who would otherwise be high school dropouts. In general, these are students who are working full time and who have had difficulty in adjusting to the usual high school atmosphere and curriculum. The program is tailored specifically to their needs, and is less academically oriented than the day school.

The experiences of Urban High and Adams High indicate that among high school students in many communities—and among high school dropouts—there exists a clientele for late afternoon and evening schools. Although in any given school system there may be only a modest *percentage* of students who would be involved, the total *number*, particularly in a medium or large-sized city, could equal the enrollment of one or more high schools. The large cities are beginning to take notice of the possibilities inherent in late afternoon or evening schools. For instance, the urgent need to find additional high school seats has prompted Superintendent James F. Redmond of Chicago to begin studying a plan to hold classes up to 10 PM at selected schools. Similar programs are being planned in New York City.

The Extended School Year Using a school for a full year is not really a new idea in education. There have always been sum-

mer schools of all varieties, with remedial to accelerated programs running during the vacation periods. Although this use of
school buildings is valuable from an educational point of view,
it brings with it little in cost savings, since it is simply a supplemental experience and does not address itself to the problem of
overcrowding. In Joliet, Illinois, the Valley View School, when
confronted with a population explosion and no money to spend
on school construction, came up with the distinctive 45–15
continuous school year plan, which works this way:

All pupils are divided into four groups. Each group attends
school for 45 class days and then has a 15-class day vacation.
The District determines which group a pupil will be assigned to,
and since this is a *compulsory* plan, parents are not allowed to
choose the group to which their children will be assigned. Each
group has four 45-day sessions per year, thus fulfilling the 180
school days per year requirement. With the starting dates for the
4 groups staggered at 15 day intervals, when the fourth group is
starting the first group is just going on vacation. This means
that at any given time only three of the four groups are in school.

Thus, the capacity of each school has been increased by
one-third. For instance, a school with a capacity of 750 would
continue to serve 750 pupils *at any one time.* But over the school
year 1,000 pupils are accommodated, and all pupils receive just
as much time and attention as before. In addition to their four
15-day vacations and the usual legal holidays, *all* pupils have a
week off at Christmas, another week off at Easter, and from 7–
11 days off around July 4th.

Administrators of Valley View School District estimate that
so far the 45–15 plan has saved the district $6 million, an amount
equivalent to the cost of building two 30-room elementary
schools. They feel that the plan has been so successful that it will
be applied to any new schools that may be built. So, for every 3
schools built in the future, the 45–15 plan will give the district
the equivalent of 4.

And three schools will not need as many administrators,
custodians, or cafeteria employees as would four. For this reason,
Paul F. Swinford, Assistant Superintendent, estimates that the
year-round schools will save $80,000 a year in salaries since the
district will not have to provide personnel in these categories
for a fourth school.

Valley View finds that operating schools year-round does not affect the total cost of teacher salaries. Each pupil still attends school for 180 days a year, and teachers are paid according to how many days a year they work. Thus, some teachers are paid more (because they elect to work more than 180 days). But the net cost in teacher salaries to the district is the same as it would have been had the decision been made to handle increased enrollments entirely by building new schools and hiring a new set of teachers to staff them.

Valley View however believes that significant cost savings will be realized by virtue of the fact that textbooks, audiovisual items, and classroom furniture are shared by a larger number of students, thus cutting down on the need for additional purchases.

Valley View's year-round schools have generated some additional expenses, but these are negligible when contrasted with the savings. Obviously, greater use of school buildings means more wear and tear, resulting in higher maintenance costs. But such school building costs as insurance—not to mention the basic investment—remain fixed regardless of the degree of utilization.

Other school systems are currently using the year-round school. The Francis Howell School District in the St. Louis, Missouri, metropolitan area has put all its elementary schools on a mandated year-round schedule. Francis Howell administrators estimate a savings of more than one million dollars in new school construction over the next 5 years. The only increased expenses they anticipate as a result of adopting the year-round schedule are for building maintenance.

Other systems which use some form of year-round schedule are Jefferson County (Louisville, Kentucky) and Hayward, California. The Utica Community School District, 20 miles outside of Detroit, Michigan, with an anticipated doubling of the school population in the next 10 years, has suggested all existing schools and all new schools go on a 4-quarter year-round schedule. As a consequence, according to George D. Glinke, director of Utica's year-round school study, the District could save nearly $100 million in construction costs over the next 10 years. When the year-round plan was presented to the voters, 80 percent of them rejected it, despite the savings, preferring to stay with the familiar 9-month school year. Apparently in this case the voters preferred to spend the extra money.

As a result of his study, Glinke strongly emphasizes the need for a long period of very careful planning on the part of school districts interested in year-round schools. He estimates that it should take over 3 years to assemble information, communicate the plan to the community, and restructure the curriculum. Even after that, he believes, several more years should be devoted to a pilot project before the year-round schedule is adopted on a systemwide basis.

The fully used schools should experience no drop in educational standards, no change in student–teacher ratio, and no loss of educational experiences. It in no way resembles the double session that many of us are familiar with because no subjects are lost and there is no stripping down of the curriculum to make room for the next batch of students to come in. Year-round schools are not only an extremely economical method of accommodating increasing student enrollments, but they are also attractive to students and teachers. Youngsters tend to become bored long before the end of the 3-month summer vacation, and prefer shorter and more frequent vacations. Moreover, recreation facilities tend to be overused during the summer and underused during the rest of the year. Teachers, on the other hand, can teach the traditional 180 days or, if they want to earn more, can teach the full year of 225 days. It must be remembered, however, that while year-round schools have advantages they cannot be put into operation without the cooperation of the professional staff and the community. Perhaps the greatest motivation for year-round schools and extended school days will be the financial crisis. Once seeing the advantage of fully utilizing the schools, the typical community and the professional staff may be ready to accept the program.

FINDING OTHER SPACE FOR SCHOOLS

Most of us have been convinced that only a school building can be a school and that learning can take place only in a school building. That notion is rapidly disappearing. We know that learning takes place all of the time and that formal learning does not need a school building. Space, wherever it is, can be turned into a learning environment—from space in a factory to a church to a supermarket to an arsenal. Often, the space is waiting there to be used. It may not be necessary to select sites, acquire land, and become involved in all the other problems of building new schools. School systems are finding that using existing space can be less expensive than building anew, that the cost of acquiring and adapting existing hidden space is a fraction of what is needed to acquire land and to build; and that "putting life" into an old building very often has a stimulating effect on the local community.

The City of Boston, having neither land, time, nor money for a new school building, took half of an underutilized public bathhouse and renovated it into a 60,000 square foot high school annex. The modernization was accomplished over a summer. Since September 1970, the bathhouse has been accommodating 450 ninth grade students from South Boston High School.

The 40-year old concrete building was structurally sound and had a satisfactory heating system. The major work required was interior refinishing and partitioning, including installation of flexible walls and acoustical ceilings. What was a big open space is now 16 classrooms and a 90' by 110' gym. Included is a cafeteria that converts from four classrooms by opening operable walls. The school has a fairly flexible plan, opening off a single-loaded corridor. Next year, a solarium on the second floor will be renovated for use as a student lounge.

The total cost to turn this portion of the bathhouse into a school was about $650,000, or $11 per square foot. This may be contrasted with the current cost of new school construction in Boston, which is about $40 per square foot. The cost per student, given the 450 student enrollment, was about $1,450.

Similarly, in California, the "Other Ways" program began, in 1968, as an open classroom spin-off from Berkeley High School. Anticipating an expanded enrollment of about 100, the school needed flexible open-plan space in a hurry. It settled on 5,000 square feet of vacant office space in an industrial building. The space was available on a short-term basis and could be had rent-free for a year in exchange for remodeling, with $1,500 per month rent thereafter.

The necessary remodeling was minimal and mainly involved bringing the building up to fire-code standards: sheet-rocking walls, electrical work, removing partitions, and rebuilding a stairway. The total cost for renovation was $13,000—$130 per student, or less than $2.50 per square foot.

P.S. 211 in New York City is a 647-student elementary school that has been housed in a converted factory since September 1969. The building, with a total of 45,000 square feet, has four floors plus a gym. Because it has no corridors and is all open space, it has a net to gross ratio of 80–90 percent.

The total renovation cost was $600,000, or $13 per square foot. This does not include the carpeting on three floors which cost an additional $36,000. The building's owner agreed to assume the cost of the renovation required to meet New York City Board of Education specifications. The city rents the building for $133,000 per year ($3 per square foot), a figure which includes amortization of the renovation cost. During the last 5 years of the lease, the rent will be reduced to $56,000 per year. The city can obtain renovated space more quickly through this process because capital budget approval and other time-consuming bureaucratic procedures are not involved.

The Philadelphia Board of Education has successfully converted several old buildings, including a supermarket, a ware-house-loft building, and a former arsenal. All of the buildings have been purchased, except for the arsenal, which was a gift from the Federal government. The school department has consistently found itself "ahead of the game," because most of the conversion costs have come out lower than new construction costs.

In 1968, the school department was able to take over surplus United States Government property—the Frankford Arsenal Gauge Building—adjacent to a recreation center, a public library, and an elementary school, and just several blocks from the overcrowded Olney High School. The subsequently renovated building, operated as a completely autonomous secondary school (grades 10–12) for 300 students, has helped to relieve pressure on Olney High School.

The building, of heavy masonry construction, is structurally sound. Originally, the interior featured high ceilings, loftlike spaces, heavy circular columns, and many windows. Renovation took 9–10 months to complete; the job involved gutting, repartitioning, and refinishing the interior; installing carpeting, additional plumbing and electrical fixtures, rewiring, and generally meeting fire-code standards for stairwells and corridors. The existing power and waste disposal system as well as the HVAC system was satisfactory.

The 81,600-square-foot school, now in its second year, is a complete high school except for shop facilities. It includes 20 general purpose classrooms, two science labs, 3 business education rooms, 3 art labs, a home economics suite, a graphics area, a health education room, an instructional materials center, a little theater, and an area for food service and dining. Gym space was provided by converting an adjacent high-ceiling garage into a 3,600-square-foot recreation/physical education room, plus lockers.

The total conversion cost was $547,500 or $6.74 per square foot. Dr. Glen I. Earthman, Director of the Philadelphia School District Facilities Department, estimated that it would have cost $32–35 per square foot to construct an equivalent new building on the same site.

A similar conversion, involving a 6-story warehouse which was purchased and renovated for use as a demonstration school and computer center, cost only $9.55 per square foot. The job included gutting and repartitioning, and the installation of lighting, carpeting, and a new ceiling. In general, Philadelphia's experience with conversions has revealed average costs of $12 per square foot or less, including both acquisition and rehabilitation. Heartened by past success, the Philadelphia School Department is presently looking for several more buildings to convert.

The Chicago School Department has over 10 years' experience with factory and warehouse conversions. In 1958, the department modernized a 50-year-old factory and its adjoining offices—about 620,000 square feet—to house the Washburn Trade School, which has a present enrollment of 3,304 students. In 1964, the city bought a wholesale grocery warehouse and garage for $1 million. The resulting 264,000 square feet of converted space now houses 1,481 students at St. Simeon Vocational High School. Since 1965, a former candy factory has provided space for the Westinghouse Vocational High School, a comprehensive high school, a Headstart program, and an adult education program. This ample building provides 400,000 square feet of space.

All of the above buildings were reinforced concrete structures which required extensive remodeling. The interiors were gutted completely. New services—plumbing, heating, electrical, firealarm systems—were brought in, and new interior partitioning was installed. All interior spaces were limited by column grids; for example, the Westinghouse building had a 20' x 20' grid.

The renovation costs of these buildings have been fairly low, ranging from $6–12 per square foot. Washburn Trade was acquired for $1.6 million, and the cost of modernizing it was about $2.3 million. The total development cost was, therefore, about $7 per square foot. Development costs for St. Simeon were about $1.6 million, or about $6.50 per square foot. The conversion cost of the Westinghouse Building, acquired for $750,000, was about $12 per square foot.

There are many other examples of noneducational space being used for educational purposes. In Detroit, an unused, 4-story Catholic academy was converted to an elementary school for 1,472 pupils. In Philadelphia, several garages are now used for vocational training, and a former bowling alley adjacent to a high school has found new life as an automotive shop. In Washington, D.C., schoolmen currently are using former churches for kindergarten and special experimental programs for prekindergarten.

In Los Angeles, several commercial buildings are used for elementary, secondary, and Manpower Development Training Program purposes. Perhaps the most dramatic demonstration of this type of conversion is the addition of 350 nonschool locations for adult education. These are used for adult education classes of all types and supplement the Los Angeles education classes conducted in 28 schools for adults. Just imagine multiplying the number of school sites by 12, from 28 to 350. People who are tired after a day's work need not travel again to a school. It is almost within walking distance. Adult education school attendance has doubled since multiplying the number of locations.

Storefront schools are operating successfully in many parts of the country. One of the most interesting, from a facility standpoint, is the Harlem Prep School in New York. It is housed in a former supermarket, cleverly designed to house the program for 150 high school dropouts. Harlem Prep's new home (formerly housed in a New York State armory) provides an environment which is open, exciting, and conducive to real and intense involvement with the educational process.

The ultimate extension of the noneducational building idea is, perhaps, the Parkway School in Philadelphia. There is no building here. The complex of private and public buildings located along the Benjamin Franklin Parkway is the campus. This experimental school is in its second year and is so popular that applicants are chosen by drawing their names out of a hat. Each school area is permitted a predetermined number of the limited vacancies.

The academic curriculum consists of three parts: institutional offerings, basic skills offerings, and electives. The institutional offerings program consists of those classes offered by participating Parkway institutions, with the classes located in the facilities of the appropriate participating institutions and taught by institutional staff members. Biology might be taught by one of the curators in the Museum of Natural Science; or an art class could be conducted in the Philadelphia Art Museum. The possibilities are limited only by the number of participating institutions. The basic skills curriculum is that required by the state of Pennsylvania and is taught by the Parkway faculty. The same is true, for the most part, of the elective offerings. In addition, each student is encouraged to participate in a program of individual study in an area of his interest.

The headquarters of the communities are in converted office space. The only indications that this is a "school" are the home base lockers from the district's central repair shop. To erase even this memory of "school," the lockers are individually painted by the students.

And so our concepts of schools are changing. Experimentation makes it obvious that our old notion of what is a schoolhouse no longer holds. As we change our attitudes on what is education, we change our attitudes on where that education should take place. We are searching both land and sea for new ways to incorporate space as places to build schools. We also see that we do not have to go it alone—partnerships are cheaper and often better. We are beginning to make better use of our existing schools and to look for schooling space all over the community. Although facilities alone will not do it, they contribute greatly toward merging the schools with the real world by enlarging the environment in which the schools are housed.

School Maintenance and General Support Services

I recently visited a large university in France—so large, in fact, that it took one hour by car to drive from one end of the campus to the other. There were 63 buildings, hundreds of acres of grounds, 17 separate colleges and catalogues, 23 eating areas, and 3 different transportation systems to connect the colleges. After touring the grounds and some of its schools, I spoke with the provost and asked him how one manages such a vast institution. He went into much detail as to its problems but emphasized the fact that no matter how good its educational program might be or the quality of its professional staff, the key to operating a university of that size was the control and management of the noninstructional activities, those functions required to bring students, teachers, and materials together in an environment that facilitates learning.

Noninstructional activities (in addition to capital investment for school space that we discussed in the previous section) include custodial and maintenance services; personnel administration and labor relations; purchasing, storage, and distribution; transportation; and a host of other activities. In a way, they are the supports to the educational process, whatever form it takes. If these are not managed properly, students do not get to school on time, buildings are in disrepair, supplies are slow to move into the classroom. On the other hand, if noninstructional activities are maintained expertly, all kinds of benefits can accrue.

Generally, throughout the country, these activities consume a reputable portion of education budgets. Efficiency in management not only can improve service but also can free funds for direct educational uses. However, even more important is the fact that through certain management practices new forms of education can take place.

We have already discussed one major item at some length and that is school space. Many economies can also be realized if we apply the new technologies to school maintenance as well.

A study was made for New York State by Peat, Marwick, and Mitchell on possible savings in the noninstructional budget. They focussed on the three money-eating items which could release millions of dollars for a more creative education if savings were possible. These are pupil transportation; purchasing, storage, and distribution; and operation and maintenance of plant.

Much of the information in this section is drawn from their study.

In the state of California, for example, savings of only 5 percent in these items of the noninstructional budget could release as much as $100 million for other purposes. The same percentage of savings, applied to New York State, could save $80 million. The ability of individual school systems, then, to save only 5 percent of their noninstructional budget could mean the difference between giving the teachers a raise and facing a job action; it could mean the difference between bringing children into the school system at the age of 4 and waiting until the mandatory age; it could mean having a community college or an open-campus high school. In a way, that small edge of 5 percent could make the difference between meaningful, exciting education and confinement to the same old conventional methods.

Let us take a look at the situation as it is at present. Except in the big cities, many school districts are small; some enroll fewer than 2,500 students in all. Usually, each district handles its own noninstructional support activities, sometimes through an assistant superintendent for business or a business manager. By tradition and status, these individuals were teachers first. Having reached their current positions via the instructional ladder, they are amateurs in the situations that comprise the noninstructional activities. They have had neither the training nor the experience needed to manage those activities. The opportunity for qualified business personnel to enter school–business management is extremely limited. This is ironic because teachers, so well aware of the need for professionalism in their own positions, should be equally accepting of a similar need for the noninstructional support positions. It is even more ironic that a principal or superintendent will bleed off all his precious time and energy from the pursuit of the academic goals the *entire system* is designed to achieve, because of his involvement in the nonacademic phases.

Another problem these communities face is typical of all small-scale purchasing units. The economies attendant on large-scale purchasing power are not available to small systems. For example, a transportation service for 50 children will generally be more expensive per unit than one for 500 children. A school district of 2,500 pupils, for example, is simply not large enough to have any leverage in buying.

Another problem with smallness is that superintendents face personal pressure from local individuals and groups. For example, if giving Mr. X the maintenance contract for a few buses will ensure his and his family's vote for the new elementary school, it may be the better part of discretion to give it to him. It may cost a little more, but it will make life a lot easier, and the children will have their new school.

As a result of this type of relationship, local vendors tend to view local school systems as outlets for their wares even though their prices may be significantly higher than those of larger, more distant competitors. To be sure, in most cases they may deliver the services called for and the higher price may even be marked by a higher level of service. Nevertheless, that level of service may be unjustifiably costly, since the threat of competition is absent.

PUPIL TRANSPORTATION

There is hardly a school system in the country that does not use some form of pupil transportation, whether it be a rural school system that buses children up to 50 miles or a large city system that, for the purpose of integration, buses children only 2 or 3 miles. The traditional objective of a pupil transportation system is to ensure an adequate, safe means of transportation for children who, because of poor health or school inaccessibility, cannot easily walk to school. Another major objective is to enlarge the social environment by moving children outside their immediate neighborhood. Integration, of course, is one phase of this goal. How do we achieve these two objectives in the most economical and efficient way?

First of all, how can money be saved in the purchasing of buses? After all, they are an expensive item ranging from $3,000 to $8,000 per vehicle. Under the present system, as we have said before, small school districts usually pay much higher prices because of the nature of small-scale purchasing and, in some cases, because of local pressures. There are two ways to combat this problem. First, school buses can be bought from a list of companies supplied by the state. Many states subsidize much of the cost of transportation for school districts, and are, therefore, concerned enough to maintain lists of reliable companies which sell vehicles at competitive prices. If a state does not have such a list now, the school district should press to have one adopted. Even where such subsidies exist, however, local purchasing must be supervised and controlled by the state, in order to check the temptation to extravagant buying. This does not necessarily mean the districts will pay too much for what they are getting. It means that buses purchased may be far more luxurious—and expensive—than is necessary. Examples are paneled station wagons, carpeting, larger seats, and fancier bodies.

Mail order purchasing of buses through state contract is not a complicated procedure. A committee defines and refines vehicle specifications, taking into account such factors as special terrain and climatic conditions. The transportation system administrators then determine the number of new buses they will require and inform the State Education Department of their requirements in sufficient time for delivery by the start of the fall term. Most likely, notification in the fall of the prior year will meet this requirement. The bidding process and letting of contracts would be conducted by the State Education Department, and penalty clauses for late delivery would be included. The regions (or districts) would process their orders through the state contract and make payments directly to the vendors. To anticipate possible emergency, the contract should also provide that, subject to the committee's approval, the region may call for extra vehicles beyond those listed by the state.

As an estimate, a savings of from $1,000 to $2,000 can be achieved on each vehicle by purchasing through a single list. If applied to approximately 1,000 vehicles a year (not an unusual number in statewide purchasing), the potential saving is one to two million dollars a year. Furthermore, since purchasing through state contract would permit uniformity in bus types over the years, a "bonus" may appear in the form of reduced maintenance costs. This would come from limited inventory needs, simplification of the inventory process, and reduction in the amount of maintenance training required. Another "plus" would be the increased safety resulting from standardized training.

An objection frequently raised against buying from a state list rather than locally is that local vendors give better service. Since vehicle maintenance is largely performed inside the community and delivery problems can be minimized by exercising the penalty clause, there is little substance to this contention.

The other alternative to local purchasing and maintenance of buses, less sweeping than the state contract route, is the creation of a regional pupil transportation system. This is an extremely viable alternative, especially in states where there is no setup for state purchasing. Regional ordering would mean that the responsibility for operating transportation activities would be removed from the districts and placed with regional transportation authorities. The intent is threefold: to permit all transportation service to be provided from a base large enough to enjoy the elements of professional management and economies of scale, to relieve local administrators of what has been a troublesome burden, and, most important, to provide a system large enough to encompass many districts so that children will become psychologically oriented to moving into alternative educational environments. There is no doubt that, as we begin to seek out more varied educational experiences for students, a high degree of mobility will be required. With appropriate scheduling, a regional service, because of its greater vehicle and driver resources, can better support any substantial requirement for movement from one site to another.

Pupil transportation regions could vary in accordance with such factors as pupil density and dispersion; nature of the terrain and roads; the number and location of the schools, other institutions, and agencies that will use the buses. Although regions would have to encompass entire school districts, it would make no sense to create a region so geographically large than the vehicles could not traverse the area within a reasonable time. On the other hand, transportation in some large, densely populated districts may already be substantial and efficient; this type of district might be considered a region by itself.

The pupil transportation regional centers would provide the transportation to and from school for all eligible children residing within the region and for other purposes as required. Utilizing self-owned and operated or contracted buses, these regional centers would be responsible for purchasing, scheduling and routing, staffing, training, maintenance, and managing. The center would bill the participating districts for the pupil miles provided the districts' children on a use basis. To provide a degree of accountability, it could be stipulated that if the quality of service deteriorates and a district no longer wants to continue with the center, it can withdraw. Of course, in that case it would have to arrange for some other means of transportation.

Operating cost savings would depend upon the number of

districts that could be brought into the regional unit. In the Peat, Marwick, and Mitchell study made for New York State that we referred to before, it was estimated that enlarging a pupil transportation system could reduce per pupil mile costs by as much as 50 percent. It has been found, however, that after a certain point, as districts increase in size either by virtue of enrollment or area, the per pupil mile cost savings is reduced. There is still reason to believe, however, that even in districts with more than 2,000 pupils, sizable savings can result from regionalization. For example, studies indicate that, nationally, 65 percent of the route miles service districts fall between 2,000 and 5,000 transported pupils and between 50 and 150 square miles. The operating cost curves developed from the statistical data demonstrate that a cost reduction of from 5 to 10 percent is a conservative estimate of what can be achieved by enlarging transportation operations.

In addition to dollar savings, there are substantial noneconomic benefits. Regions can more easily support professionally trained transportation managers. The larger systems can also afford such things as modern and well-equipped maintenance facilities and computer scheduling and routing. This in turn means safer transportation and better service for children. Safer transportation also results from the mandated purchase of buses from the state contract list, since standardization facilitates improved maintenance and training. Regional control also removes local vendor pressures and may relieve parental and political pressures. These influences have been among the most troublesome noninstructional burdens that school districts have had to face.

The busing of children, for whatever purpose, will probably continue long into the foreseeable future. It is important, therefore, that school systems give it full consideration from an efficiency–economy point of view as well as for its value in varying the education of children.

PURCHASING, STORAGE, AND DISTRIBUTION SYSTEMS

Nationally, between 1955 and 1969, the volume of annual purchases by school districts has increased fourfold. With inflation and the accelerating demands for new teaching aids and materials, the figure is expected to continue growing at least at the same rate well into the 70's. Despite this tremendous growth, the manner in which districts handle the purchasing, storage, and distribution (PS&D) function has changed very little. They still follow what is essentially a three-stop process:

1. Users in each unit within the education system specify their various needs on "budget requisition lists." A very limited number of items—only about 10 to 15 percent of all purchases—are "prespecified": a single brand and type of item can be used to satisfy all units. Requisitions are consolidated, first at the school level and then at the district level.

2. The district business manager sends out requests for bids on all items over a dollar limit specified either by the local school board or by the State Legislature. He selects the lowest responsible bidder and places orders for the entire year's requirements to be delivered in the fall at the beginning of the school year.

3. The vendor delivers the order usually by drop-shipping to individual schools or buildings, where they are stored until needed. A few districts operate warehouses, but even these districts often accept single annual shipments rather than spaced deliveries because the vendor can obtain his money only when the whole order has been delivered.

The problems are many. In most districts, for instance, the system is fragmented and the responsibilities are discharged by a myriad of people, none of whom is trained to cope with the work. Inadequate advance planning results in numerous small orders, and incomplete specifications for special one-time purchases lead to innumerable small problems. There is little control over vendor, product performance, or receiving. Inventories and the space they require are immense. Since schools are not designed for storage, pilferage shortages run into untold thousands of dollars.

There are three other major problems. First, the link between the budgeting cycles and purchasing. School boards usually approve budgets in the very late spring and orders for the fall term are not given until early summer. Because of this, vendors cannot schedule inventory build-up gradually. They must often hire extra personnel to get the entire annual shipment to the schools before the beginning of the school year. In addition, with the fiscal year on school budgets beginning on July 1 and the many bureaucratic steps that must be taken before orders are approved and payments validated, school systems most often lose out on cash discounts. All these are expensive and avoidable extras.

The second problem is that, despite potential economies of scale, districts still strongly resist consolidating needs. Yet a school district simply does not represent a powerful enough buying force to obtain purchase price concessions. Even cooperative buying, which requires no great shift in policy or operation, has not gained wide acceptance for anything except food purchasing and a few other very basic items. The reason is that districts have felt little or no incentive to consolidate. Just as in the transportation area, any suggestion to consolidate is a red flag suggesting deprivation of control.

Finally, the districts face unrelenting pressure from local vendors who feel—rightly or wrongly—that the district should be a source of income. They contend that they pay its taxes and their interests coincide more nearly with those of the schools than do those of some remote impersonal supplier.

Again, these problems are not dissimilar to those of transportation. Communities are loath to surrender the privileges and power of local autonomy. Yet, in view of the urgencies of the budget crisis, districts must choose between their immediate personal satisfaction and the benefits to be derived from long-range economies. As with transportation, such economies can be realized by purchasing in combination with other school systems, either on a regional basis or by ordering through the State Education Department.

It is estimated that price savings of as much as 6 percent could result if a sufficient number of districts were to take advantage of statewide ordering. This does not include the savings on the clerical and administrative costs of bidding. A recent study conducted by the New York State School Boards Association conservatively estimates the cost of each bid process conducted by a district as approximately $150. If the use of state contracts should reduce the number of bids in each district from 28 (the present average) to 18, statewide administrative costs could be reduced by an additional $1.2 million.

The regional approach likewise offers substantial savings, much like those in regional contracting for transportation. It introduces cooperative bidding by centralizing the purchasing function of several districts to gain price advantages. It centralizes the receipt of purchases from vendors, both to gain further price advantages and to achieve better control over receiving, quality, and service; and it expands the purchasing entity to a size large enough to justify the cost of introducing needed professionalism in purchasing activities.

Regionalization of purchasing and distribution is a logical facet of cooperative bidding, with two special advantages. First, because regional agencies are established throughout the state to purchase for the component districts, they can receive bulk purchases and then redistribute the individual requirements immediately to the various drop-points. Secondly, the regional agencies exercise control over vendor and product performance, maintain open orders, and process accounts payable centrally on behalf of the participating districts. A recently concluded study entitled "Report of the Massachusetts Business Task Force for School Management" by the Massachusetts Advisory Council on Education, September 1970, reported that for all the school systems in Massachusetts a 17 percent price reduction could be achieved through centralized purchasing.

District workload savings would also accrue through eliminating the need for each district to carry the burden of preparing specifications, maintaining lists of bidders, advertising, analyzing bids, preparing purchase orders, preparing correspondence, and all of the other activities related to purchasing and receiving.

As with pupil transportation, the two most appropriate alternatives are to expand the use of the state contract and to regionalize the system. The net savings are almost 10 times greater than individual purchasing. There are also noneconomic advantages. For instance, the substantially greater purchasing power generated by combining several districts can be used to leverage tailor-made products from vendors. Presently, we take what vendors offer. It has often been said that three major book publishers set the curriculums for the nation. Within the last few years, publishers and general school suppliers have made attempts to become more responsive to schools' needs, but even then nothing has made them *more* responsive than large orders. Tell the suppliers what your specifications are, offer them a substantial contract by means of regional or statewide ordering, and, for the first time, school people, not vendors, will be "calling the shots."

If children are to receive instructional materials and equipment of desirable quality and interest, as and when needed, we must have a purchasing, storage, and delivery system that is very different from what we now have. In a regional center quality would increase markedly, since it would be staffed and equipped to count, inspect, and test shipments, and make returns if necessary. The computerized inventory and ordering systems now emerging would also help improve quality by facilitating analysis of vendors and products. With the merchandise no further away than the regional warehouse, delivery and service could be exceptionally good. Finally, the whole tone of purchasing would improve as the large entities start to bring on board the kinds of buying personnel that truly know how to serve their clientele while resisting vendor pressures.

MAINTENANCE SYSTEMS

When budgets are presented for the building of schools, they sound astronomical—5 million dollars for a 20-classroom primary school, 40 million for a 4,000-student high school. The costs not only sound astronomical, they are. Nothing has risen so much in these inflationary times as construction costs. Couple with that the slow, cumbersome process of site selection, land acquisition, bidding, and you often have a delay of several years between the time the budget for the new school is approved and the awarding of the contracts.

Over the past 5 years, there has been an average increase of 5 percent each year in building costs. Translated into practice, this means that because of the time gap between allocation of funds and signing of contract there could easily be an increase of 15 percent in cost. All of this adds up to the fact that building schools is expensive and, therefore, whether the schoolhouse be a new one or an old one, it is important that it be maintained well so as to preserve the investment.

A sound operation and maintenance system is imperative not only to get the most for our investment, but also to enhance the physical environment in which learning is meant to occur and to keep the facilities safe, sanitary, and attractive. Nothing is more depressing to both teacher and student than sitting in a school with broken furniture, missing window panes, toilets that do not flush, water fountains that do not work. A learning environment that is deteriorating has a negative effect on learning. A well-run, attractive, functioning environment, although it does not guarantee learning, at least makes things physically comfortable and often affects one's attitude toward school.

In order to achieve a well-maintained school, it is necessary to provide efficient operational or custodial services that will keep the physical plant open and ready for use, and the buildings, grounds, and equipment must be kept in good repair.

Although operations is, in most cases, technically a district responsibility, the custodians are generally assigned to individual schools and, for all practical purposes, report only to the school administrator. The skills required are diverse, but not highly technical. The operations personnel obtain them through apprenticeship. As a result, the quality of training depends very much on the senior man on the job during the apprenticeship—and not much else. Training programs are rare and seldom comprehensive where they do exist. The standards for staffing levels have been set on the basis of custom and practice and are determined solely by the size of the building. The Custodians Handbook, last published in 1955, is both out of date and out of print. Finally, standards of quality do not exist. In some areas, custodians have virtually no ability; in others, they themselves operate as the in-house maintenance crew, performing all but the most difficult maintenance work.

However, such things as disparities in performance from district to district, the lack of properly defined scheduling and staffing procedures and guidelines, and the absence of training, are all no more than symptoms of the problem. A more basic problem is the difficulty of finding and retaining capable people and the lack of sources to tap for training assistants. Good people are hard to come by and usually maintenance budgets are kept low in an effort to pare capital costs. Maintenance budgets are often among the first to be cut. It usually creates less furore to cut maintenance items than to cut the teaching staff.

This is compounded by the fact that industry frequently pays far better salaries than school systems do, and it is, therefore, difficult to lure personnel away. Although salaries have risen recently for many of these positions, there are just not enough capable applicants to fill the vacancies. As a result, the individual responsible for the school plant is frequently a promoted subordinate or one with very little academic training in the area.

Another problem is the need for equipment repair and replacement. Students today are "rougher" on their schools. The repair of broken windows, clogged plumbing, and countless other school facilities is expensive in terms of both material and labor. Even though, according to most superintendents of building and grounds and school construction specialists, "easy-maintenance" materials cost only an estimated 5 percent premium, newly constructed school buildings may prove no more maintainable than the old ones. Besides, in these times of limited fiscal resources, administrators, boards, and taxpayers shortsightedly opt for lower construction costs even though it means substantially higher operations and maintenance costs for their successors.

What, then, can be done about the problem? Are we destined to perpetuate the rapid deterioration of buildings, or are there ways out? One alternative is to supplant the regular custodial staff with part-time employees. This would address itself to two problems: one, cost; and the other, the shortage of full-time custodians. Because the job requires relatively little skill, two part-timers can serve as effectively as one full-timer and for less cost. Part-time staff can include students. This has particular value because it not only saves money and gives students a chance to increase their earnings, but it also provides an opportunity to improve relations between students and supervisory custodial people. Student involvement may also help to reduce vandalism.

Under this alternative, students of working age would have the opportunity to apply and be paid for custodial work, e.g., sweeping, waxing, cleaning boards, carpentry, plumbing, electrical work, etc., in the schools. The number of full-time custodians would be kept at a minimum, and the work would be scheduled so that as much of it as possible could be done after school by students and other part-time workers.

It is quite possible that the use of students could be coordinated with an official work–study program. Work–study programs allow high school students to work a limited number of hours per week, while attending school. Just as some students are employed by industry, others can be employed by the school system to perform custodial or other maintenance functions. To encourage employment of this type, educators should seek to impart a sense of status to the position. The post of part-time custodian should not be treated as menial, any more than would the position of IBM secretary or stewardess on TWA. The image the position presents can be an important incentive.

The cost of implementing a program such as this would be minimal because the hiring and supervision of the part-timers could be handled by the same individuals who engage the full-timers. The potential savings, however, could be substantial. For example, if one full-time custodian can be replaced for an equivalent number of hours by part-time employees, the cost savings can be calculated as follows: A custodian earns about $3.75 an hour or $30 for an 8-hour day. On a 40-hour per week basis, his compensation is $7,500 per year. If his 8 hours' work can be performed by 4 hours of student work and 4 hours of another part-timer's work, the daily cost would be about $6.40 for 4 hours of a student's time and about $9.60 for 4 hours of another part-timer's, totalling $16 for an 8-hour day.

These part-time hourly rates are realistic because the student will usually work at the minimum rate without any fringe benefits, while the other part-timer will also draw a reduced hourly rate with little if any fringe benefits. In fact, there are a variety of Federal and state programs that provide funds for just such work-type projects. Even without supplementary funding, and at these rates, the annual cost would be $4,000 per year, which could be a $3,500 per year saving in each school. To carry these figures a little further, if there are 4,000 schools in a state and $3,500 can be saved in each school, the total saving would come to 14 million dollars. Even if we reduce this figure by about 25 percent to account for part-timer's lack of skills, higher turnover, and initial training, we still have a total of about $10.5 million in reduced costs per year. Further, while some smaller schools cannot discharge a full-time custodian, this would probably be balanced by the larger schools, which could replace more than one.

In addition to generating cost savings, this would also provide financial assistance to some students and would enable schools to tie together the experiences of education and employment—a task many fear they are not doing too well.

One major problem with this approach might be union opposition. Although spokesmen for custodial unions have said they would not oppose such a step provided custodians are not "fired" but are eliminated by attrition, it would be advisable, before any unionized school system attempts the approach, to enter into prior agreements with the union.

In any event, school systems should see to it that custodial maintenance measures are kept up to date whether their schools are staffed by professional custodians or part-time helpers. Rapid changes in product and operating equipment technology have reduced the value of on-the-job training. Most supervisors don't know enough about procedures and products to manage their activities efficiently and to impart the knowledge required. Some school systems are producing manuals that provide information on management techniques for the operations and maintenance functions. They offer specific instructions by which a district can determine and set cleanliness standards, and schedule the required personnel; directions on how to perform specific operations and maintenance tasks.

Estimating the savings potential inherent in such measures is difficult, but it is reasonable to assume that the improvement in management and operating techniques and the availability of a training and reference source will result in better standards and schedules; these should bring about a reduction in total costs.

Until a manual is prepared, or for that matter even after it is prepared, it is important to develop training programs that would encompass a variety of training requirements and situations. Some would instruct supervisors to train their own staffs, while others would train custodian and maintenance personnel directly. Some would be for new staff and some would be refresher courses. Also, they would be continually updated to incorporate the uses of the new equipment and materials that are constantly becoming available. Most important, they would be practical rather than theoretical. The programs could be held either within districts for large cities, or centrally for a number of smaller districts. Still others could be given on a statewide basis or even under contract at a state university location.

To motivate employees to take in-service training, it is important to build incentives into the programs. The training should take place during regular hours and those attending should be paid. In fact, it might be wise to provide a bonus or an upward movement on the salary scale for those who successfully complete the training sessions.

Just as with pupil transportation and purchasing, more efficiency can be obtained and dollars saved by regionalizing or centralizing maintenance services. A maintenance organization would have to be set up, and the maintenance technicians would be employees of this organization. Working out of a central location, each would have a fleet of maintenance trucks to service all the schools on both routine and emergency tasks. The organization would develop and use computerized scheduling techniques for preventive maintenance. Some of the large city districts already possess centralized maintenance groups and have been experimenting with some forms of computerized scheduling techniques.

Centralizing maintenance would provide savings in the following areas: (1) labor, through more efficient manpower utilization; (2) maintenance equipment, supplies, and materials, through centralized purchasing, storage, and warehousing; and (3) other new equipment costs, through professionally run preventive maintenance programs.

This alternative might have the additional advantage of eliminating the tendency to postpone preventive maintenance by lifting it out of the local budgeting process. The central organization could also employ multicrafted maintenance persons, who are virtually impossible to obtain through local contracting. In this way, jobs requiring two or three skills could still be performed by one man.

Perhaps one of the most reasonable and sensible ways of reducing maintenance costs is to pay for better construction and to buy readily maintainable standardized materials. Yet the nature of the school district financing practices impels Boards of Education to minimize today's costs despite tomorrow's penalties. This is particularly true in new construction where districts are tempted to forego easy-to-get and low-cost-maintenance materials simply because it may mean an initial premium of about 5 percent. Yet, over the long run, it is more economical to consider the total life-cycle costs including operations and maintenance. This is analogous to the "total package" and "life-cycle" procurement practices of the Federal government, which considers the whole spectrum of costs rather than the initial cost alone.

As sensible as this sounds, it admittedly brings with it higher initial costs for construction. In view of the ultimate benefits, however, the state might be willing to increase its contribution to encourage this type of purchasing. Perhaps the state and district would split the additional cost on a sliding scale, the state paying an increasingly larger percentage of the total construction cost as the districts include more and more "maintainability" features.

The state would rank the floors, walls, and roofs, for example, according to the materials used for each of these items. As part of its normal approval procedure for new construction, it would evaluate the materials and score the construction on a basis of maintainability. The higher the ratio of designed maintainability to optimum maintainability, the greater the reimbursement rate would be. Knowledgeable people estimate that the incorporation of these "ease-of-maintenance materials" would reduce the cost of operating and maintaining a building by 10 to 15 percent.

In most states, legislation would be required to establish the principle of an incentive formula for construction. The theory is a far reaching one and it will be difficult to convince legislators to reverse the "do it now and pay later" strategy. The eventual cost savings, however, should be a vital factor in their considerations.

The above analysis of noninstructional activities shows that feasible alternatives exist that can provide considerable cost savings to schools and school systems. Since the technical requirements for such changes are not overwhelming, and since schools and districts can no longer afford the price of inefficiency, it is essential that school administrators now take the hard road of greater efficiency rather than the easy road of extra funding.

Furthermore, it should be apparent that the notion that local autonomy must exist in all school matters is a fetish, with no necessary application to noninstructional activities. Such activities as transportation or building maintenance can be withdrawn from the local districts with no detrimental effect on the quality of the educational program. In fact, relieving the district administrator from involvement in noninstructional activities permits him to spend more time on the educational program—and to bring it closer to his community.

It is to be expected, then, that regional service centers will be large, complex, business-type entities. They can provide the anticipated cost-savings and service *only* if they are managed by persons who are truly specialists in their fields. Both school administrators and legislators must find a place in education for people with this special competence.

INSTRUCTIONAL ACTIVITIES

People—New Educational Roles

The largest continuing item of expense in all school budgets is for professional personnel. Although construction costs as represented in capital budgets are large, they are only a one-shot expenditure and can be amortized over a 20- to 40-year period. But professional salaries must be figured on a yearly basis—there is no deferred payment or budget plan. Most school systems spend as much as 85 percent of the tax budget on personnel: teachers, administrators, supervisors. This means that if we spend $800 per year per student, about $700 goes to salaries and the rest to teaching materials, health services, maintenance, and other fixed charges. Therefore, unless we can do something about reducing the cost of the most sizable slice of the budget, we will be making only insubstantial inroads in our expenditures.

The traditional method of cutting personnel costs is to reduce the size of the teaching and administrative staff. In other words, fewer people to do the same things. This is unsatisfactory because everyone loses. The remaining teachers are overburdened, and the students become the victims of overcrowding and of resentful teachers. Administrative tasks pile up because fewer people are there to do them. Some school systems, therefore, elect not to reduce their professional staff but, instead, to work a shorter school year and pay their professional staff accordingly. Others are moving into half-day schools so that they can cut their personnel costs in half. Whichever of these methods is used, it is un-satisfactory. It penalizes both teacher and student, and certainly does not make for a relaxed atmosphere when teachers feel that at almost any time they may either lose their jobs or have their jobs curtailed. The student may be unconcerned, since for many youngsters staying in school for a full day or for a full term has no particular appeal.

The question, then, is whether there are ways of making education more attractive and meaningful to students while, at the same time, cutting the cost of the personnel budget. The an-swer is that it can be done in various ways. First, of course, we can increase the productivity of the existing staff by fixing more precisely our educational goals and objectives and training the kinds of people we need to achieve these goals. Professionals will, no doubt, have a major role to play here, but not entirely. That is the difference. Those parts of the curriculum and of the school experience that must be performed by teachers and ad-ministrators should continue so. But examining all that goes into these experiences or all that *should*, one can see much room for people who are skilled in aspects of education that do not require the talents of professional teachers or administrators. These run the gamut from management experts to paraprofessionals.

Let us first talk about administrative costs and how they can be cut. School administration in this country is the largest and most costly of any in the world. The State of New York, for example, is reputed to have more administrators than all of France. And whereas in Great Britain, a school might be man-aged by one headmaster and a secretary, a school of equal size, in this country, appears to require the part-time services of an over-all superintendent, a full-time principal, assistants to the principal, a maintenance man, a business manager, a curricu-lum supervisor, and a half dozen counselors. Why is this so?

The point is made that the complicated nature of modern educational and budgeting problems demands specialists of many different kinds. For example, a superintendent will often have on his administrative staff, in addition to the customary financial and building specialists, a person to prepare Federal and state reports because of the flow of monies and the accom-panying accounting procedures, and another person to negotiate with teachers because of complicated contracts with teacher organizations and unions. And yet, unless the district is exceedingly large, it is unlikely that either position is a full-time assignment. It is still more unlikely that one person can serve in both capacities since each has its own peculiar skills. Therefore, we employ two people and fill up their spare time with whatever busywork can be found for them. Eventually, this work becomes so burdensome that there is not enough time for the original assignment, and, with the inevitability of Parkinson's Law, the employment of an administrative assistant and an additional secretary becomes essential. Thus, many of these positions are superfluous and the product of sloppy management.

I know of no district where there are not far more administrators than are really needed if personnel were used efficiently. Actually, the situation is so bad that in some districts over half of the certificated (professional) employees are in nonteaching assignments. And all, or nearly all, are frozen into position by a combination of tenure and tradition.

Let's go back a bit now. If our objective is heightened productivity, certainly the example stated here will never achieve it. Schools and school systems continue proliferating staff, adding, always adding, at costs that are going up each year. Some school systems, panicking at the skyrocketing costs, run to specialists, hoping that they can come up with a cure. Some management companies perform this service, and more and more of them are beginning to enter the educational management field. In the long run, management studies may really pay off. But there are many problems in this approach.

In the first place, these specialists are usually called in after the damage has been done. The school system is in the red, teachers are demanding better working conditions and more money, and the State Education Department is threatening an audit. The people in the system who hold the "management" type jobs feel threatened and very often the system "clams up" and "outsiders" have a tough time obtaining information. Everyone feels "under investigation" and the climate of the schools deteriorates.

Besides, usually by the time the study is completed, the school board that originally let out the contract has been replaced, and the new board, since it was not its idea in the first place, may seek to evade the obligations for outside consultation incurred by the prior board. Many a potentially good study has been aborted for this reason. In addition, even if the study is completed and recommendations are made, the implementation remains. It takes courage to put efficiency studies into practice. It has been said that only 5 percent of all "efficiency recommendations" are ever put into practice. It is understandable that the tendency to resist change is greatest when jobs are at stake. Then, too, management studies are in themselves expensive and often do not resolve anything but only add to the existing costs.

It has been suggested that a more effective approach would be to replace the existing administrative structure with a management firm working for the school board under contract. This firm would take care of all the administrative tasks currently under the jurisdiction of school superintendents. What would some of the benefits be of such an arrangement? First, there would be the economy that would result from competitive bidding. The Board of Education would specify in broad terms the character of the administration they desire, and competing firms would bid for the contract. Thus, instead of appointing an administrator at a tenured or traditional salary for which there is little room for negotiation, the board would select the firm from which they would get the most value for their money and would be tied to that firm not for life as with tenured personnel, but for the life of the contract only. This advantage would seep down the administrative ladder. Right now, an administrator, be he superintendent or principal, is obliged to accept an administrative staff he knows little or nothing about and cannot dismiss or transfer except at great peril to himself and the system by which he is employed.

Under a management contract, much of this would be avoided. The director (superintendent) might or might not be designated in the contract. In either event, he would be appointed by and responsible to the managerial firm, as a school-building architect is responsible to and paid by the architectural firm that assigns him to a specific job. In other words, he would not be an employee of the school board but of the contractor or management firm. Those who work under him would also be employed by the management company, and presumably would be hired because of their competency and they, too, would have no claim to lifelong employment.

It would be incumbent upon the management firm, in order to meet its contractual obligations and build its own reputation for competency in the field, to hire the most able administrators they could find and pay them whatever is necessary to retain their services. This approach is in contrast to the current practice of salaries and promotion based upon length of service in a school district or the attainment of an advanced degree.

Another advantage is that an individual would no longer be given an all-inclusive title with dozens of duties to enable the board to get its money's worth. Some of these functions he is not competent to perform and some are just a type of "busy work." A firm would not employ a business manager, a maintenance supervisor, a personnel director, a data processing director, and a teacher negotiator for every school district it serves. Rather, it would have specialists who would serve many districts. Unburdened by rigid tenure laws and seniority rights, the management firm would employ only the minimum number of executives necessary to get the job done properly. And their executives and the personnel they employ could very easily come from the ranks of teachers who want to be administrators, and administrators who want to specialize in educational management. For example, a teacher interested in administration would train specifically for employment with a managerial firm. Here he would gain experience in a variety of administrative capacities. No longer would he be thrown directly from the classroom into a full-scale administrative assignment for which he may have had little training, experience, or talent. Current administrators, too, would have the same access to educational management positions as would teachers.

Educational management firms are springing up throughout the country. The talent is available but school people and board members have to seek it out. A start has already been made by a number of large consulting firms who are admirably staffed by ex-administrators, college professors, architects, data processors, and a host of other specialists. Many of these firms presently have the training and competency to take over the management of a school district of any size.

There is little doubt but that such a management firm, operating on a contractual ad hoc basis, can bring greater efficiency into a school system at less cost than it now spends by misusing its professionals as administrators. A large New York firm,

now engaged in handling a major assignment in a good-sized
California school system, has cut their administrative costs by
20 percent. Similar programs are in existence in Cleveland and
in a group of schools in the suburbs of Galveston, Texas.

Regardless of which form of management a district employs, there are two items of business that are basic to any administrative approach. These are budget preparation and school-
wide scheduling. Each of these can usually be handled more
efficiently. Let us look at the budget first. A budget is initially
developed on a school basis and eventually ends up on a districtwide basis. Ideally, a budget should be a cooperative venture, a
product of the pooled thinking of the educational and administrative staffs. The budget is a projection, in dollar form, of the
values they attach to the various items that go into the educational process. Hence, the greater the involvement of those who
contribute to the formation of the budget, the greater the likelihood of positive achievement and of final acceptance of the budget by the taxpayers.

Since the preparation of a school or district budget is a
complicated, time-consuming process, it has been found that an
effective means of combining such involvement with administrative time-saving lies in the use of the computer. The potential
in this field of this relatively new electronic tool has not yet been
fully appreciated, but there is a growing awareness of its value.

One example of how a computer can be used in budget formation has been demonstrated by the Littleton Public Schools in
the Denver, Colorado metropolitan area. In 1971, they launched
a computer-based budget development program. They found
that it was feasible to program the computer so that almost
all the detail work, formerly handled by individual staff members, could be processed by use of the computer. In fact, the time
saving was estimated to be at least 40 percent. Since completing
the budgeting cycle, for the first time, in the preparation of the
1971 budget, it has been learned that the total staff time saving
was even greater than the original estimate. It is difficult to
generalize what the dollar saving would be because of different
salary scales, but even 40 percent is a substantial figure, regardless of salary ranges.

After placing the 1971 budget on the computer, staff members have recognized the following advantages in this new

process.[1] First, each person is identified by a code number and is held responsible and accountable for his area of responsibility—the superintendent, assistant superintendent for administrative services, assistant superintendent for instruction, director of personnel, etc. Then, by using a computer-printed budget request form that includes historical data (actual expenditure of prior years), many specialized budget forms have been eliminated. Also eliminated have been problems of incorrect account numbers and erroneous totals in budget requests. Also, a single form makes it easier for the central staff to review budget requests.

Having the computer do calculations and provide printouts of the budget saves a significant amount of clerical time. Also, storing the budget narrative in a data file reduces clerical time spent in typing this same narrative each year. Since the final budget document is printed by the computer, there is no need for a secretary to type the budget document or a linotype operator to set type for the document if it is to be printed.

Numerical totals, carried between object, function, and fund, are obtained by computer, thereby reducing the possibility of manual calculating and typing errors. Placing the budget on a computer provides flexibility in changing any object or series of objects in dollar amount or by percentages.

Then, too, as board of education and employee groups negotiate for salaries, a program geared to proposed salary changes provides immediate information about the dollar impact of these changes on the budget, and a computer program with projected variables and constraints can forecast future budgetary needs and resulting revenue needs. As the United States Office of Education and state departments of education move toward more detailed program-budgeting requirements, computerized coded account budgets appear to lend themselves to the flexibility needed for setting up programs the districts desire. Such programming facilitates identifying budget election items and other specialized programs.

A word of caution: it should be recognized that the implementation of such a system requires a close working relationship between budgeting and data-processing personnel. It is essential

[1]Albert D. Link, "District Budget on a Computer," *School Management*, December 1971.

to select budgeting and data-processing supervisory staffs who are capable and willing to develop a computer budgeting system.

Realizing that the modern budgeting process is in its infancy, the Littleton, Colorado, staff members have indicated that they feel the assitance provided by the computer has been a major contribution in the preparation of the budget. At a recent meeting, one principal remarked, "For the first time we are taking less time to accomplish the same ends."

Computers are entering the educational field by performing many other functions. Among them are payroll, record keeping, research calculations, counseling, library information retrieval, and student testing and evaluation. The use of computers for direct instruction to students will be discussed later in the chapter.

Every dollar spent for more efficient administration, be it by a management firm or a computer or a combination of both, is likely to produce more tax savings for the other needs of the school system.

Much of what has been said about effective management in the district can be applied equally to the school level. In a way, the principal's role is more complicated than that of central administration. He is closer to the firing line. He deals with people, students and adults, every minute of the day. School board members, the professional staff, dissatisfied parents, and students, increasingly turn to the principal as the key to the improvement or deterioration of education in a school. In addition to being constantly harassed by the demands of his constituency, the principal is burdened with the everyday demands of the administrative tasks and the "fire-extinguishing" jobs that are part and parcel of every administrator's day. The question, however, is whether this is really what school principals should be doing.

Often, when educators are asked whether or not they are fulfilling their role as they originally envisioned it, they will say: "That was a dream. I only wish I could do all the things that should be done in the school, but I am too busy with day-to-day problems, with trying to 'recapture' the students who are truants, with trying to accommodate angry parents, demonstrating community groups, teachers and students demanding their 'rights.' The list can go on and on." Days could be spent just listening to the principals, the "educational leaders," tell of their daily problems. The moral may be pointed up by the story of a prospective young employee in a logging camp. A strong and willing young man approached the foreman and inquired about a job felling trees. The foreman, even after finding that the youth had had no experience, decided to give him a chance. He handed him a razor-sharp, double-bitted axe and briefly instructed him as to the how's, do's, and don'ts of felling trees. The first day the young man felled 200 trees, the second 150, and the third only 100 trees. The foreman, after looking over the logger's performance, decided to check with the young man regarding his declining performance. Arriving at the site, the foreman asked the young man if he had been working as long the last few days as he had the first, to which the young man replied, "Longer." "Have you been swinging the axe as fast?" asked the foreman. "Faster," replied the young man. Bewildered, the foreman picked up the young man's axe, only to find its cutting edge dulled and chipped. "When did you last sharpen your axe?" asked the foreman, to which the young man replied, "I've been working so hard that I haven't had time."

The above situation exists all too frequently in education. Principals, like the woodcutter, continue with a multitude of activities but with "dulling" performance in the areas that really count. School boards are becoming increasingly aware of both the salary and the function of the principal. As the highest paid educator in the school, he is in many ways the least productive. While his burdens, unfortunately, increase, his skills and attitude remain essentially the same as those of a decade ago.

When we talk about productivity, we must think not only in terms of saving money but of how we can make education more effective. One way is to free the principal so that he can pay more attention to what happens in what is more properly his province. What can be done about the day-to-day problems, about low achievement, faculty disinterest, community hostility, student apathy, and bureaucratic inertia? The principal has several roads open to him, but, first, he must release himself from many of his "burdens."

In the field of administrative tasks, as many activities as possible can be farmed out to a management firm, as suggested previously with reference to superintendents. In fact, it becomes economically ever more feasible on the school principal level since several schools can combine to share the services of a single "team." As to budget, a school system can install a computer budget system, as just described, thus releasing the principal from many of his chores. The next on his list of burdensome tasks is the school schedule. It takes not only some of the principal's time, but also much of the time of members of his staff. Yet it is a vital and important function and cannot be shunted off. As one high school principal says, "The master program is to the high school principal as the musical score is to the concert director, for in either case a soundly planned program, harmonious and tightly knit in all of its component parts, will determine the effectiveness of the individual staff members and his entire organization." Another administrator put it more starkly: "The schedule is in many cases the principal, if not the only, bulwark standing between the administrator and chaos." For a given school year, the master schedule tells you who will do what and when—this includes teachers, students, and units.

In many high schools, teachers are removed from teaching assignments and are replaced by substitutes as early as May to formulate the next year's schedule. Other schools employ teachers in the summer to do this. Both are costly procedures from the point of view of time taken away from students as well as actual dollar cost. Substitutes are expensive; paying teachers to work during vacation time is expensive; the principal's time is expensive. Yet today there exists a computer program called Generalized Academic Simulation Program or GASP that creates a school schedule in a fraction of the time and at a fraction of the cost of teacher–administrator produced schedules. Certain information is gathered by the school, such as: a list of all instructors, by name and subject area; a list of all rooms, giving capacity and special purpose, if any; a list of all students and subject requests or a sampling thereof; permissible time patterns e.g., Monday–Friday first period, Tuesday fourth and fifth periods, etc.; a list of all subjects, and for each one: the number of sections indicated, and all other relevant information, such as the maximum number of students per class, the type of time pattern available for each subject e.g., "five days a week," "twice a week," etc., instructors available for each subject (and any preferences), and the distribution of rooms available for each subject (e.g., for English the list might specify any standard classroom, but for physics laboratory periods "physics laboratory only"). Once this is done, the information is punched on IBM cards, and then the computer goes to work. To produce a schedule using GASP takes only about one quarter of the man hours required to produce a schedule by hand.

The basic cost of GASP falls into two categories: (1) purchase of computer time; (2) salary or fee for expert help. The program itself—the actual tapes and related instructions—costs nothing (in keeping with the special freemasonry of computerdom). GASP requires the use of a large IBM computer (a 709, 7090, or 7094), plus a smaller computer (1401) operated in tandem. In the present state of the art, programs are not adaptable to all computers—they work only on the computers or family of computers for which they were designed. (It would take up to several months to recode a program like GASP for use on another kind of large computer.) Many sizable school systems now rent, by the year, 1401's or comparable computers to do their own data processing.

A school wishing to embark on GASP should shop around for a good buy in computer services. A nearby university is the logical first choice; in most universities, however, computers run on two or even three shifts, and are booked solid for months ahead. Another possibility is any good large scientific laboratory (a thousand employees or more); some of these institutions charge only for large-computer time and throw in the 1401 time free since they have relatively small need for the vast print output which is 1401's specialty.

Outside of such nonprofit sources, the school's best bet is a commercial data-processing center or the nearest big plant of a research-oriented industry such as aircraft, petro-chemicals, communications, defense industries in general.

In GASP's brief history, costs have varied widely—from $1 to $10 per student. Some of this cost is fixed, and does not depend on the size of the school. The variation is a function of many factors: the complexity of the school program in question, the accuracy and completeness of the data the school provides, the unit price of computer time, the extent to which the school requires expert assistance, and the amount of output that the school wants. For instance, GASP scheduled one school with 2,500 students at about $3 per student, and a school with 400 at about $7 per student. In both cases, the cost included *expertise* plus multiple outputs, including grade reports and attendance records, as well as all the standard and optional GASP outputs.

Besides computer time, the other basic GASP cost is for expert help. Here again there are various ways to "skin the cat." A school may already employ a computer man, or it may hire one when it undertakes GASP, probably part-time or in conjunction with other schools. Or the school may retain a consultant for a month or so to manage the technical details of GASP and work with the scheduler, who would then plan to spend twice that much time himself on the feed-in and reading. The school may be able to buy the GASP scheduling service as a package from the company or institution from which it buys computer time. (The McDonnell Automation Center in St. Louis, and International Telephone & Telegraph in northern New Jersey, for instance, are both currently servicing GASP in this fashion.)

However, costs can be reduced most sharply if someone on the staff learns from the consultant the ins and outs of computer scheduling. In Ridgewood High School, in Norridge, Illinois, after only one year's experience with GASP, a staff member now handles pretty much the whole process with minimum outside help, up to the actual computer runs. And Ridgewood's "expert," an administrative assistant to the principal, was formerly a teacher of industrial arts, with no great background in mathematics, who learned about GASP "without too much trouble" — mainly by working with the experts and brushing up a bit on digital computers. He spends no more than one-fourth of his time on scheduling matters, including GASP.

Computer scheduling is currently in use in San Jose, Stockton, and Sunnyvale, California; as well as Marshall High School in Portland, Oregon; Wayland High School in Wayland, Massachusetts; Ridgewood High School in Morridge Illinois; and Cohasset High School in Cohasset, Massachusetts; Pascack Hill High School in Montvale, New Jersey; two high schools in Quincy, Massachusetts; Centennial Joint Schools in Bucks County, Pennsylvania; and a high school in Charleston, West Virginia.

The use of computers to relieve the professionals of some of the time-consuming administrative tasks of scheduling is just one example of how to bring down the cost of personnel. Another of its time-saving functions can be the setting of salary schedules. At least once a year most school administrators are tagged with this ordeal. The long hours of exhausting work have been known to produce ulcers, emotional trauma, and four or five service calls from the desk calculator repairman. Perhaps, after salary ritual time is over, some administrators will claim the process was worthwhile. However, any administrator who has been in the business very long will attest to the fact that, despite all his efforts and the most skillful application of talents, the new schedule will please very few, if any, staff members. Yet, come what may, the schedule must be ready for the opening of the new school term.

Today there exists a computer program, SSS—Super Salary Schedule. All it needs is a terminal connected to a computer. Almost any local data-processing company has the facilities for a programming language that can use the Salary Scheduler. With the use of the SSS program, all of the necessary data can be entered into a computer in less than 5 minutes; once entered, the data setup is available for all future program runs. Changes are easily facilitated to contend with differing forms of salary scheduling.

It should be noted, too, that a complete scheduling run, including schedules and analysis, takes less than 20 minutes of terminal time and a complete run uses less than one minute of computer time. It is estimated that one run of the program is equivalent to 40 or more hours of work using traditional manual methods.

And what a saving of professional salaries! Depending upon the salary schedule of a school district, it has been estimated that from $50,000 to $500,000 can be saved by using a computer. And, most important, aside from the ease of computation and the money saved, the computer will do the job with over-all greater efficacy. Some of the more obvious advantages over the traditional methods are:

The element of human error is appreciably reduced.

Minutes are required to create a workable salary schedule instead of hours, weeks, or, in some cases, months.

New salary schedules needed on a crisis basis are quickly and accurately available.

Analysis-in-depth is enhanced.

Numerous different salary schedules are available, literally at the push of a button.

Computational readouts are available for validation and/or verification.

Administrator's time can be released for other important activities.

In addition, as with the school-scheduling process, the salary-scheduling program is not difficult to understand. Even a person with limited computer experience can use the terminal with ease; after one round with the help of an expert, the task can be taken on by a lower-paid employee.

Thus, cumbersome and expensive administrative tasks can be taken away from the school principal and his staff, time and money can be saved, and more information can become available more quickly.

Principals repeatedly maintain that relief from administrative loads would be among the greatest of possible blessings. Then, they say, they could "get down to the business of education." Let us suppose, then, that many of the "managerial" tasks were removed from the principal's agenda—would life really be so idyllic? Probably not, unless he could discard the traditional concept of his position. Although principals complain that their burdens are all administrative in nature, they fail to understand that many of them are psychological, a matter of how the principal views himself and those who work for him. The principal too often sees himself as a father figure, the one to whom all problems flow—and as the ultimate decision-maker, responsible, too, for putting those decisions into effect. This approach is self-defeating. By depriving his staff of all power and responsibility, by requiring that they clear everything with Mr. Principal, he emasculates them and destroys the motivation that a sense of sharing will inspire.

Let him not, then, simply decry his burdens. Both he and the school would benefit if he would divest himself of many of them. The school environment would improve and education would become a more exciting and involving experience. It only requires that he be ready and willing to share his responsibilities for decision-making with members of his staff, and permit them to face and resolve some of the problems that affect them.

Furthermore, by calling upon the staff to share in the decision-making process, the administration does much to allay the resentment often created when new regulations or practices are sent down from above. Also not to be overlooked is the fact that such allocation of responsibility helps develop the staff's ability in problem-solving and decision-making, and in personal development.

In a recent article for the *National Elementary School Principal*, William Wayson, Director of Urban Education, The Ohio State University, describes the "new kind of principal" as one who, by decentralizing the decision-making process in his school and setting a climate of cooperative planning, opens the door to a whole new concept of priorities for himself and his school. Teachers and parents join him in making decisions.

This new collaborative approach can sweep in the fresh winds of divergent and unorthodox practices. The length of the school day might vary; children may be in school at 5:30 PM or on Saturdays. Staff comes in on staggered schedules. There may be no textbooks, or at least fewer textbooks, but other kinds of educational materials. Parents may teach classes. All of this because teachers, parents, and students are involved in composing the programs. These are their programs, not his alone. This new principal, through the process of participatory decision-making, may now introduce new practices and seek more solutions; he may discard the rituals of tradition and policy that obscure his view of education's ultimate goals.

Once a school can be opened up in this way, then, instead of having one overworked, unproductive principal, you have many professionals who divide the work and responsibility. It no longer operates as a monolithic entity. The principal coordinates and orchestrates all of the elements in his school. Costs, too, are reduced because of higher productivity on everyone's part.

If this new kind of principal really produces a better environment and, therefore, a better education, we may appropriately ask if he should not be compensated for it? No industry will operate efficiently unless it provides an incentive motive for its employees. This brings us to another factor in cost reduction.

Would principals "produce" more if there were incentives, or bonuses, if you wish? Is this possible in education? Why is it that with much the same type of population some schools are better than others; students, parents, teachers are happier and achievement is higher? How can you get all schools in the district up to those standards? What kind of incentive can you offer the chief administrator so that his school becomes as productive as the others?

The Chicago school system was one of the first in the country to develop and put into operation, in March 1971, an administrative compensation plan for principals and all other supervisors based on performance. Although it is considered a new approach in a large urban school system, the plan is based upon tested and accepted business management practice. The procedure is based upon the appraisal of an individual's achievement of performance objectives, mutually agreed upon by him and his superior. Performance appraisal is put into terms of the actual achievement of objectives which are specific and meaningful—objectives which the administrator and his superior have agreed upon at the beginning of the review period and have discussed during the review period. Specifically, this approach involves measurement of actual results accomplished during the review period in relation to the objectives previously agreed upon.

Basic features of the plan call for selecting the key functions so as to underscore the most important areas of individual responsibility, determining performance objectives described in specific terms within the framework of these key responsibilities, preparing accomplishment reports as a brief statement of results achieved in the accomplishment of individual objectives, setting up interim reviews as an ongoing report of progress toward achievement of objectives, and, finally, the performance appraisal, made by evaluating results achieved in comparison with objectives.

Principals and other supervisors, such as curriculum directors, guidance counselors, and office administrators, are then compensated according to the appraisal of their performance. High performance—meeting all one's performance objectives—brings with it higher salary. Low performance not only brings lower salary but gives both the employer and employee a common basis for either changing positions within the system or leaving the system. Firing an administrator is no longer one man's opinion of another or even a group of opinions of a person. Staying, leaving, advancing, are now based on appraisal of performance by stated criteria.

This method is too new to evaluate. Its purpose is not to cut the cost of education by giving some administrators less than others. That would defeat its intent. Its real purpose is to get "more for the money," greater productivity. Hopefully, by comparing the relative performance of the individual administrator with the objectives previously agreed upon, there will be improved instruction resulting in higher student achievement, which is recognized as the basic responsibility of any administration.

A somewhat similar approach is being taken with teachers and parents in San Antonio, Texas. Teachers and parents of pupils at an elementary school are being offered cash rewards—up to $1,200 for instructors—if the pupils show "greater than anticipated" progress in math and reading this year. Parents could receive incentive payments up to $100 under the Federally-financed pilot project approved by trustees of the San Antonio School District.

The project was designed to determine the "change process" that occurs in terms of pupils, teacher, administrator, and parental behavior while working under defined incentives. The rewards will be presented after the pupils are tested at the end of school next spring. Parents are being offered the stipends to "encourage them to give proper supervision to studies within the home." The program will work this way:

About 600 pupils at Washington Elementary School will be tested by an independent agency before and after the program. Pupils at another grade school, comparable to Washington in terms of socioeconomic and ethnic backgrounds, will also be tested and will serve as a control group. The progress of the pupils at the two schools will be compared at the end of the year to determine the effect of the incentive program. Teachers and parents will receive stipends in varying amounts depending on the rate of "accelerated achievement." What is being said is that incentives to produce are important to all concerned with education, not to administrators alone.

This brings us to where the largest amount of the educational dollar is spent, teachers and teacher salaries. And for that matter, the largest impact on education is made by teachers. Teachers' salaries, because they represent the largest part of the operational budget, are the first item to be sliced from the budget when the crunch comes. Incidentally, there is nothing wrong with cutting the cost of teacher payrolls, if it is not done at the expense of approved educational objectives. If the same goals can be achieved with fewer professional teachers, there is no reason why an already overextended system should maintain excess positions. On the other hand, if we cut the teaching staff by, say, 10 percent, solely because of a budget crisis, we not only undercut the teachers but we overburden the remaining staff with more students and more class work. Although this is the prevailing method of cutting costs, it may not be the most productive.

Are there ways of economizing that give promise of being more creative than "across the board" cuts? Should we not be taking a new look at what kinds of jobs have to be done in education and who are the best people to do them? Are we chained to the idea of the professional "teacher" being the only person who can facilitate learning, and are all teachers equal in their ability to do even that? Should we not consider differentiating assignments among our professionals, bringing into education people other than professional educators, such as specialists from industry, central agencies, and the outside world generally, parents, even students both from the colleges and from those now within our schools? Should we not be looking at new ways of sharing services, both within the schools and in conjunction with agencies outside of the schools? Perhaps some of the following ideas will not only help in cutting the cost of education by economizing on the number of highly paid professional teachers we employ, but, equally important, by introducing new and exciting people into education. Let's brush the cobwebs aside and see what we can do.

When we look about us, we see that in almost every business or profession, people are paid according to their particular skill; no one person is expected to do everything. Yet in education, teachers are all assumed to have the same role, and no salary differential is established regardless of what service they perform. Admittedly, any deviation from a uniform salary scale may lead to abuse; and the teachers' very real fears on that score should not be minimized. Favoritism by the principal or any other potential abuse from subjective selection should be precluded in every way possible. And yet, we cannot afford to neglect this approach as a major economy.

Differentiated staffing is new to education. The first pattern was carried out in Temple City, California, in 1966. The Temple City program takes the form of a stairstep, or hierarchical model. Starting at the top and going down are echelons of master teachers, senior teachers, staff teachers, associate teachers, and three types of paraprofessionals—teacher aides, resource center assistants, and lab assistants. Responsibilities and salaries for these positions are varied, though the staff teacher and associate teacher are tenured. The associate teacher, a novice, has a "learning schedule" and less demanding responsibilities; the staff teacher has a full teaching load and is aided by paraprofessionals; the senior teacher is a "learning engineer," or methodological expert in a subject; the master teacher is a scholar-research specialist who translates research theory into classroom possibilities.

This model is the forerunner of many attempts to break the mold in which all teachers are treated as equal in ability and in pay. As do most differentiated staffing models, it provides teachers with the opportunity to work themselves up a career ladder without having to leave the classroom in order to be recognized both professionally and financially. It allows good teachers to

TEMPLE CITY MODEL (Salaries as of 1966)

Tenure $6,500-9,000	Tenure $7,500-11,000	Nontenure $14,500-17,500	Nontenure $15,500-25,000
Associate Teacher	Staff Teacher	Senior Teacher	Master Teacher
A.B. or Intern	B.A. Degree and Calif. Credential	M.S. or Equivalent	Doctorate or Equivalent
100% Teaching	100% Teaching Responsibilities	3/5's Staff Teaching Responsibilities	2/5's Staff Teaching Responsibilities

Academic Assistants A.A. Degree or Equivalent
Educational Technicians
Clerks

maintain their contact with youngsters, instead of being "kicked upstairs" into administration when a promotion is in order. It increases the incentive factor and recognizes creativity and dedication.

This model has been adopted by many schools. The objections of those involved have been minimal, probably because it has not displaced very many people. Note that no matter what step or level one is on, one is still a teacher or about to become one. Even the paraprofessionals are professionals in their own right. They do not fall into the familiar category of people with low-level skills. The professionals range from interns to those with B.A.'s, M.A.'s, and Doctorates. The salaries are commensurate with responsibilities, and tenure applies only to those on the lowest level. Once you start to rise on the ladder you trade security for greater responsibility and a higher salary.

This model, although attractive because it does not take on the dragon of introducing nonprofessionals or paraprofessionals into the teaching hierarchy, is nevertheless a concept that has been fought vigorously by labor organizations in the educational profession. It is seen by them as a grandiose subterfuge for implementing "merit pay," which opens the door to favoritism and encourages faculty separation and divisiveness. However, over all these objections, this and other patterns are evolving and are meeting with success in communities where teacher organizations are not too active.

The answer to the merit pay objection, according to proponents, is that, under differentiated staffing, teachers are paid differently for different responsibilities, as opposed to traditional merit pay setups where people are paid differently because they are judged to be performing similar tasks at different quality levels.

Unquestionably, the most extensive proposal for differentiated staffing is found in Florida, where, in 1968, the state legislature issued a mandate requesting the state department of education to "develop and operate model projects of flexible staff organization, in selected elementary and secondary schools, based on differentiated levels of responsibility and compensation for services performed." As a result, a comprehensive feasibility study was completed, along with a plan that included role clarifictations and cost analyses. Pilot projects are now set to begin in these three counties: Dade (which includes Miami), Leon, and Sarasota.

The Florida model has more levels than the one in Temple City, California. Starting from the top, there are: a teaching research specialist, equivalent to the principal, teaching curriculum specialists, senior teachers, staff teachers, associate teachers, assistant teachers, educational technicians, and teacher aides. Each position has a different salary range and certain educational requirements.

The first break into research responsibility comes at the senior-teacher level, though the senior teacher will still spend four-fifths of his time in the classroom. Personnel at the two highest level positions will teach about three-fifths of the time. Within the salary brackets, each position from associate teacher up has a range of $1,500, divided into 3 yearly increments of $500 each. The lower positions have a range of $1,000, divided into 4 yearly increments of $250 each.

In addition to some earlier models and the Temple City and Florida models, many local districts have certain aspects of differentiated staffing (team teaching, flexible scheduling, etc.) already built into their programs. A substantial number are said to be considering full-blown programs. And the states of Wisconsin and Massachusetts appear to be boosting the concept through changes in state certification regulations.

Since teachers are most affected by differentiated staffing, the Association of Classroom Teachers conducted a conference

FLORIDA MODEL

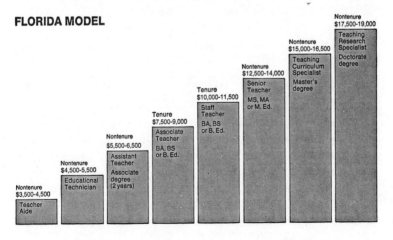

of representative teachers from all parts of the country to compile opinions. Conference participants cited these advantages:

The concept appears to provide a more meaningful educational experience and climate favorable to the development of each child.

It fosters good teaching techniques, such as flexible assignments, modular scheduling, matching of instructional resources with learner needs, individualized learning experiences, and a clinical approach to meet student needs.

It provides for more effective use of human resources.

The opportunity is there for interaction among teachers, administrators, teacher aides, parents, and the community.

On the other hand, they foresaw some obstacles:

A tendency on the part of some persons to move too quickly. The roles of administrators must change at the same pace as the roles of the classroom teachers.

Insufficient funds for an adequate program.

Personnel not prepared to operate within the new framework.

The tendency to bill differentiated staffing as a cure-all for educational ills.

A fear that assignments will be used as a means to cut school budgets by paying higher salaries to a few teachers who reach top brackets and lower salaries to the vast majority.

Inadequate public relations and biased information programs.

It was admitted, however, that all these "obstacles" could be overcome by judicious planning. These evaluations, both positive and negative, are familiar and can be raised against almost any new program.

Now, let us take a look at the cost of these operations. First, has it improved education so that we can reduce our losses in human resources? Both experiments, Temple City and Florida, felt they were better able to meet their educational objectives through differentiated staffing. Teachers became "individualized" by matching their talents to a level of performance. Students gained by having a greater variety of teaching personnel rather than a single teacher or a prescribed set of "professionals." They are closer in age to the interns and feel that they get "expert" instruction from technicians. They also have a sense of belonging to a team—a sort of school within a school. Students interviewed said there was an intimacy generated by the new structure that they did not feel before—all this to the good.

Now, what about the dollar cost? When Arthur Shapiro, assistant superintendent of schools in DeKalb, Illinois, who helped write a differentiated staffing simulation kit for the Center for the Study of Educational Personnel Policies, Inc., was asked this question, he responded: "Differentiated staffing is going to make us much more efficient, but I don't think it's going to reduce costs." But is this really true? In both Temple City and Florida, the total personnel costs with differentiated staffing came to 5 percent less than the conventional mode of staffing— hardly a significant saving. But let's look ahead. To begin with, even with the present models which are limited, fewer teachers reach the top payscale. As more unnecessary high salaried, but tenured, teachers retire, they will be replaced by new teachers, operating at different steps on lower salaries. Any plan that can be a positive force in education *and* still reduce the number of high salaried, tenured teachers has promise even if we cannot see startling results in the immediate future.

Another modification of differentiated staffing is that of pooling of resources. Some states are instituting cooperative education programs whereby teachers are shared by two or more schools. For example, a topnotch science teacher on the highest rung of the pay scale can head up a differentiated staffing team and service more than one school. This has advantages because not only are expert teachers hard to find, but they are expensive. Why not share their talents and skills by having them serve two schools or a cluster of schools. Either the teachers can travel to several schools or the students, certainly on the secondary level, can attend school in different locations. One day, for example, they may go to a school for science, another day to a school for social studies. Not only would the experience of moving around be interesting for the students, but it could be extremely productive financially. Money could be saved on materials and equipment since it is less expensive to equip one social studies or science laboratory than two or three. The cost of the teachers' salaries would also be shared. This could be done, of course, most effectively in schools with small registers, where there are too few students to keep a particular teacher or team occupied for the full day. It can also be done in situations where new curriculums are being offered, such as environmental education or urban and ethnic studies, and where the course can then be shared by many schools on an experimental basis. If the course becomes very popular and highly effective, an individual school may institute the course on its own.

Those subjects which are not basic or required subjects often are not attended daily by students and resident staffs, and are expensive additions to the payroll. Sharing of personnel and facilities is not a complicated process. It takes cooperative planning on the part of teachers and administrators and an understanding of the purposes of such an approach on the part of parents and students.

Although most cooperative education plans are currently in operation in small communities, large school systems are beginning to move in that direction also. In Chicago, Los Angeles, Philadelphia, and New York, students are now being offered a comprehensive high school program. Rather than having to select an academic or vocational school, they can go to an academic high school for basic subjects and then, for part of the week, to a vocational high school for automobile mechanics, beauty culture, food trades, or any other vocational course that is offered. This avoids expensive duplication of services and equipment and allows the student to have many more experiences than any self-contained high school could possibly afford to give him.

Another approach to utilizing personnel in a cost benefit manner and also to inject new blood into our schools is to employ students to work with students. Informally, children have always helped their friends with homework, and older brothers have tutored younger siblings. Children teach each other chess and Monopoly. Peer counseling and rap sessions in college dorms are normal and accepted practice. What is not generally recognized, however, is that the learning that is taking place is a two-way process, that the teacher–student learns as much as, if not more than, the student–learner.

Mobilization for Youth, a New York City antipoverty program, reports that over a 5-month period in which older children tutored younger childron with reading difficulties, those tutored gained 6.0 months, while the tutors themselves gained an extraordinary 3.4 years. This virtually doubles or triples our profit. Both learn, the student and the teacher. Jerome Bruner, in *The Process of Education*, says on this subject:

> I went through it [the quantum theory] once and looked up only to find the class full of blank faces—they had obviously not understood. I went through it a second time, and they still did not understand it. And so I went through it a third time, and that time I understood it and so did the class.

What could be more natural than that children, faced with the task of tutoring others, should learn to grasp the strategy of learning by dint of having to master materials well enough to teach others? Forced to figure out why another child might be floundering, the tutor achieves a new insight himself. The seventeenth-century Comenius said:

> The saying, "He who teaches others teaches himself," is very true not only because constant repetition impresses a fact indelibly on the mind but because the process of teaching in itself gives a deeper insight into the subjects taught . . . The gifted Joachim Fortius used to say that . . . if a student wishes to make progress, he should arrange to give lessons daily in the subjects which he was studying, even if he had to hire his pupils.

In our schools we have literally hundreds of students who could become "teachers" of others. Naturally, there would be no compensation since it is all part of a mutual learning process. In some situations, remediation in reading or math could, with minimal assistance from a teacher, be administered by student "teachers." Advanced science courses, foreign languages, instrumental music, are just samples of the kinds of learnings that could be joint ventures between student–learner and student–teacher–learner.

Furthermore, there is another advantage that we derive as a spin-off from this type of programming. Urie Bronfenbrenner's perceptive analysis of the isolationist effect of the tendency within American society to grade and segregate by age makes one realize that the idea of peer teaching may be a revolutionary step toward maintaining communication in a society where the forces of urban organization, of mass production, and indeed of mass education, are all centrifugal. The contemporary effort to reconstruct our schools is part of the general effort to reduce isolation, to re-establish mutuality and exchange. Sharing one's skills and knowledge with others, being teacher as well as learner, is conducive to that end.

The student–teacher–learner relationship has been around a long time. Now we are suggesting institutionalizing it. It offers few problems; it is a threat to no one on the professional staff and it can be utilized whether or not there is differentiated staffing. It adds no costs and it does increase services—a good measure of productivity.

The techniques of differentiated staffing and sharing services are performed primarily in the educational community. Even in differentiated staffing, rearrangements are made within the realm of professionals with some few additional experts and technicians. Shared services and cooperative education ventures are usually exclusively among school people and school institutions. There is, however, another approach to shared services and differentiated staffing that extends itself outside of the school community, and one that shows much promise of cutting costs of personnel and revitalizing education.

In Cambridge, Massachusetts, a manufacturer of hi-fi equipment has just set up a demonstration day care center for children of his employees, in cooperation with the United States Children's Bureau, and with the cooperation of the employees themselves. The KLH Child Development Center, Inc., as it is called, will be owned and operated by the children's parents. It will run from 7 AM to 3:30 PM to coincide with the parents' work day. It will take children between the ages of 2 and 6. Mothers will be free to come and eat with their children during their own lunch hours.

This school provides many of the functions of public education, although in a specialized situation. The parents hired the teachers, some of whom are the professional teachers, but most are other parents or college students. They also hired a child psychologist and a nurse. The "rent" or space is provided by the company, since it is to their advantage to make it possible for mothers to work. The parents bear the rest of the costs. The costs are $300 per year per child. This is opposed to a range of $600 a year in some of our poorest and most backward school systems to $1,500 a year in our richest systems. What a difference in costs! Three conclusions may be drawn from this type of arrangement. One is that education can take place anywhere and not exclusively in a school building. Secondly, that education is everyone's business, and school boards would be wise to team up with industry, labor, church organizations, parents, college students, as a means of sharing the costs. Thirdly, it explodes the myth that we must employ only professional, highly paid nursery school teachers. The parents and college students received 40 percent of the going rate for professional nursery school teachers.

There is a tendency to believe that some mystique attaches to the training methods for the early childhood years and that specialists are needed to apply them. Actually, there is nothing so esoteric in the education of these youngsters as to preclude the aid of kind and intelligent laymen.

Informal schooling of this type can be made available in any convenient location within the walking capacity of children. The schools can be housed in renovated tenements or in newly built "pocket" type construction or placed in mobile units if land and buildings are not available. By placing these tiny schools throughout the community we not only make it possible for children to walk "around the corner" or "next door" to school, but we also relate the culture of the school to the culture of the community. Each such block school, largely administered by its own staff and parents, could have a resident staff consisting of professional teachers, paraprofessional teacher aides (neighborhood parents), student teachers, big brothers and sisters, who would work in the schools as part of their education—a truly differentiated teaching staff. A visiting staff might consist of artists, musicians, and representatives of local cultural institutions who would extend the experiences of the children. They would, in fact, be an extension of the home; and, through constant parent interaction and involvement, the home in turn would become an extension of the school.

In supporting this concept, Paul Goodman, in *The New York Review of Books* (January 4, 1968), wrote of the practical aspects of budgeting such schools:

> *The cost saving in such a setup is the almost total elimination of top-down administration and the kind of special services that are required precisely because of excessive size and rigidity. The chief uses of central administration would be licensing, funding, choosing sites, and some inspection. There would be no principals, assistants and secretaries. Curriculum, texts, equipment would be determined as needed—and, despite the present putative economies of scale, they would be cheaper: much less would be pointless or wasted. Record-keeping would be at a minimum. There is no need for truant officers when the teacher-and-seven can call at the absentee's home and inquire. There is little need for remedial personnel since the staff and parents are always in contact, and the whole enterprise can be regarded as remedial. Organizational studies of large top-down directed enterprises show that the total cost is invariably at least 300 percent above the cost of the immediate function, in this case the interaction of teachers and children. I would put this 300 percent into increasing the number of adults and diversifying the possibilities of instruction. Further, in the conditions of New York real estate, there is great advantage in ceasing to build four-million-dollar school buildings, and rather fitting tiny schools into available niches.*

Let's extend this concept a bit further. Can we bring other kinds of people into the education process at levels other then preschool and kindergarten? What about primary or elementary education? It is perhaps on this level that most progress has been made in bringing in outside people. Five years ago, the term "paraprofessional" meant some sort of poorly compensated person, preferably from the local community, who took over some menial tasks that the teacher had to perform—lunchroom duty, putting on snow suits, policing the toilets. Today we define a paraprofessional as someone who performs a necessary function within an agency but who does not require professional training.

For example, paraprofessionals, today, include school aides, such as cafeteria employees, clerical assistants, building helpers; teachers aides who help teachers in classroom chores; and teacher assistants who actually assist teachers in instruction.

Throughout the country at least 116,000 such teacher and school aides are employed. Of these, 30,000 work in New York City alone.

Most of these paraprofessional programs are built on the concept of career ladders. A person can enter at almost any rung and move up. Mobility is a key factor. Unlike teachers, who are paid up to $12 an hour in some school systems, paraprofessionals earn from $2 to about $4.25 an hour. Those systems that use them are usually more than pleased with the results. Teachers are relieved of the multitude of tasks that they consider unprofessional, and children get more attention because adults are assigned to meet their specific needs. Paraprofessional programs, however, are only a saving to a school system if they serve to reduce the regular teaching staff. Otherwise, they simply swell the payroll (which is the complaint of most school systems). It is most important, therefore, that before hiring more teachers because of increased enrollment, an analysis be made of objectives—tasks and programs and the kind of people needed to do them. The principal is then in a position to say how many professional teachers he needs and at what levels of competency, and following that, the number of paraprofessionals he will require and for what purposes.

In Ulster County in New York State, paraprofessionals were incorporated into a brand new high school of 2,500 students that opened in September 1971. The program was launched in cooperation with the AFL-CIO State, County, and Municipal Employees Union. A study was made of the number of students to be enrolled and the curriculum that was being afforded them. Then the soon-to-be principal and the community had to make some hard decisions. Were they going to be guided by the customary pupil–teacher ratio, one teacher for every 30 students, or were they going to use some other formula? They decided on a modified form of differentiated staffing plus a large infusion of paraprofessionals. They were able to do this because they worked closely with the union. Even though it was not the teachers' union, it was respected and accepted by the professional organizations. According to a projected figure of one million dollars allowed for salaries, they were able to hire an instructional manager (principal), 3 teaching research specialists, 20 senior teachers, 43 staff teachers, 22 associate teachers, 15 assistant teachers, 3 educational technicians, and 30 teacher aides (paraprofessionals).

If they had used the 30 pupil to 1 teacher formula, the school would have had a complement of about 83 teachers. Using the differentiated staffing approach, plus technicians and teacher aides, they opened with 140 adults—almost twice as many "teachers" as they would have had with the conventional formula. With all of this personnel, they spent $900,000 instead of one million dollars. It is much easier to introduce this concept in a situation that either calls for more teachers or one in which you are opening a new school than in an already existing one. To "let teachers out" is not only difficult and unwise, but in schools that are unionized it is almost impossible.

Another approach to incorporating new kinds of people in education is to reach outside the school to its environs for some phases of education. This brings with it a double bonus, new places to learn in and people with new faces and skills to learn from. Forward-looking school boards and high school principals are beginning to realize that, in some instances, students learn more when they are teamed up with the "people who do it" —rather than the middleman, the teacher. Most of this is happening in the career areas, and is a natural response to some of the shortcomings of our vocational schools. Generally, students enter a 4-year course in a vocational school, expecting to graduate with a marketable skill; yet within those 4 years the specific skill for that job may change or the skill be eliminated because a machine has replaced the manual worker.

An example of this may be seen in the food trades. Thousands of young people throughout the country were being trained as meat cutters. By the time they were ready for employment, manual meat cutting was largely eliminated and machines had taken over the job. Obviously, the skills required to build and operate these machines fell into an entirely different category; the vocational schools had no facilities to teach those skills.

Industry, on the other hand, is geared to change. The incentive of competition will produce the ideas, the instructors, and, most important, the constantly changing equipment. It is almost impossible for any school to secure sufficient funds to change equipment as often as industry does. The cost factor, combined with the special expertise that only industry has, raises questions as to what education's role should realistically be in vocational training.

School people and industrialists should together survey specifically designed industrial programs to determine what parts are appropriate to a school curriculum and what parts are so highly specialized that they can and should be taught only "on location." This would remove many obsolete practices from school programs. And it would help maintain student interest in achieving the specific goal of getting a job.

Today's young man often cares little for long-term goals. He wants immediate satisfactions, realistic results at an early age; he is aware of the value of money and he wants a "piece of the action." Programs that build on this measure of success and hold promise for realization in the very near future have a better chance of capturing such students than do those with long-range goals. Industry can offer such programs.

And, what is more, this combination of industry and education offers advantages beyond the obvious one of joining a receptive youngster with a functionable skill. A competent career training costs public education about $1500 per year, per student. A.T.&T., R.C.A., and IBM estimate the cost of their training programs at about $1200 per student. One reason for the difference is that "trainers" in their institutes or educational programs are practitioners and are skilled in their specific area. Their salaries are far below those of professional teachers in the vocational high schools. And, what is more, about 80 percent of the young people stay with the program to the end and pass the examinations. Of course one must allow for the fact that in private industry a screening process takes place before a person is accepted. This often eliminates the "hard-core" unteachables. On the basis of these figures, it would certainly appear that we can get more for our money both in the development of human resources and dollarwise if we turn over some of the school functions to appropriate agencies.

For others who seek an education in the "outside world," another idea has been introduced. The Human Resources Administration in New York City has begun by taking 200 high school students to work part time in welfare agencies, senior citizen's centers, and in child care centers—a sort of urban peace corps. A curriculum is developed for them by the agency and the school. Similar programs are in operation in Cleveland, San Diego, Chicago, and Houston, among other municipalities. In these programs, teachers are really "other professionals," and the students in the program learn as they work for social workers, nurses, physicians, psychologists. In the New York City program, it is not costing the schools anything because the Human Resources agencies are delighted to get the help of the young people. They, too, need resources.

In suburban St. Louis and Atlanta, similar programs are in operation within the judicial system. Students are programed into police precincts, courthouses, jails, and into the offices of the corporation counsel and the district attorneys. Together, students, teachers, and "other professionals," plan that part of the school year that will be spent in these activities. A city environment is not necessary to launch such a program. Every community includes industries, businesses, houses of worship, service agencies, and the like. The environment and its components can become the curriculum for schooling.

The school systems that have instituted these programs have found that the students are fascinated by their work experience outside of school, that their achievement in school subjects is no worse and in some cases far better. In many cases, attendance has improved; discipline cases have been fewer. Some students say they feel "uncaged"; others say it's fun; still others feel "they are doing something for others"; but almost all like the freedom of being in an adult world.

Does this cost the schools any less? Most certainly it does. A Cleveland high school, facing increasing enrollment, has been able to avoid increasing its teaching staff by 5 percent or $100,000, by programing students into the community agencies for part of the school day. It is almost impossible actually to reduce the teaching staff by introducing the program. Job elimination is too difficult a personnel problem. It is far simpler to freeze all increases in staff.

The Parkway School in Philadelphia was able to run on a fraction of a regular high school budget by programing the students into the city rather than into a school. However, much of the Parkway Project, like the program mentioned above, depends for its survival on the good will of an agency director or a city administrator or a corporation president. Such tenuous status is risky. When positions and people who fill them change or are subject to political whim, it can play havoc with a program such as this. If this type of program is to be made attractive, provision must be made within the school budget to insure services no matter where they come from.

Many schools both within the public school system and outside of it are utilizing some of the personnel practices suggested in this section. Computers, management teams, productivity scales, differentiated staffing, new kinds of teachers, new partnerships for education are currently being experimented with. The chapter on Alternatives in Education will describe in detail how schools are using these approaches.

Technologies for Learning

Traditionally, in American education the teacher is the dispenser of knowledge and the students the recipients. Like fledglings, the students depended upon the teacher for all learning functions until they could walk on their own. It was assumed that as the child progressed through the school years, he would become more independent and eventually would be able to apply the learning skills by himself. This assumption, however, has not been borne out by fact. Too many "graduates" today have neither the knowledge they were to have acquired through this intravenous method nor the skills for acquiring it when needed. Too many youngsters have been left crippled by the method and unable to function when the crutches were removed. They acquired neither the skills of learning nor the interest in it that self-help would have inspired.

If formal education is to be the official launching pad for a lifetime of interest in learning, then a teacher's highest goal should be to instill a sense of independence in his students. Today, we have come to realize that as soon as the child enters school he must learn *how* to learn. Teachers must, from the very beginning, harness the child's natural curiosity and imagination to the formative tools of education. To do this a youngster must learn not only how to learn but how to do it on his own.

Independent study permits a child to develop, often with delight and sometimes with frustration, his own power to seek out information, organize facts, master material, and generally accept responsibility for his own learning. Independent study is not new to children when they enter school. It begins in the home, where the child through practice learns to do such things by himself as dressing, tying his shoes, using the toilet, playing, looking at books, counting, and, in general, performing the daily functions of living.

In the preprimary school, this at-home learning can be strengthened by an even richer environment. Montessorians and behavioral scientists like O. K. Moore have demonstrated that very young children get tremendous satisfaction from self-correcting devices from which they can learn at their own pace without the intervention of an adult. Specifically, nursery and kindergarten children should have the opportunity for free exploration of materials, paints, books, and blocks, as well as slides and short films.

The same process can continue through the primary school, with the child independently investigating the library corner of the classroom, perhaps deciding to play alone at recess or to work alone in a setting arranged to enhance his particular project. Learning to read looms large during these early years, and a child can acquire this basic skill faster if, in addition to regular reading instruction, he uses devices such as sandpaper letters, typewriters, films, tapes on reading readiness, and magnetic recording cards to practice his newly acquired skills.

As the child moves ahead, he acquires increased self-reliance in the library-learning center, and he can pursue his personal interests there. Through the use of programmed materials, he can proceed at his own pace in mastering some materials, and can even test his own progress and determine how much drill, remedial work, or other extra work he needs. A wealth of multisensory equipment can come into play here: single-concept films on cartridges, microfilmed materials, slide projectors, audio- and videotapes, maps and globes, books and other printed materials, and individual filmstrip viewers. To this we can now add the computer as an instructional device in almost every subject area. A systems approach to such resources, through the audiovisual information retrieval system, would make their impact even more powerful.

By the junior high or middle school years, a student needs more specialized materials and equipment for independent study; for example, laboratory tables for math and science experimentation, simple computers to operate, as well as computer instruction, art materials and facilities, industrial arts machines. Schools can deploy them for students to use, safely and profitably, without continual supervision by an adult. The teacher becomes even more the facilitator, the collaborating person who supports self-examination and the growth of personal responsibility for the student. The teacher drops his role as dispenser of knowledge from on high. Authority now resides in the self-instructional curriculum and in the learner who controls these materials.

In all of this, the underlying purpose is to get the student engaged in managing his own education, setting his own goals, devising his own procedures, learning from his own mistakes. Through this approach many of the stumbling blocks that so often exacerbate the frustrations of the instructional process can be removed. Without having to sense the teacher constantly hovering over his shoulder, the student can proceed at his own pace, responding to the challenge implicit in the task and to its impersonal demands for diligence, care, and imagination. It becomes clear to the student that responsibility for success is his. For example, a student who has decided to skip over all or part of a unit of instruction will be expected to evaluate his decision in the light of performance outcomes, confronting the reality of himself as learner in the process. Thus, it is unlikely that a student will perceive, reactively and passively as many now do, that "she marked it wrong" or "it's right." He knows when he succeeds or fails, not because an adult judges his work, but because a "responsive environment" tells him. This is, of course, an ideal of such independent study arrangements. But it is an ideal worth aiming for, particularly in view of the discouraging environment existing in so many of our schools.

If our primary objective is to focus on the independence of the learner, we must ask ourselves how we can best achieve our purpose. The teacher remains a key ingredient in this process. The teacher becomes the facilitator, the broker, the one who matches the skills and the materials to the needs of the learner. He is indispensible in this role. However, one recognizes that this is not the traditional role of the teacher; certain functions will have to be removed and replaced by others; still others will be "taken over" by some of the new technologies of education. These technologies not only relieve the teacher but, even more important, help the student in the essential area of gaining independence and learning how to manage knowledge.

In order to do this, however, one must know one's goals and how the component factors intermingle and work toward fulfilling those goals. As important as the new technologies are, if they are bits and pieces, if they are fragmented gadgetry, they will do more harm than good because they will give the student only the illusion of having mastered the strategy of learning. Perhaps the best example of this has been the media of the last 20 years—filmstrips, record players, 8mm cartridges— all supplementary tools of education. Whether it was a map, a slide projector, episcope, tape, or film, it was no more than an incidental study aid. There was no over-all strategy whereby these "aids" fitted into the curriculum.

Strategic thinking was not a factor in this approach to educational technology. Yet strategies are regarded as absolutely essential in the new view of the teaching/learning process. They are in fact a consequence of the systems approach to educational technology. Systems analysis identifies the elements of the teaching/learning process and their interrelationships; the development and implementation of learning systems which follow this analysis call for a plan of action, i.e., a strategy. There is ample evidence today, for example, that one of the reasons why educational television was not initially successful is that the potentialities and limitations of this unique new medium were never properly analyzed.

Included in this analysis or systematic approach to educational technology is the need to fix the place or function of technology in the education process. Today's technologies, as opposed to those of the last 20 years, are not primarily supportive in nature. Many of them do not "reinforce" a lesson. The medium itself has become an autonomously functioning instrument of information. Language laboratories, TV educational programs, and "classical" as well as "modern" learning machines can be programed so that they themselves take over the teaching process. If certain accessories are used, e.g., accompanying texts, then these media can assume an interactive relationship with the pupil which is independent of the teacher, though, of course, the degree of freedom in the relationship is controlled and limited. Under these circumstances, the teacher no longer remains the main conveyor of information.

This, of course, is a key difference in this new teaching/ learning process. As one can well imagine, this image of a teacher substitute is not easy for professional educators to accept. It arouses apprehension that computers will replace teachers, that education will be dehumanized. Before weighing the merit of these fears, it may be well to consider what this area of technological instruction has done, what it can do, and what its effect is on the learner and on the budget.

To begin with, technological learning systems or prefabricated course materials are utilized by the student independent of the constraints of space, time, and personnel. Computers, programed instructional materials, television can be used anywhere. A computer terminal can be placed in a storefront, a housing development lobby, a public library. In fact, there is a new development in computers that makes use of your home telephone and television set as a terminal. This will be described later in the chapter. The latest development in television teaching permits you to tape a program when it is being shown and to replay it when it is convenient for you to see it, either at home, at school, or in a friend's living room. As to programed instruction, this self-contained teaching and testing device is now in the form of a paperback and can be carried by a student wherever he may be going. As one can see, with none of these new media is a school or schoolroom necessary. This does not mean, of course, that one does away with schools; it merely means that learning can take place in space other than school buildings— not all of it, but certainly some of it. Time is another element affected by the new media. There are no prescribed times for learning. A terminal, a TV set, programed instruction books can be used any time, day or night, summer or winter. And not only can programed materials be read any time, but also for any length of time. It is no longer necessary for the fast-moving students to stay with a lesson for 45 minutes because that is the prescribed time of the class period. Nor will the student who moves more slowly be spotlighted before his classmates as "dumb" because he cannot keep up with the rest of the class. This revises another constraint on the learning process.

A third constraint is that of personnel—the role of the professional teacher. These learning systems or new media transform the functions of the teacher while releasing him from his traditional duties. A teacher may take on several new roles.

Most importantly, he must be aware of and must be able to handle new instructional facilities, programed materials, electronic media, etc., and should render them available when necessary. In a sense, it may be said that he is an expediter of the materials of learning. This new role frees him from the static position of expositor in front of a class and allows him to move among his students, to talk with them in small groups and individually, and to depart from his position as a one-dimensional teacher.

In any consideration of the various uses of technology in education, one should keep in mind the need for a return to the Socratic method of individualizing teaching (the sitting-on-a-log approach), in which there is a continuing dialogue between teacher and student, whether it be a real live teacher or a mechanized one. Equally important are the need for immediate response and reinforcement of instruction, individual control over the pace and content of the material, the means to stop and start the material whenever the student desires, and facilities that will permit the student to proceed at his own pace. Fundamentally, formal education should be convenient, responsive, and interesting, and it should be totally disassociated from the "lockstep" features that so many of us have grown to abhor.

Learning systems or the new technology take many forms. It would be impossible in a section of a chapter to describe all types of educational technologies and their applications. This section, therefore, will describe only three of the new technologies: programed instruction, television, and computers for instruction—always keeping in mind their effect on the learner and whether or not they are economically feasible.

Programed Instruction The principles on which the "programing" of instruction are based are not new. The research of Pavlov, Poe, Spence, and others has demonstrated that when a stimulus-response-reward pattern is repeated often enough, learning takes place. Pigeons, for example, have learned highly involved patterns of behavior (pecking a specific number of times on different colored buttons to receive food) by application of this psychological principle. The results of these animal-learning studies were formalized by experimental psychologists and applied to human learning.

In programing, each step is broken down into discrete bits of information. The student reads an instruction, a question, or an incomplete sequence; he then responds by filling in a blank; he checks his answer to see if it is correct, and then moves on to the next step. Each question or item is called a "frame." Each answer is called a "response." Programers have given the name "cuing" to the technique that is used to insure a correct response. A cue is a subtle hint which suggests the correct answer. There are different types of cuing, the limit depending on a programer's ingenuity. When a response is being introduced, a programer maximizes the number of cues. We know that a student knows his subject when he responds correctly without any cues. Cues are withdrawn gradually; the term for withdrawing cues is "fading."

To insure that the student has really learned what has been taught, the terminal behavior should be repeated several times at intervals in the program. A good program reviews and tests as it proceeds.

There are two important names associated with programing. One is B. F. Skinner, Professor of Psychology at Harvard. He developed linear programing whereby learning tasks are presented in many small steps and with many varied learning cues so that correct answers become expected and nearly always obtained. However, the ultimate objective is eventually to use as few cues as possible so as to force the student to derive his answers from an understanding of the frames. Reinforcement of correct answers is the primary concern. The program must be completely self-contained, adequate to carry the student from start to finish without aid from other sources. In linear programing, adaptation to individual differences is not carried out by the program itself, but rather by allowing each learner to take whatever length of time he requires to complete it.

All students are required by the program to complete the same items in the same order of progression. Linear programing is only one form of programed instruction. Another is adaptive programing. Adaptive programing provides techniques that allow for individual differences. One form of this type of programing is called "branching" and was first developed by Norman Crowder.[2] Under the branching pattern, students are required to recognize and to choose correct answers;

[2] Norman A. Crowder, "Automatic Tutoring by Intrinsic Programming," in A. A. Lumsdaine and Robert Glaser (eds.), *Teaching Machines and Programmed Learning*, Department of Audiovisual Instruction, National Education Association, Washington, 1960, pp. 286–298.

if their responses are incorrect, they must take "relearning detours" or "corrective assignments." When ready, they may skip program portions for which they have indicated they already possess sufficient skill or knowledge. Branching programs are provided in books ("scrambled books") or on machines (which use filmstrips and present information and tasks on individual frames). Either way, the student responds to a question and is directed to another page or frame where this response is evaluated. Which pages he must turn to is dependent on his response. There, if his response is incorrect, he is given further information, usually including some explanation of why he was wrong. He may be told to return to the original page and try again, or he may be asked to go to a new page for more information before trying a somewhat different version of the same question.

Branching questions are not always dichotomized as "right" or "wrong." Some questions or problems call for opinions or troubleshooting decisions and so have more than one appropriate answer. In the event that responses reveal some fundamental lack of knowledge considered necessary to proceed with the program, students may subsequently be "branched" into side studies to prepare them to take the next steps in the "main line" of the program.

The more varied the program, in both its details and its alternative learner paths, the more "adaptive" it is. Thus "computer-assisted instruction" (CAI), with its computer capability to produce almost instantaneous responses to inputs and its almost infinite capacity to store information and to manipulate it in ways that lead to learning, is potentially highly adaptive and seems to offer great promise for the future. CAI is discussed in more detail later in this chapter.

A linear program may be presented on paper, on film or filmstrip, by computer, or by a teacher. A branching program may also be carried by any of the same media. In addition, either one of these programing strategies may be presented through a combination of media.

Decisions about which media are to be used in program presentation are made primarily on the basis of what is available, their comparative costs, and which one medium offers the best condition for learning. While it is probable that programed instruction as a mode of teaching will be presented primarily through *printed* materials for some time, the concepts of programed instruction are influencing many processes of teaching and student learning. More and more attention is being given to individualized study, and the concept of adaptive programing is helping to extend the uses of multimedia resources in education.

Before we get into the advantages and disadvantages of programed instruction, how it can be used and what it costs, let us see if by going through just a few "frames" we can get the feel of learning by means of this invisible teacher.[3]

While several styles of programing are currently in use, and other styles are being developed, it is possible to divide most existing programs into three large groups.

Linear programs—in which the sequence of frames seen by one student is identical to the sequence seen by all other students.

Adaptive programs—in which the sequence of frames seen by each student is determined by this responses to questions asked in the program.

Combination programs—in which the program is a combination of linear and adaptive programs.

To see whether we have made this point clear, we are now going to ask you some questions based on the above information and give you alternative answers from which to choose. Your response will determine the frame you will see next.

QUESTION. This frame is an example of:

(a) a linear frame . . . (Page 2)*

(b) an adaptive frame . . . (Page 5)*

*Explanation. Turn immediately to page 2 or page 5 (depending upon your choice) to check your answer and to receive further directions.

Page 1

---

[3]James W. Brown, Richard B. Lewis, and Fred F. Harcleroad, *AV Instruction: Media and Methods*, Third Edition, New York: McGraw-Hill Book Company, 1969, pp. 118–119.

A. *The first frame is not a linear frame but rather an example of an adaptive frame. Understand, you were given a choice of two alternative answers to the question, each of which led you to a different page. Your selection of alternative (a) caused the program, in a sense, to adapt to your need for further explanation. When the content adapts to you in this way, we call it a/an* _____ *ive program.*
Adaptive

B. *When a program presents a fixed sequence of frames which is identical for all students (like the route of a trolly line), we call such a program a/an* _____ *program.*
Linear

C. *Once again, a program that modifies itself depending on the response of the student is called a/an* _____ *program.*
Adaptive

D. *The sequence which you are now working through is a/an* _____ *sequence.*
Linear

Page 2

E. *"Branching" is a term which, when applied to programing means that the student is "branched" to the next part of the program based on his response to the last part. A branching program is thus a/an* _____ *program.*
Adaptive

F. *In a "scrambled book" each frame presents information and a multiple choice question. Beside each alternative answer is a page number. When the student selects his response, he does so by turning the indicated page. There, based on his answer, is the next step in the program. What are the two names for this style of programing?* _____ *and* _____
Branching and Adaptive

G. *Adaptive programming, because of mechanical limitations, must be multiple choice, a program in which the student writes in his answers (a "write in" style), is normally* _____
Linear

H. *The sequence through which you have just worked could thus be described by two terms:* _____ *and* _____
Linear and "Write-in"

I. *You have just completed an example of a linear sub-sequence and have arrived at a criterion checkpoint. Here you could be*

Page 3

given a test of several items and according to your score, sent on, sent to another sub-sequence, or directed to a remedial program. Here, for the purposes of this sample, is a one-question test:

The first frame you read (the one which brought you to this sequence) is an example of

(a) a linear frame . . . . Page 6
(b) an adaptive frame . . . . Page 5

Page 4

You answered that the first frame is an example of an adaptive frame. Right. Your response to the question dictated what frame you would see next and the program thus adapted to you.
(Here the program might proceed to a discussion of other points, but whatever point is next, it will be treated as a unit to be taught, and the well-constructed program will require the student to respond to the point and demonstrate mastery before he can proceed to the end.)

Page 5

Sorry, but the first frame is an adaptive frame. Your response indicated that you need some background before this program will be meaningful. May we suggest that you read several items in the bibliography for this chapter?
(The above response would be designed for the student who clearly is not ready for the program; its intent is to discourage the student from proceeding at this level without further background.)
The program could, however, assign outside reading by utilizing the "criterion programing" idea of Mager. An example of how this might work would be:

Instruction
READ Cram, p. 72, and return.
_____

Criterion Test
(This would be a test question based on the reading assignment, and each answer would direct the student to specific "outside" activities (reading, for example) designed to correct wrong notions, explain unclear ideas, or advance his understanding of the topic. Other uses might be to direct the student to review a particular part of the program or be directed to another part of the same program. At the end of each outside assignment the student returns to the program for another criterion test and new assignment.)

Page 6

If you have come through these few frames understanding the way one uses programed instruction, your next question might be, "If I were a student, when would I use a programed instruction course?" You would use it when the subject matter was such that dialogue with a teacher or a fellow student was unnecessary, or otherwise when the forming or changing of opinions were not involved. Programed instruction is effective in the basic skills of mathematics and English, and more recently has been used in social studies. Patterns of use of programed materials vary widely: they may be presented in class for the purpose of keeping all students moving ahead together or for the purpose of fostering completely independent, individualized student progress; as out-of-class study assignments, with or without teacher assistance; or in correlated large-group classroom activities.

The lessons are self-administered and self-checking. Learning becomes a private affair, a solo relationship between the person and what he has to learn. If he is correct, he continues with the program. If he is wrong, no one sees his errors. He works until he is right and then moves on at his own pace, on his own time, and wherever it is convenient for him to work. The constraints of time, place, and people are removed.

Programed instruction, which started in the early 1960's, has been most prolific. Programed texts are available in almost every subject matter from the time the child learns to read through college and graduate studies. Whole courses are given at colleges by means of programed instruction. Programed materials are also used extensively in industry. Workers who come to learn a trade, or those who need retraining, most often use programed materials.

Although there is this plethora of programed materials, schools are using programed instruction in a limited way. Programed texts are inexpensive, in many cases one-third the cost of traditional texts, because they have few if any illustrations or charts. They have tear-out pages and are consumable. When the student answers all the questions, he has exhausted the book. Like newspapers, magazines, and other "disposable" printed material, they must be inexpensive. There is no easy way, as in a textbook, to amortize the costs over the years.

With all of the cost advantages, school systems are still

slow to incorporate programed instruction into their way of teaching. This in spite of the fact that programed instruction is especially adaptable to teaching small groups and to individualized instruction, both goals that school people espouse. Why, then, this reluctance, exceeding the aversion to most of the other new technologies? Perhaps it is because programed instruction competes with a textbook on its home grounds, in its own medium. The textbook in this country is as American as apple pie. It has become part of our tradition. Anything that shakes the sanctity of the textbook becomes suspect. Couple this with the general reluctance to change and you can understand the slow process of acceptance.

This has generally been the history of technology in education, despite the fact that students are demanding it and are tired of the traditional teacher. Perhaps the students' demands, in conjunction with the reduced costs that technology can bring, will compel the educational establishment to take technology more seriously.

Television For an educator to ignore the impact of television on our lives would be the ultimate in petrifaction. The number of homes with color television passed the 30 million mark in 1971. Hours of reported adult viewing showed a steady increase over the past 10 years to a median of 2 hours and 47 minutes per day by the typical adult.[4] Estimates of time spent by children in front of the television set range even higher, although few if any research studies have scientifically measured this statistic.

Today's children have never known what it was like to live in a world without television. Instantaneous worldwide communication has changed a whole generation's outlook and is one of the primary reasons why educators have revised the curriculum, re-examined teaching methods, and taken a new look at how children learn.

There are three major categories in television: commercial, educational, and instructional. Somehow our schools tend to focus mostly on the values of instructional and educational TV and far less on commercial television, the category that is most widely viewed and has had the greatest impact of all. It is simply

[4]Burns W. Roper, *A Ten-Year View of Public Attitudes Toward Television and Other Mass Media, 1959–1968*, Television Information Office, 745 Fifth Avenue, New York City, 10022, March 26, 1969.

a myth that commercial TV presents only soap operas, violence, and variety shows. To the contrary, commercial programs bring home to children many of today's social, economic, and political realities. School children today are viewing, on the screen, the dynamics of economics and political science and contemporary social problems, such as the influx of rural populations into the cities, the confrontations between the races, and the war in Vietnam.

Literature and drama have been revitalized through television. The classics were once taught in so soporific a fashion that students closed the covers of books forever when they left school. Today, television has brought a new dimension into literature—old and new, from *The Last of the Mohicans* to the History of Civilization to the plays of Harold Pinter. In science, we need only reflect on the awe experienced by millions of viewers who traveled vicariously with the astronauts on the moonflight of the first Apollo spacecraft. How many inspired young scientists were born of that spectacle!

For the past decade KMOX-TV, a CBS commercial television station in St. Louis, has provided, as a public service, an educational link between its programs and the classroom. The link is the *Viewer's Service for Schools,* a monthly bulletin describing the coming month's programs of educational value and offering back-up ideas for reading resources.

In 1961, KMOX-TV executives had invited a group of librarians and curriculum workers to form a committee to help develop the service. At that time there had been widespread concern that "television would kill books," and the television station management and committee of educators devised an experiment to determine whether the use of selected television programs could, on the contrary, motivate reading.

From the beginning, programs ranged widely, but each was clearly justified as contributing to the educational process. With very rare exceptions, programs were those scheduled after school hours and on weekends, and it was expected that students would view the programs at home. Concerned with parents' attitudes, the committee set evening cut-off times for various age levels, and late shows were not recommended, no matter how excellent they were. KMOX-TV's policy from the start was that the service would be measured in terms of genuine benefit to the schools, not as a promotional vehicle for the station. The service was, and is, free for the asking—but schools must renew requests for it each year.

The station continues to be guided by the judgment of the committee members on program selection, and depends upon the members for the related resources for each program.

A continuing evaluation has been made of the program by the television station's consultants through surveys of the schools. Over the years, the pattern of school usage of the program has changed. The most recent digest of purposes stated by teachers using the service stresses "motivation," "extension of material," "reinforcing basics," and "introducing concepts," as much as or more than the original purpose of encouraging reading. Looking back, we see that the fear of killing books was unfounded, as library circulation has steadily continued to increase.

Each year, about 200 programs are listed, supported by over 750 resource suggestions. It is still the consensus of the committee that the service should describe programs logically related to education, should suggest class discussions and individual projects where appropriate, and list related resources. Many imaginative ways are used by teachers in the St. Louis metropolitan area for putting these suggestions to good use.

The increasing stress on television as a tool for building concepts—as a means of motivation, of "hooking learners," and of leading to a search or quest—speaks for the growing importance of television as a tool for learning.

A review of the literature on commercial television for classroom use indicates that the Missouri program is unique. Few schools or school systems, if any, utilize commercial television. Yet it is the best produced, most sophisticated, most available, and can be used at no cost at all to the viewer. The superintendent of a Diocesan school system, which has felt the budget crunch perhaps even more than the public schools, has requested that for the coming year no new instructional materials be ordered for his schools. First, he wants better use made from existing materials, and, secondly, he has suggested that television will save the cost of the usual yearly ordering of expensive social studies and science books. Nothing, he said, could be more current, or, for that matter, more exciting and stimulating, than to see history being made before your eyes. What would happen if public school boards placed a moratorium on the ordering of all textbooks for one year and asked that television be used instead? The costs would run no more than a few pennies per student. What might this do for the budget? What might it do for capturing the students' interest?

Educational television as opposed to commercial television is beamed directly at a specialized audience—students. Those stations that dedicate their programs to educational telecasts operate under special channel allocations by the Federal Communications Commission. Some stations broadcast direct, formal instruction as part of local school or college curricula. Some carry programs of special interest to children and adults on hobbies, recreation, community welfare, and related topics.

From the earliest days of educational television in the United States, broadcasting values played a major role in setting policy for the new medium. It was those persons having a broadcasting orientation who convinced Washington-based representatives of the professional education organizations to give their verbal support to the reservation of channels for education.[5] Once the channels were reserved, it was *not* the American educational establishment that gave leadership. It was the Fund for Adult Education and a number of cultural leaders in local communities who put ETV on the air. Only a few professional educators were involved.[6]

As nonprofessionals entered the field,[7] professional educators began to eye the stations and their programing both critically and enviously. This group picked at the "broadcast" content and style, and decried the lack of articulated curriculum planning and the "pedantries" with which educators themselves had long entranced their prey. These educators resisted the contention of the Fund for Adult Education that education was too important to be left to professional schoolmen, and lamented that they had lost control of ETV to the Fund. And indeed they had, but how much of a tragedy is this?

[5] Robert A. Carlson, *The Creation and Development of Educational Television as an Institution of Adult Education: A Case Study in American History,* An unpublished Ph.D. dissertation, University of Wisconsin, 1968, Chapters 4 and 5.
[6] *Ibid.,* Chapters 7–9 and 11.
[7] By March of 1958 there were 31 ETV stations on the air, all of them assisted by the Fund for Adult Education.

For a variety of reasons, mostly to cut costs, a national network was formed, NET (National Educational Television), which now controls educational TV as we know it. In addition, smaller networks are springing up all around the country in the form of regional networks. Although some exchange programs are on tape, others are establishing electronic interconnection which permits live program exchange. In some instances, stations receive programs from others in the network by "off-air pick-up," a "one-way" participation in the regional program. Numerous states are also developing in-state networks, including Alabama, Kentucky, Nebraska, New Jersey, and Tennessee.

Primarily, educational TV, be it via NET or state or local networks, is concerned with audience-attracting cultural and public affairs programing, with literature, art, music, and instruction of the kinds that "exercise the mind." This emphasis has not set too well with conservative educators.

Variety, the show business magazine, credited NET's drama programs in 1966 with "making a sizable cultural contribution."[8] Such notices from show business gained NET little prestige in education; neither did attacks on NET by the drug industry and the militant United States right wing.[9] Instead of applauding the kind of educational programing that disturbed America's troglodytes and led to examinations of NET programs and personnel by the Federal Communications Commission and the United States Congress, professional educators quivered in fear and quoted the gospel of curriculum planning.

In the February 1967 issue of the *New Republic*, David Walker of Yale University attacked the public affairs and cultural emphasis of NET and expressed disapproval because such broadcasting values were becoming dominant on the national level of educational television. Walker called for professional educators to champion more articulately the role and importance of instructional TV.[10] His plea for educators to argue for "truly

<hr/>

[8] Murray Horowitz, "Drama-Promises, Promises," *Variety*, Dec. 7, 1966, p. 31.
[9] Robert Carlson, Interview with Harry McCarthy, producer of NET's "Dollars and Sense" series, New York City, July 6, 1966; John White, "A Report to Affiliates," speech to the 1965 Spring Meeting of the NET affiliates, Boston, Mass., April 12, 1965; Edwin R. Bayley, NET vice-president for administration, speech at Lawrence University Alumni College, Appleton, Wisc., June 11, 1966; and *ETV Reporter*, IV, March 6, 1970, p. 3.
[10] David Walker, "Who Runs Educational TV?" *The New Republic*, 156, February 11, 1967.

educational" TV, i.e., *instructional TV*, gained response during testimony before Congress on the future of the educational televison medium.[11]

Schoolmen in 1970 continued to complain that educational TV was a failure. Nevertheless, they have been unable to wrest control of national-level programing from the influences that initiated it. The educational establishment does continue, however, to be a millstone around the neck of educational television.

It is a matter of interest to see what is happening on the local level. By August 1967, there were 136 educational television stations in operation (73 VHF and 63 UHF), reaching approximately 80 percent of the population of the United States. In addition, 60 stations were then under construction, and 14 additional applications for new stations were pending. By 1971, there were 310 ETV stations in operation.

It was anticipated that from its inception, ETV would have tripled its number of stations by 1972; each week ETV reaches more than 8 million homes and nearly 20 million individual viewers. At any given weekday evening hour, ETV is probably being seen by an audience numbering about 1.5 million people.

As for instructional TV, it differs from commercial and educational TV basically in the fact that it presents *formal* courses. This includes portions of in-school courses for direct instruction or for facilitating lecture-demonstrations. Instructional television may be distributed by open- or closed-circuit systems, or by both simultaneously. As attractive as this should be to the professional educators who protest their loss of control of ETV—it still has not been accepted by the education community. This despite the fact that the educational value of television can no longer be questioned.

In his comprehensive analysis of the evidence as early as 1962, Wilbur Schramm, director of Stanford's Institute for Communication Research, concluded:[12]

> *There can no longer be any doubt that students learn efficiently from instructional television. The fact has been demonstrated now in hundreds of schools, by thousands of students, in every part of the United States and in several other countries. . .*

[11] United States Senate, *The Public Television Act of 1967*, pp. 267–288 and 558–579.
[12] Wilbur Schramm, "What We Know about Learning from Instructional Television," *Educational Television: The Next Ten Years*, Institute for Communication Research, Stanford, California: Stanford University, 1962.

Instructional television is at least as effective as ordinary classroom instruction, when the results are measured by the usual final examinations or by standardized tests . . . [And] employing the usual tests that schools use to measure the progress of their students, we can say with considerable confidence that in 65 percent of a very large number of comparisons between televised and classroom teaching, there is no significant difference. In 21 per cent, students learned significantly more, in 14 per cent, they learned significantly less, from television.

Why, then, have educators resisted it?

In an evaluative report of the status of television in instruction, *Learning by Television,*[13] Alvin C. Eurich states in the preface:

The findings reported in this study indicate that there are two prime causes for instructional television's limited acceptance: the quality of the transmitted instruction, and the way it is used in the classroom.

Whereas instructional television is ignored by the majority of educators and schools, there have been and are some exemplary programs. It is important to note them, since, in a way, they have answered Dr. Eurich's finding that LTV is of poor quality and poorly used. One of the dramatic experiments in instructional telecasting is the Midwest Program on Airborne Television Instruction (MPATI). Its educational and organizational problems and technical requirements stagger the imagination. MPATI broadcasts its instructional programs to schools in a 400-mile radius, from an airplane flying 23,000 feet over Montpelier, Indiana. Within this area are 17,000 schools and colleges enrolling 13 million students in parts of 5 states (Illinois, Indiana, Kentucky, Michigan, and Ohio), as well as smaller portions of Wisconsin and Ontario, Canada.

Programs broadcast by MPATI were 15 and 20 minutes in length for elementary schools and 30 minutes for secondary schools; program transmission is 6 hours per day. Most elementary-level tele-lessons were twice-a-week programs (except first-year French and Spanish, which are broadcast 4 days per week). Secondary school lessons were about equally divided between 2-day- and 4-day-per-week schedules; there were no transmissions on Fridays.

[13]Judith Murphy and Ronald Gross, *Learning by Television,* Fund for the Advancement of Education, New York, 1966.

Originally, MPATI was financed by the Ford Foundation. It was then supposed to become self-supporting on a membership basis. It is estimated that annual costs for operating MPATI are in the range of $1½ to $2 million a year. Unfortunately, as is the case so often after "outside" money has been withdrawn, the member schools and school boards did not pick up the tab.

Faced by limited funds, a large population of school-age children, and an inadequate supply of fully qualified teachers, South Carolina has undertaken to solve some of its educational problems through development of a statewide closed-circuit instructional television system, in cooperation with educational television stations. In 1966, the South Carolina ETV Network was in its seventh year of operation. It is of special interest since it combines both open- and closed-circuit distribution of programs for instruction and reaches into all counties of the state. The closed-circuit system serves 213 schools, 5 private universities or colleges, 13 hospitals, 6 technical-education centers, 3 private schools, and 3 other state institutions. There are 3 open-circuit stations (in Greenville, Charleston, and Columbia) which reach approximately 60 percent of the state's population. The state plans eventually to reach all of its citizens with open-circuit television and to extend closed-circuit service.

WGBH-TV, in Boston, telecasts to 205 public, private, and parochial schools and school systems in Massachusetts and parts of Rhode Island, Connecticut, and New Hampshire participating in the "21-inch Classroom." Most of these programs were produced by WGBH-TV in Boston, but some were borrowed from other sources. Their productions are supported by member schools systems, which pay 25 cents per-pupil to participate in the development of the lessons and study guides.

The Byrd Elementary School in Chicago was built to contain closed-circuit television facilities, with well-equipped studio space and television outlets in all instructional, administrative, and work areas. As installed, the television system permits a wide variety of television instructional techniques: direct teaching to several classes simultaneously; in-class use of television for image magnification; potentially, 12 simultaneous television programs, plus 2-way audio intercommunication channels from classroom to studio and classroom to classroom. Programs from off the air are also received and distributed. The school plant does not have an auditorium and depends on closed-circuit television in lieu of a meeting place for all students. The school's location adjacent to a large public housing project makes it possible to explore ways of improving school-community relations and of providing parent education and preschool education.

In the October 1971 issue of *Educational Technology*, a report was given on the Broward County, Florida, public school system's use of instructional television in an innovative school setting. It places emphasis on a major program of individualized instruction in many new "flexible" schools. Introduced in part to meet the educational needs of a spectacularly growing population, the program has already begun to produce an enriched curriculum, replete with a wealth of easily accessible learning materials and geared to highly personalized instruction.

As a result of combined county-bond and state funds totaling $146 million for a 5-year construction program, Broward County now has 16 flexible elementary and 5 middle schools where interdisciplinary teams of teachers guide students in numerous activities in huge classrooms without ceiling-to-floor walls or partitions. Success of the innovative educational program depends in part on a countywide instructional television system through which a vast amount of instructional materials are made available to assist in the implementation of the instructional program.

The Instructional Television Fixed Service (ITFS) system, which began telecasting in January 1968, also is used extensively for compensatory instruction, for in-service training of faculty, for supplying teacher-aid materials, and for parent-teacher-administrative community relations. Much of the transmitting, receiving, and distribution equipment was provided and installed under turnkey contract by Jerrold Electronics Corporation, Philadelphia. The system was designed by Adair & Brady, Inc., Lake Worth, Florida, a consulting engineering firm.

Programs are received on some 1,500 TV sets in the various schools. These receivers are both 23-inch and 12-inch to accommodate individual, small-group, and large-group viewing (30–35 students). In conventional buildings, many sets are equipped with listening centers containing eight earphones to accommodate small-group or individual viewers.

The system began by transmitting on four 2500-MHz

channels to 32 schools in the southern half of the county. The schools are equipped to receive programs from the four ITFS channels, from two educational stations and two commercial stations in Miami. The ITV Center broadcasts 34 video-taped series, 27 of which are produced at the Center and 7 supplied by the state. Each series consists of from 17 to 37 programs. Most of the programs are 15 to 20 minutes in length, and involve the viewing students during the telecasting.

Twice each school year, ITV personnel meet with one representative from each school as well as with administrators and supervisors. The purpose of these "Committee of 2500" meetings is to evaluate present programing and plan future series.

Comprehensive lesson guides have been prepared for many series. Weekly program guides are distributed to all teachers receiving ITV. These weekly guides contain synopses of the programs, broadcast times and channels, and other pertinent information.

The system has begun to be used also as a means of instant administrative communication on subjects of vital interest to the entire school system.

The Broward County system is not only interesting because of its imaginative use of ITV, but also because of its ingenious and systematic combination of commercial, educational, and instructional TV. The competition has been removed and the best of each combined to meet the educational objectives.

Perhaps the ultimate in the use of instructional television is the United States government-supported contract to develop and operate instructional television services and facilities in American Samoa. It was started in 1961 on a large scale. The principal purposes of the program were to improve the quality of instruction and to raise the achievement levels of children in both elementary and secondary schools. Significantly, maximum use of television supported by reinforcement activities that take place in the classrooms provides the core of instruction. Instructional planning and teaching were cooperative enterprises involving teachers from both the United States and Samoa. A complete redesign and construction of curriculum and methods to meet the very special needs of the Samoan people have been a major effort of the project.

Central studio and production facilities in Pago Pago are

operated by Samoans under supervision of technical, production, and education specialists from the United States. Transmitters for six channels serve the villages and schools of Eastern and Western Samoa.

The importance of this program is that through the use of television thousands of children and adults in outlying areas where there are no teachers or schools now receive an education. Again, however, because of a lack of local funds after United States government funds were withdrawn, this program has been greatly curtailed. Yet it has been a forerunner of similar ones in Indonesia and India. Egypt is now using instructional television for outposts on the desert.

TV, like computers, 8mm film loops, and cassettes, is an insistent presence as a medium of instruction. Whether or not we decide to use it, budget demands compel us to scrutinize it seriously. With growing enrollments of students and diminishing funds for teachers, television can be a major economy in education.

Videotapes, too, require consideration. They are now relatively inexpensive, and small videotape machines are available for use in schools. Tapes of commercial, educational, or instructional broadcasts can be made, and, of course, used over and over again. Because of their proved usefulness, school systems will markedly increase their use of these closed-circuit facilities (programs distributed by coaxial cable or by 2500 MHz transmitters), which are now available at comparatively low cost.

One such closed-circuit facility is a community antenna system (CAT). In this system, sidebands or unused channels have been allocated for school television programs, thus providing closed-circuit interconnection for the schools of an area at a reasonable cost. In Meadville, Pennsylvania, the CAT system is originating local news, features, and documentaries. The technology of this operation, which has won the praise of teachers and parents, as well as that of the youngsters, includes mobile units and a studio worth a quarter of a million dollars. *TV Guide* called the Meadville system's origination "a country newspaper of the air." Local residents are far more complimentary!

In Coachella Valley, California, the CATV system has been originating color programing for several years now, and its stated credo is to be a mirror of the community and a source of local expression.

The concept of program origination is also a prerequisite for successful local advertising. This concept has been strongly endorsed by officials of the Ottawa (Illinois) TV Cable Company and the LVO Cable system in Tulsa, Oklahoma. The Tulsa cable operation, for example, provides local programing facilities for local educators and students. In Casper, Wyoming, the cable system is now programing instructional courses as well as originating community programing.

"This type of programing gains local recognition and public acceptance as a valid medium in which advertising dollars and subscriber dollars might be safely invested," is the evaluation of economist Sukor Sandor.

In addition to locally produced programs, various syndicated materials are now available at relatively low cost. For example, National Telesystems is offering its "Green Valley Nursery School" as a sort of CATV version of "Sesame Street." Foundation and independent producers will be moving more rapidly into this area now that the FCC appears to have removed the restrictive log jam against CATV's growth. New York, Chicago, and Denver are three of the large urban cities that are currently using CAT for educational uses.

There are no exact figures on how much commercial, educational, or instructional television is being used as part of the school program, but generally the use is spotty. For those who feel that introducing the outside world of culture and public affairs into the schools is a key to modern learning and living, it should be a welcome innovation. Educators should bear in mind, however, that television, as part of the curriculum, is a one-way medium; as such, it will require teacher–student interaction both before and after programs are viewed. On the other hand, it offers major benefits: it can either supplement or supplant the buying of expensive, commercially produced instructional materials; it can free teachers to do other professional tasks since no set pupil–teacher ratio is required to view a program; and it can make learning a more exciting and instructive experience.

Computer Instruction There are uses for computers in all phases of the educational structure. We have already discovered how they may help in administration. Now, their application to direct instruction is becoming increasingly significant. New York City, Chicago, San Francisco, and smaller systems in over 23 states are presently employing some form of computer instruction.

It may be well to have a look at this relatively new teaching form in order to evaluate its budgetary and educational advantages. Normally it employs an individualized approach whereby a series of problem materials or questions ("items") is presented to the student automatically. Seated at a terminal, the student types in his "number," and within the time it takes for the student to type four digits, the computer "finds" this particular youngster's program, greets him with "Good morning, Johnny," and then proceeds with a mathematics or spelling or language arts program. If it is a master lesson, the program will proceed in the form of a two-way conversation. The computer gives examples and asks questions, and the student answers. The computer may ask a child to multiply 2 by 7. If he answers "12," for example, the computer will type out, "No. Try again." If he gives the correct answer, the computer will go on to the next question. Should he be wrong twice, the computer will tell him the correct answer, and then ask the same question—to make sure that the correct answer has registered with him.

The advantage of this kind of step-by-step instruction is that it provides a built-in check system—a combination of teaching and testing. When a student, reading an assignment in a textbook or doing homework on his own, fails to understand an idea or principle, a gap may result that can interfere with his understanding of other related problems. Computer instruction, on the other hand, virtually eliminates this possibility because a student is not allowed to go on to more difficult examples until he has proved that he understands the simpler material. A bright youngster, however, will be spared the more elementary questions, since the computer considerately analyzes each student's performance automatically, and skips those sections of the program which the youngster has already mastered.

After a lesson has been completed, the computer types out the percentage of questions the student has answered correctly and the amount of time spent on the lesson. The pupil is free to keep his "lesson" (the computer print-out sheet) to show to his parents.

Mathematics is by no means the only subject suited to

computer instruction. Particularly promising is a remedial reading program for junior high school students. Educators are fully aware that reading is the most basic of all academic skills. A student who does not learn to read well is almost certain to do poorly in every other subject. Unfortunately, the older a student gets the more difficult it is for him to overcome reading problems. Many junior high school students who have not learned to read well are embittered by past failures and refuse to make any effort to improve. But the novelty and the privacy of computer instruction is often enough to induce a reluctant student to try again.

The computerized remedial reading program gives each student the individual attention he must have if he is to make any progress. A student is never ridiculed or made to feel stupid. He works at his own pace without anyone looking over his shoulder to tell him whether he is right or wrong. And though it is too early to judge the success of the remedial reading program, it is encouraging to note that the school attendance of these youngsters has improved by about 70 percent since they started it.

Programs for computers—software—are being produced by traditional textbook companies, such as Harcourt, Brace, and Jovanovich, and by companies formed for the specific purpose of developing computer software, such as the Computer Curriculum Corporation in Palo Alto, California. Researchers are now working on the development of more sophisticated programs designed to stimulate the student to think critically and to answer open-ended questions with phrases or sentences.

One intriguing experiment, called the "doctor" program, has been written by scientists at the Massachusetts Institute of Technology. In this program, the computer assumes the role of the doctor and the student pretends that he is a patient. The dialogue begins when the computer types out, "Tell me about your problem." The student might reply, for example, "I have a terrible headache." Next, the computer might ask, "Do you know of any reason why your head should hurt?" The dialogue can go on in this manner—the computer replying each time to the student's response with an appropriate question or comment.

Of course the doctor–patient relationship was not supposed to be taken seriously. The subject was picked merely because it attracted students to the computer. What is significant about the doctor program is the fact that the computer is able to pick up key words and certain combinations of words in the student's reply and then to react with whole thoughts and leading questions. A program of this type does more than a simple question and answer lesson. It forces the student to think and to become involved by the dialogue.

Another more complex computer system is a vocational and educational guidance program now being used in the Newton School System in Massachusetts. One important part of the system is a program designed to help students select a college. The computer questions each student at length, asking his grades, his class rank, his occupational goals, and what he wants out of college. After the questioning is completed, the computer compares the student's abilities and desires with its stored information on colleges in all parts of the country. Just a few seconds later, the computer lists a number of colleges which seem appropriate for the student. At this point, armed with a list of suitable colleges, it becomes profitable for the student to discuss his plans with a guidance counselor.

All of these programs, proven and in experimentation, are tailored to meet the needs, abilities, and learning styles of the individual. The material allows the student to progress according to his own motivation and knowledge, stimulating inquiry and, in some instances, creativity.

Computer-assisted instruction is available in subjects ranging from Basic English to Remedial Reading; Language Arts—Grades 7, 8, 9; and Mathematics—Grades 1–6. Programs are currently being developed in Social Studies, Guidance and Counseling, and Sex Education. Costs vary; a large system, such as Chicago's, can cost up to $60 a year per student for one-half hour of computer instruction each day, regardless of the subject matter. This includes the use of a large IBM 360-type computer plus terminals placed in each school plus the telephone lines that connect the computer to the terminals. In a large school system where thousands of students are on terminals and the system, probably, owns or rents a large computer for administrative tasks, it may be most economical to tap in or share time on the computer it already has.

If a computer is not available, there are many commercial

companies that will rent out time on their own computers. The process is convenient and not particularly costly. Since most commercial work can be done at night, the machines are often available during the day. It may also be possible to purchase a small low-cost computer system. This is a viable method for an individual school or a group of schools that wants to share a system. It is completely self-contained, requiring no communications costs or special environmental controls. A small system generally includes computer hardware, the computer program, and eight student terminals. The purchase price of such a system is approximately $30,000 and can be paid off at the rate of about $1,000 a month over a 3-year period.

It is extremely difficult to figure per pupil cost because, once again, it depends upon how regularly one uses the system. If a system is driven to full capacity— 10 months a year, 10 hours per day (5 for regular school students, 2 hours for remediation, 3 hours for adult education, or any other combination), the cost per pupil can be as low as $20 a year.

However, these figures are meaningless from the point of view of economy *if* they are added on to the current expense budget. Only if a school or school system is willing to analyze its instructional needs not only in terms of personnel, such as differentiated staffing, but also in types of learning techniques, can economies be realized. Computer instruction is all too often a feather-bedding device, and for that reason may be too costly a venture. Professional teaching staffs can be cut up to 25 percent if educators and school board members are willing to take a giant step. Teacher organizations will fight them as they fight against differentiated staffing and performance contracting. Parents, and scholars like Henry Winthrop,[14] will deplore the computer as dehumanizing, and will proceed to rediscover all the fine qualities of the human teacher: he is multitalented; having many disciplines, he imparts values; he is able to conduct high-minded conversations with his pupils, thus drawing upon the best in him and in them; and so on. All one can say is, granted, if only one can multiply such a person by the 2 million teachers needed in American schools today. Indeed, the reply of Gordon McAndrew, Gary, Indiana's Superintendent of Schools, is, ap-

[14] Henry Winthrop, "What Can We Expect from the Unprogrammed Teacher? *Teachers College Record*, Vol. 67, No. 5, February 1966, pp. 315–29.

propriately: "If there is anything we're doing that's dehumanizing, it's allowing generation after generation of children to go through school and fail."

Lewis Mumford[15] talks about the threat of domination by a "technostructure," the subordination of the individual to the environment of a managed marketplace. Unquestionably, in education, as in science, government, and business, one must face up to the existence and challenge of a technological age. The cost saving and, in many instances, increased efficiency of computer instruction must be weighed in the balance against the advantages of the human factor.

Less threatening to personnel than computer-assisted instruction, which to a large extent can be used independently of a teacher, is computer-managed instruction, which not only relies on the teacher but is a support service to the teacher. It is a system in which the student, instead of taking his lesson directly from the computer, interacts with his teacher on the basis of information the teacher receives from the computer. Today's teacher presents most information herself and personally administers most tests; she also depends upon her own resources to answer a variety of procedural questions. For example, she daily considers: "How much review should I give on this lesson?" . . . "Are my students grouped for most efficient learning?" . . . "What materials or procedures should be changed to make this lesson more effective?" She bases her decisions on a collection of remembered observations of students at work, reactions during group lessons, or performance on work sheets or informal tests.

Computer-managed instruction would change her role and would guide and advise the teacher as to how to proceed with each individual student. The system would minimize the teacher's need to rely on her memory as to where each student is in the curriculum; it would provide her with detailed performance data to diagnose individual student weaknesses and would suggest a variety of resources for remedial instruction. It would enable the teacher to continually study each student's performance record, and adjust her procedures until her prescriptions improve that performance.

[15] Lewis Mumford, "The Automation of Knowledge," *AV Communication Review*, Vol. 12, No. 3, Fall 1964, pp. 263–4.

Let us take some examples of how this would work in a classroom. A test is given and the results are diagnosed by the computer. These results are picked up by the teacher (or a messenger) from a central site. The computer-produced reports summarize student-performance data collected the day before, and suggest procedures and schedules for the current day's lessons. It would take some time to study these reports, noting first the students who progress normally from one unit to the next, and posting work assignments for those who should continue in self-directed units or modules. The computer report might list several students who are ready for a film, a group presentation, or a progress test. The daily report might also flag students who face special problems, such as sudden changes in score patterns, unreasonable time spans in particular units, too many student choices in one content area, or special program-planning problems.

Not only does the computer diagnose and spot special problems, but it also prepares lesson sheets for the individual student or a group of students. Upon completion, the lesson sheets are collected and sent to a central terminal station. When it has digested the results of each student's performance, the computer composes the next lesson: it notices, for example, that a concept that had been adequately mastered 2 weeks before was not thoroughly understood in its relation to the concept presently being taught. The computer, therefore, selects, for inclusion in the next lesson, frames that sharpen the principles constituting the relationship between the two concepts; then it goes ahead with frames on the new work. That the class or the individual needs this more careful review of the material is, of course, noted, for the benefit of the teacher and the learner.

The frames selected for the next lesson are assembled from storage capabilities of the computer and placed on pages, with the identifying information added to each page. Included with the lesson pages for each student are whatever ancillary materials (diagrams, tables, photographs, etc.) he may need for this lesson or may want to keep for future reference. In addition, whatever material is designed for the teacher's use (visuals for class display, descriptions of relevant experiments, questions for quizzes, etc.) is also included.

Once all the material is assembled, the computer then

connects the storage unit to the long-distance image reproducer at the terminal, wherever it is located. The lesson pages, reference material, and teaching aids are then reproduced, so that the terminal staff may pick them up and do whatever collating and stapling are required. The cycle then starts again, with the materials being picked up and presented by the teacher to individuals and to groups. At the end of the day the teacher spends another short period organizing tests and observation or ratings for submission to the management system, so that her computer aids to planning will be ready for the next day.

Several million dollars and 4 or 5 years have been spent in the research and development of management systems to accommodate this teacher role. AIMS (Automated Instructional Management System) was developed by the New York Institute of Technology. CAM (Comprehensive Achievement Monitoring) was jointly developed by staff members of Stanford University and the University of Massachusetts. IMS (Instructional Management System) is a product of System Development Corporation (SDC) and the Southwest Regional Laboratory for Educational Research and Development. IPI (Individually Prescribed Instruction) began at the University of Pittsburgh's Learning Research and Development Center. PLAN (Program for Learning in Accordance with Needs) is the product of the American Institutes for Research, Westinghouse Learning Corporation, and several cooperating schools. The Teacher's Automated Guide (TAG) is a system developed by the Portland, Oregon, schools; and, finally, various management systems exist to monitor instruction at Job Corps Centers.

The University of Buffalo has developed a Computer-Based Resource Unit Service (CBRU) which became available in the school year 1972–73. It includes information for teacher curriculum planning in the areas of Drug and Health Education, Special Education, General Education, Migrant Education, and Vocational Education, and is geared to students from kindergarten through high school. For example, courses in Environmental and Public Health are available from kindergarten through grade 12, as is Drugs, Mood Modification, Disease Prevention and Control, Nutrition, Speaking and Listening, and some very interesting programs written for the perceptually handicapped. In all there are 25 computer-managed units available.

These systems are similar in their components—each one defines instructional objectives, measures student performance on the objectives, and provides reports for the teachers. Some of them, not all, provide materials of instruction. They have differences as well as similarities, however. CAM, IMS, IPI, and CBRU define objectives in a modular fashion, and test students as frequently as once or twice a week. They are heavily test-oriented, with CAM having a strong item-analysis capability. PLAN and TAG define content in broader units, but PLAN allows learner characteristics to help determine the unit each student takes, while TAG's emphasis is a careful coding of lesson materials for easy retrieval by teachers. Some systems have been primarily concerned with orienting teachers on how to use the information provided by computers (CAM, IMS). IPI is particularly strong in the development of instructional materials and presentation procedures, and both IPI and IMS have detailed remedial prescriptions for pupils who do not achieve. Finally, certain management systems are adapted for special class levels. PLAN is operating in both elementary and high schools; IMS, IPI, and TAG have operated for the most part in elementary schools; CAM has been used primarily in high school math; New York Institute of Technology has done its work at high school and college levels; and Job Corps systems are for special education.

Teacher reaction to computer-managed instruction is mixed. Although they find that the system makes physical management of the classroom easier, lightens the load of lesson preparation, and helps explain the progress of students to parents, early system evaluation data showed that there are some problems, too. Pacing of instruction is often related to the school's socioeconomic status as well as to test scores; that is, pupils in high socioeconomic schools tended to complete more of the work than those in low socioeconomic schools. In addition, some of the teachers used the system's test items directly as teaching objectives, completely molding instruction to them. Sometimes teachers move low-scoring pupils through instruction just as quickly as some of their higher-scoring counterparts. Finally, the prescriptions and remedial or reinforcing activities are not always administered, or clear indications for regrouping students are not always followed.

Teachers find that they need training in how to interpret the daily computer reports and lesson plans using them. They need practice in relating pacing of instruction to test scores, in regrouping children on evidence of similar performance, and in selecting and administering suggested prescriptions. A second problem that must be overcome is the threat imposed upon teachers when large amounts of data suddenly become available. It is difficult to sort out and use information, and if the teachers do not use this information, they are vulnerable to being accused of not being responsible. Again, teacher training must be the answer.

A third limitation of development of computer-managed instruction is the variety of materials and approaches made available to the teacher. In most systems the materials are meticulously keyed so that the students get a carefully balanced program tied to specific teaching objectives. But to help a child who fails, the teacher needs more than one approach; she needs the total school resources at her fingertips. She needs an easily queried catalogue of supplemental texts, workbooks, films, tapes, games, tutorial procedures, community resources—in short, every known resource that is both available and relevant to the current instructional needs of the students. She must be able to call for the items in the catalogue by objective, or simply by describing student performance and receiving a series of appropriate instructional alternatives. Although IPI and IMS do provide remedial prescriptions, and the TAG system is designed for easy retrieval of lesson materials on particular learning objectives, no one of the existing management systems combines both of these capabilities as fully and completely as they should.

Whatever the limitations, they will eventually be worked out. Computer technology in education is, after all, a new service. When the bugs are out and the processes further developed, CMI can be invaluable in coping with mass enrollments and in contributing to the equalizing of educational opportunity. No longer will students suffer because of weak teachers. Computers will support the teachers so that their own inadequacies will be minimized. Computer-managed instruction can reach larger numbers of students by centralizing the curriculum process. Good sequential learning materials can be made available to almost everyone who plugs into the system. Eventually, teachers will have totally different roles. They will manage the materials of instruction rather than instruct. They will be facilitators as opposed to pedagogues; guides as opposed to mentors.

What do students make of these systems? In interviews with young people in Pittsburgh's Oakleaf School, their reactions ran the gamut from "too much classroom confusion" to "school can really be exciting." While those who move faster in the curriculum like it better than slow learners, actually not too many were aware of the computer and its role in their instruction. Since they had no contact with the machine or a terminal, they had little feeling about who or what produced the tests or the materials. Professor Oettenger, in his 1969 publication, *Run, Computer, Run,* calls the computer a "transparent tool—so skillfully engineered as to be foolproof, to disappear from view."

What are the financial implications of computer-managed instruction? In CMI, the costs are far less than in computer-assisted instruction. To begin with, there are no individual terminals and no communication costs. The large "central" computer "takes back" the child's work, corrects it, and prepares his next lesson for him on a sheet of paper. It substitutes for communication costs by using human managers, teachers, and messengers, and it does away with expensive repairs.

The University of Buffalo did a study of several existing systems. The cost per student varied from $1.35 to $25 a year, depending upon the extent of the service and the number of students enrolled. For example, in a population of 1,000 students it might reasonably cost $1.25 per student or $1,250. In a population of 6,000 students it would be $.57 per student or $3,420. A population of 4,000 students would cost $.65 per student or $2,600, etc. In other words, fees are based on the number of students in the program in a given area.

In addition, there can be other cost savings in CMI. If computer-managed instruction suggests hiring classroom managers rather than professional teachers because the kind of person that is needed is a facilitator as opposed to an imparter of knowledge; if it enables students to take work home for part of the day and do without expensive adult guidance; if, in addition, more schools buy into the system thus spreading the cost among many, then computer-managed instruction will become an important factor in reducing the price of education.

It is difficult to compare CAI and CMI. Each is valuable. CAI provides for individualization, whereas CMI, except in a very rough fashion, does not. CMI involves the teacher more than the more personal computer-assisted system, which has tremendous spin off in teacher acceptance, in developing teacher capabilities, and in providing for interaction between student and teacher. CAI, on the other hand, has the tremendous advantage of truly individualizing instruction, something we always speak about but have never really been able to achieve.

It would be ideal, of course, to have both—computer-managed instruction in the school and some form of terminal that can be placed almost anywhere, where the child could plug in and receive individual instruction or reinforcement of what he learned in school.

In a sense, there are two types of such terminals in most homes today. They are not thought of as "teaching machines" or computers and, in fact, except by special adaptation, they are not presently used as such, but their potential is now being harnessed. They are the common telephone and the common television set.

Patrick Suppes, a professor of mathematics at Stanford University, has initiated a new program for the computer, termed Dial-A-Drill. Dial-A-Drill is unique in the field of computer-assisted instruction in that it brings lessons directly into the student's home by telephone. Each day at a scheduled time the computer calls the child (if the line is busy, he loses his lesson that day) and gives him a set of questions which the student answers by pressing the appropriate key on a Touch-Tone telephone. The problems are automatically selected by the computer and presented to the student as a verbal message.

In areas where push-button dialing is not available, a Touch-Tone pad may be connected to a normal telephone. The Touch-Tone pad resembles a 12-key adding machine, connected to the telephone. The keys are numbered 0 through 9 and include an asterisk and a number sign. With these symbols the student is able to communicate to the computer the answer to any problem contained in a Dial-A-Drill curriculum. The computer recognizes the key which has been pressed and responds with an appropriate message.

Dial-A-Drill's mathematics program includes curriculums

for students in grades 2 through 6 in addition, subtraction, multiplication, and division. The curriculum is organized according to a system which insures that each lesson will contain a mixture of problems. For example, lessons for a second-grade student would include problems in addition and subtraction. A fourth-grade student would have a mixed lesson of addition, subtraction, multiplication, and division problems. The lessons follow a drill-and-practice format and last 5 minutes.

The computer keeps an updated summary of the work of each student. As the student proceeds through the curriculum, his performance is continually evaluated. When he has difficulty with one set of problems, he is automatically given easier ones. Students who perform well are given increasingly more advanced work, insuring that the difficulty of the drill always matches the student's capabilities.

The mathematics program was first used in the homes of 2,450 New York City school children from a variety of backgrounds, including deprived neighborhoods. Some children were homebound because of physical handicaps. Others were patients in hospitals. In addition to providing students with instruction in mathematics, Dial-A-Drill helps stimulate an interest in learning among other members of the family by extending the influence of the school into the home.

Dial-A-Drill is just in its beginning. It is estimated that it would cost about $4 a month for a student to have 5 minutes of telephone instruction every evening—about a dollar a week. Is it worth it? It would certainly seem so. It brings with it a whole new world of possibilities. Education need no longer take place only in the schools. Education can take place anywhere—even in one's own home and without a teacher coming to instruct and without "buying" equipment. This pioneer program has tremendous potential for schooling in the future, when the actual centers for learning are scattered within the total environment. It makes it possible to receive drill and, hopefully, instruction wherever you are, provided you are near a telephone. It makes education "accessible."

Another "accessible" machine—with almost every home in America having one—is the television set. Television has for many years been used for instruction and is discussed elsewhere in this chapter. But it has always been used only as a one-way medium. It transmits information and the viewer or receiver of the information has no way of interacting with it, no means of answering or questioning what he has just seen and heard. This often leads to frustrated feelings—you cannot differ, you cannot talk back, you have no power over the medium. But now all of this may become possible—a marriage between television and a computer.

The MITRE Corporation of Washington, D.C., has invented a new, low-cost method for delivery of computer services to homes and schools called TICCIT (Time-Shared, Interactive Computer Controlled Information Television). TICCIT combines television, video cassette tape recorders, cable television wideband transmission, and modern minicomputers. The first complete curriculum designed for TICCIT will have five full semesters of junior college courses, including freshman mathematics, English composition, and computer science.

As shown in Figure 1, interactive television has a key board similar to Touch-Tone in Dial-A-Drill. Associated with each TV receiver is a computer. The computer is programed to translate whatever key the viewer pushes into the content of whatever the viewer is watching. It may permit the viewer to participate in a public meeting straw vote by punching "yea" or "nay" or to search for a new apartment by pushing the key to designate the number of bedrooms desired, or to take a course on home repairs or a lesson in mathematics or English composition. The key board is the viewer's means of interacting with the system.

TICCIT provides computer-generated or controlled information that can be selectively received and projected by individual TV sets. Utilizing one television channel, each of 600 separate TV sets can receive separate information provided by the computer. A local signal "refresh" device which incorporates a video cassette recorder allows the TV screen to display the information at the standard television set. Using either the telephone or the cable system, each subscriber can call for any kind of information the system is designed to provide, independently of all other subscribers. Pictures and sound can be sent as well as printed text. At the present time, software programs for this system are being designed under the sponsorship of the National Science Foundation to provide individualized educational

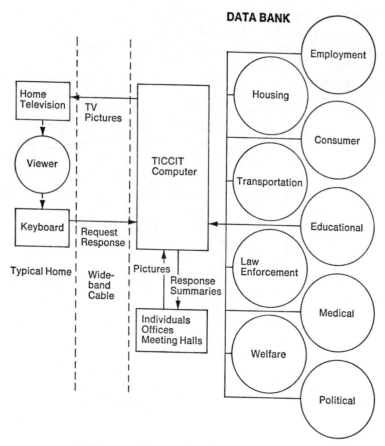

Figure 1 General Purpose Ticcit System

courses for home or school use. These types of courses could soon make it possible to take accredited courses at home, using computer-aided instructions and computer-aided grading systems, thereby permitting people to obtain a large part of their college education without attending formal classes. This approach is currently being seriously considered by the State University of New York under the "open university" concept.

The first educational program of this type for elementary schools is called "Carry" and was authored by Bob Eicholz (principal author of the best selling Addison-Wesley Elementary School Mathematics Series) of the University of Texas' Computer-Assisted Instruction Laboratory. This program teaches children who can add only two single-digit numbers to add any two-digit numbers together. (The program teaches the concepts of carrying; hence, its name.)

The other educational program in the system is aimed at fourth-grade level arithmetic students. It is a 5-day drill-and-practice course that provides both a pretest and a post test. The lessons for each day are presented on five levels. The total package consists of 27 lessons of 14 problems each; both the pretest and post-test courses have 16 problems. The material was authored by Patrick Suppes's group at Stanford University.

The TICCIT system can also provide for selective distribution of materials during "off hours" so that, for instance, a movie or book or newspaper can be sent to a subscriper's video cassette recorder to be stored for later display on his TV set whenever he might want it.

Using some version or elaboration of MITRE's TICCIT concept, the ability to "access" yesterday's edition of the world's newspapers on demand, section by section, paying only for what is used, and even to deliver mail, is, I believe, a goal that is technologically and economically realistic for the next decade. Thus the subscriber could receive and record daily news transmissions or take courses in French or mathematics, which utilize conventional filmed lectures, interlaced with one-frame-at-a-time questions and equations. In addition, the subscriber could, under his own control, request socially and politically oriented services for his personal viewing.

At election time, a citizen can have access—on demand—to information on candidates, their position on issues, an explanation of referendum items (e.g., specific political platform positions for comparison). If desired, he may review this material prior to visiting the polls.

Again, accessing on demand detailed information on job openings from the state employment agency, for example, along with photographs of the places and people employed there, could facilitate matching the needs of the applicant and the employer.

Use of the even more futuristic two-way TV-PHONE allows such services as remote control substitutes for home visits by physicians, telediagnosis and prescription, social counseling, probation checking, drug monitoring, not to mention interaction with a live teacher working in conjunction with a mechanized system.

Presently, social protocol does not encourage the use of display advertising for most social services (for example, social security information, VA information, health care information, food stamp information, etc.). However, it requires no stretch of the imagination to foresee expanded interactive "yellow pages" for these social services.

Especially for the recluse, the invalid, and the aged, but also for others, we can anticipate the machine's ability to play games with the subscriber, such as bridge, chess, blackjack, etc. One can readily imagine a cult of computer nuts growing up around such programing. Two-way games with these or other shut-ins are quite feasible. For the person who is not willing to fight the traffic and crowds downtown, the graphic capability of computer to allow tele-shopping for the latest bargains would reward business with expanded sales revenue.

Off-track betting, and other types of legalized gambling, could be handled with maximum efficiency by way of such terminals. The income derived from this could subsidize much of the interactive hardware installation used for educational or other purposes.

TICCIT has certain outstanding advantages. First, it is fairly inexpensive—conservative estimates fix a price of 25 cents per terminal hour. Secondly, TICCIT is individualized. It responds "instantly" to the demands of each viewer, permitting him to receive detailed information economically and privately. It offers search and calculation of information that might otherwise be difficult to obtain. Like the telephone and the mail service, it provides unlimited points of entry and delivery of information; in addition, it offers controlled storage, access, and unparalleled speed and convenience of retrieval. It is indeed multimedia, providing sight, sound, computer assistance, all within one system; and, with its two-way video-phone "snapshots," it gives us an interactive language.

Despite its advantages, however, media technology no matter what—programed instruction, television, individual computers and computer systems—has still to find a secure place in the field of education. It is intrinsically an artificial medium, as foreign to the teaching tradition as a plastic heart inserted in the human body. From its derivation from the Greek word "technilogia," meaning a systematic treatment, it would suggest a process whereby we analyze a problem and then develop a system of logistics to solve it. In the context of that definition, the electronic media might be considered as only a part of the total array of resources to be applied to the area of education. In a sense, then, it is, like the chalkboard, the workbooks, and the textbooks, a middleman between the learner and his environment. Unlike the others, however, it is an index of the accelerated pace of modern technology in all fields, and, as such, it is certain to have a profound effect in the field of education.

---

*Educational Facilities Laboratory, an organization dedicated to the creative use of space for education has done major studies on educational environments. A good deal of the descriptions which follow have drawn upon the E.F.L. students.

III
Alternatives to Our Present Structure

In the previous chapter we spoke about redesign within our present structure, and took a new look at school space and teaching staffs, and at the new technologies of teaching. Our assumption was that our present teaching system can be improved. There are those, however, who feel this is not so; that redesign is simply a refinement of existing machinery in a futile attempt to resuscitate a moribund system; that what we need is not a better job of alteration but a complete reconstruction. Those who call for alternatives generally fall into two groups: those seeking alternatives under the governance of the public schools, and those who say the structure cannot accommodate to total change and that we must go outside the system to achieve it. In other words, the advocates of alternative schools range from the moderate who would generate change gradually from within the current school system to the radical who wants total "instant" change generated solely from outside the system. Each of these "camps" has its supporters.

The logic of the extremists is that the human being responds more positively to completely new environments than to redirection within the ones he is used to. This concept is supported by Margaret Mead in *New Lives for Old,* largely on the basis of a study made on the island of Manus where a stone age population emerged into the 20th century within a single generation.

Margaret Mead tells the story of this seeming miracle of cultural adaptation and argues that it is far more difficult for a primitive people to accept a few fragmentary crumbs of Western technological culture than it is for them to adopt a whole new way of life at once. "Each human culture, like each language, is a whole," she writes, and if "individuals or groups of people have to change . . . it is most important that they should change from one whole pattern to another." The same thesis is expressed, in more contemporary fashion, by Timothy Leary: "No society can exist half turned on and half uptight." And Fidel Castro would have it that "Revolution and education are the same thing." These two figures may not be among one's favorites, but they do express a recognition of society's aversion to change and the need, therefore, not to prolong the process.

On the other end of the spectrum, however, are those who say, "Yes, we do need alternatives to our present educational system, but why need they be so abrasively forthright?" All over the country alternative schools are springing up that are "friendly" to our present society, that accept change but without total upheaval, without seceding. We are already familiar with some form of alternative schools—those that offer work–study programs, for example. This surely is an alternative to traditional schooling. There has been a long-standing acceptance of the notion that students may receive part of their education outside the school, so long as a specific purpose is being served. In other words, some alternatives do exist within the school structure and within public education.

However, whatever position is held, from radical to moderate, there are some basic elements that those who want alternatives adhere to. The difference is often the extent or degree of application. For example, both moderate and radical want greater participation of students, parents, and citizens; they differ, however, about where the decision-making power rests. The radicals want total shift of power to the people concerned; the moderates want to share power between the professionals and those affected by education.

Both radicals and moderates want new kinds of teachers. They both agree that new purveyors of education are necessary if there is to be a meaningful change. Yet, once again, it is a matter of degree. The radical wants "all" new teachers. The professional teacher as we know him is not generally acceptable because of the very nature of his training. The moderate will accept new kinds of teachers for new experiences, retaining the professional teacher for appropriate courses. Both are unhappy about the tenure system, but the moderate will work toward gradually modifying it by the infusion of new personnel without tenure rights, while the radical wants no part of it at any time for any one.

Both groups are calling for free choice for students, for opening up options. The difference rests in whether these options shall take place within public education or outside of it. Neither camp at this time is ready to say let there be both, with the parents having a choice as to whether they want to send their children to schools within our system or outside of it, and, incidentally, making it financially possible for them to exercise this choice.

Both the moderate reformers and the radical reformers have reasonable goals for today's world—new kinds of experiences, new kinds of teachers, new learning environments, and a shift of decision-making power from a remote hierarchy to those who are most closely affected by the educational process. The hard question is, is it achievable? Can you really get people to "turn around?" To what extent can you change institutions?

Can you, for example, expect a school or school system to create and support what it might consider a competing institution, such as an alternative school, to be housed within its own walls or even within its own system? What are the chances that the public education network, the largest institution ever run by federal, state, and local agencies, will give up some of its "holdings" to those who want to run their own schools, in their own way, without any monitoring, and with the use of public funds? Will the professional organizations and unions ever concede that by granting tenure to teachers we lock ourselves in and lose the power to decide what kinds of staff we really need, and, therefore, that tenure as we know it should be abolished? Can you really shift power from the few to the many, from a handful of people who now set policy for the schools to a more representative community-selected group? Can you really move from fiat to consensus? Let us examine the possibilities in the specific areas—perhaps they are not as bleak as they sound. How far can we really go?

Let us start with the most far-reaching and perhaps the

most difficult proposal, offering options to students of alternative educational experiences both within the system and outside of it. This chapter will devote itself primarily to the many such alternatives currently being offered within the governance structure of public education. Undoubtedly, the competitive feature of these options creates roadblocks that do not exist when we step outside the public school system. People who can pay for their children's education have always been able to select a private school. However, it is only the ability to pay that allows *them* to do so, just as the inability to pay deprives others of that choice. Is it possible, then, to give every child a voucher that will let his parents select a school, whether it be public or private? Can the poor child, like his rich cousin, be offered the same variety of choices?

Milton Friedman[1] advanced the concept of marketplace education in the early 1960's.

> Governments could require a minimum level of schooling financed by giving parents vouchers redeemable for a specified maximum sum per child per year if spent on "approved" educational services. Parents would then be free to spend this sum and any additional sum they themselves provided on purchasing educational services from an "approved" institution of their own choice. The educational services could then be rendered by private enterprises operated for profit, or by non-profit institutions. The role of the government would be limited to insuring that the schools met certain minimum standards, such as the inclusion of a minimum common content in their programs, much as it now inspects restaurants to insure that they maintain minimum sanitary standards.

Like most ideas subjected to intensive examination, the strengths and weaknesses of the proposal are being exposed. The voucher system scores as a means to stimulate diversity and create competition. On the other hand, it produces problems in supervisory quality control over the available educational services—such as, who will see to it that standards are maintained, that children achieve, that physical conditions are adequate, and so on. It poses problems in dealing with possible discriminatory practices against the poor and the blacks. It can totally ruin any attempts, as feeble as they now are, to integrate the schools.

[1] Milton Friedman, *Capitalism as Freedom,* Chicago: University of Chicago Press, 1962, p. 89.

In many communities in this country, parents of both races will select segregated schools. Indeed, vouchers are not an easy way out, yet with carefully built-in controls, they may offer a mechanism for freedom of choice. Perhaps there are others, not as yet formulated, that will allow us to remove the shackles compelling children to attend only one kind of school, in one locale, with a philosophy that may not be palatable to *all* who are made to attend, and to replace this instead with a series of options and free choices from which parents and students may make a selection.

If the diversification of education is achieved through either the voucher system or any other mechanism that may be adopted, large numbers of new kinds of teachers will be needed—new people for new programs in new types of schools, and working, perhaps, in some instances, for new kinds of "bosses." On first inspection, it may appear that the welfare of large numbers of professionals will be threatened, and the teachers' organizations for this reason will take a dim view of this alternative.

Yet, David Seldon.[2] President of the American Federation of Teachers, says that the role of the teacher has changed very little from what it was following World War II and is very little changed, he goes on to say, from even what it was following the Spanish-American War.

> *Teachers, as was the case a half-century and more ago, still teach groups of children according to a standard curriculum and under the supervision of others whose primary function is to make sure that teachers carry on their assigned tasks with a reasonable amount of diligence. Any fundamental change in role would require a change in this established pattern—teaching individual children instead of groups, use of individually prescribed curricula instead of a single standard course of study, or replacement of the present chain-of-command, line structure with new collegial and peer group relationships.*
>
> *There are many experimental programs in progress which would change one or another aspect of the teacher role, but although some of these programs are quite widespread and comparatively mature, no middle-sized or large school system has adopted any of these plans as its main strategic approach.*
>
> *Nevertheless, . despite the lack of significant change in teacher role to date, the demands for such change have become increasingly insistent. These increasingly insistent demands,*

[2] David Seldon, *Educational Technology*, February 1970, pp. 70–71.

> *however, arise primarily from the failures of American educa-*
> *tion—Don't just stand there; do something!—rather than from*
> *the demands for adoption of new discoveries in educational*
> *methods, which are not being utilized for one reason or another.*

Perhaps we tend to underestimate teachers and their leaders. Are they really as hide-bound and as resistant to change as
we seem to believe they are? Or do they, too, want new roles,
new ways of doing things, some excitement in their lives. Would
teachers not welcome the opportunity of updating themselves
to pass muster in the new schools, set themselves up as tutors,
or convert to emergent roles that are now on the drawing boards?
This will require a difficult change of direction in the thinking
of people who are now teachers. Little is being done other than
speeches being made by proponents of changing teacher roles on
all sides of the argument either by educators or by teachers'
organizations to set up any mechanisms for conversion.

A whole new thrust in personnel brings with it vital supplemental considerations. For one thing, since the new teacher
will be subjected to a different standard of accountability, it is
essential that his role be fixed more precisely. Unless there are
protections for the teacher so that he is not exploited by irrational
demands, the whole new structure would be tenuous.

Another problem is the whole question of governance and
prerogative. Both the moderates and the radicals believe that
effective education can be achieved only if we shift authority
from the currently elected or appointed school boards, who represent the so-called power structure, to those more vitally concerned with the benefits of education. Much has been written
on community control, its merits and dangers. One cannot deny
the desirability of bringing decision-making to the level of the
people who are affected by it. There is little doubt but that there
must be a symbiotic relationship between institutions and the
communities they serve. But how can we achieve this? The answer, it would appear, is that there is no one way to achieve this
relationship; different groups have done it in different ways.
Some have exercised force to achieve community control, others
have quietly and unostentatiously changed the kinds of people
who run the schools. There are still others who feel that community control in itself means little, that it is the caliber of
people who direct the educational decisions that is important,

regardless of whether they come from some remote establishment or from the bosom of the community.

In any event, it would appear that free choice for students to select the kind of education they want, the right of the overseers of schooling to choose new kinds of teachers and hold them accountable, and more personal administration, whether by community control or any other mechanism, are all essential ingredients of alternative schools, if they are to be successful.

Until now, little has been said about dollar cost. It is extremely difficult to generalize on costs for alternative schools. Schools that run outside the system may cost less because, as a rule, they do not use professional teachers. Those who work in these schools rarely get union wages. Many paraprofessionals are used. Building sites range from open spaces like farms and communes to apartments or storefronts. Generally, the cost of these kinds of spaces are a fraction of a schoolhouse. Maintenance is usually done by parents and teachers and students. Instructional materials or technologies are usually of the simplest and teacher-student-made variety. Textbooks as such are rarely used. Tradebooks, magazines, newspapers, which are cheaper, are more prevalent.

Alternatives within the system, on the other hand, can be housed in existing schools without additional cost, but then again they are required to use a majority of professional teachers and somewhat conventional educational materials and texts. Alternatives within the system usually cost more than traditional education because classes are smaller, requiring more professional teachers. In many cases, the school day is longer because that is what the students want and all-year-round schools are not uncommon to alternative schooling. As the experience becomes more interesting, both students and teachers want to stay with it; this, of course, costs more money. Realizing good alternative education within the system could very easily raise the dollar cost. But, just as easily, it can depress the human cost. Wouldn't it be just wonderful if the majority of students wanted more rather than less education? Incidentally, in those states where state aid is based on a pupil's daily attendance, school programs that "bring the students in" easily pay for themselves. In the auxiliary high school program in New York City that has attracted 7,000 dropouts back to school, the public school system

received from the state $4 million that it would have lost. There-
fore, the program not only "captured" the students and offered
them another chance, but it did this at no cost to the city.

No matter whether the alternative is inside or outside of
the system, both groups face the financial problems of survival.
For those alternative schools that are outside the public school
system, their funds must come from private sources—from either
tuition or foundation grants. This is precarious and often they
run on a month-to-month basis, not knowing whether they will
have enough money to get through the year. This brings with it
a whole group of insecurities that tend to impede good education.

On the other hand, those alternative schools that are within
the public school network receive their funds as do all other
public schools and should feel secure. But they, too, have their
money problems. They live in constant jeopardy of being anni-
hilated by the existing establishment. In most cases, the establishment does not look favorably on alternative schools. If they
are really alternative, the unpleasant implication is that there
is another and perhaps better way of doing what the rest of the
schools are doing. In much of the establishment, they are still
fringe and icing—they cater to few children and have little, if
any, impact on mass education. When the budget squeeze comes,
these items are the earliest victims of the red pencil.

In a way, this emphasizes Margaret Mead's contention
that partial change is difficult to achieve. All alternatives,
whether or not they save money, are in constant financial jeopardy. They may be able to survive if they can prove their worth
to the point that public funds are allocated for them or by their
being absorbed within the current power structure because they
no longer threaten the established way of doing things. Initially
at least, alternative schools within the system may survive by
accepting students whom the regular schools do not want, thus
relieving the schools of their problem students; or by being so
imaginative and creative as to be regarded as laboratories where
experimental methods are tried out for possible acceptance by
the larger institution. The former reason, at least at this time,
seems more likely than the latter.

Perhaps the greatest value of alternative schools lies in
their ability to show us that there are other ways of doing things,
that an education can be tailored to fit the child rather than the

reverse, so that as a result, children can become more involved in an environment of learning. This adds up to a cost saving that cannot be measured in dollars but only in terms of human achievement.

This chapter will devote itself to the two "alternatives," the moderate's more or less traditional approach which would expand the present educational system to include people and places that are now outside of and different from the existing school system, and the more extreme point of view which is the building of totally new conceptual structures wholly unrelated to those now existing. One might call the latter an alternative in the purest sense. Quite often, an alternative school combines features of both, extending existing programs and adding completely "new" components. Therefore, they are not easily catalogued.

EXTENDING EDUCATIONAL ENVIRONMENTS

Among the most intriguing, productive, and economical alternatives in use today are the wide variety of programs built around the premise that students need not spend all of their time inside a classroom, or for that matter inside a school facility; that physically the educational environment can be enlarged. For some educators and school board members this concept is hard to accept. They still believe that there is a world inside and a world outside the school, and that the school's business is its own. In a way they are right; too often there are two different worlds, the one of reality and the one of the textbook. Today, students are seeking to break out of this inside world and taste the excitement of the one outside. Instead of inhibiting this desire, and in many cases forcing youngsters to make unfortunate choices such as leaving school in order to "taste life," why not legitimatize and capitalize on outside experiences by incorporating them as part of the school program?

These "extending" experiences can, for convenience, be divided into two categories, For example, a student can take on new kinds of courses, with new types of teachers, even just "free time" to do what he wants—all within the school confines. This approach is most palatable to the traditionalists. "Give them a little leeway but not too much." As unsatisfying as this may be to those who seek true alternatives, it should be viewed, nevertheless, as affording the student an opportunity for new experiences and perceptions. In fact, most schools that have started with this limited model have expanded to allow the student to spend part of his time in activities outside the school. These activities are planned, scheduled, and accredited, and, together with the regular, ongoing in-school activities, make up a student's requirements for graduation.

Permitting students to move freely *within* the school itself and *outside* the school, usually referred to as the *open-campus plan*, is a way of extending the walls of the school. There are substantial and growing numbers of high schools across the country which have adopted—or are in the process of adopting— open-campus plans. Two basic reasons underlie the current popularity of this approach. First, as communities like Beeville, Texas, have found, open campus helps to relieve overcrowding by making needed classrooms available during the time students are out of the rooms or the buildings. Second, in communities like Brookline, Massachusetts, open campus has been introduced for the purpose of humanizing the school, making it more flexible and responsive to student needs, and to broaden educationally the scope of secondary school experiences.

A second category is an *off-campus plan* whereby the largest part of students' experiences are obtained outside of school. The most notable examples of this approach are the Philadelphia Parkway Program and the Chicago Metro High School, where most of the student's time is spent in agencies and institutions not connected with education as we usually perceive it. The off-campus schools have as their primary focus outside experiences, whereas the open-campus schools stress in-school experiences with outside activities being ancillary. At times, as the following examples will show, it is difficult to place a school in a specific category since, as one can well imagine, there is a tendency in some programs to cross categories.

Open Campus

A prime mover, as we have said, in stimulating open-campus plans is the need for added space. With industry becoming somewhat mobile, school systems suddenly find themselves with an influx of new students. With higher enrollments and, in many instances, no money to build either a new school or an addition to the old one, school boards have had to look for other means of absorbing students. One obvious solution is to extend the school day; in that way you can accommodate many more students within the existing space. But this solution creates its own problems. A student usually has two free periods a day, one for lunch and one for study. Now, with the extended day, he still has the same number of required classes to attend but he has up to four free periods. What does he do? Where does he go in those periods?

The traditional method has been to assign a large number of teachers to classrooms set aside for study purposes. This in itself can be self-defeating since it "uses up" professional teachers by making them monitors, and, at the same time, "uses up" much-needed classroom space. We are not even mentioning what happens during these so called "study" periods. Assignment to study halls has been high up on the grievance lists of students, and of teachers as well. Rather than do this, some school administrations use larger spaces as study halls, such as the cafeteria or the auditorium, thus preserving space and personnel. One or two teachers may be needed each period to supervise 50 or 100 or more students. Experience soon reveals, however, that the cafeteria and auditorium are inappropriate for study halls. There is little study and a lot of discomfort for both students and supervising teachers.

If instead of concentrating in one large prescribed space, the students were given a choice of several available spaces in the building, such as the library or an area that could be converted into a student lounge or an empty classroom or a section of the locker room, for their free time, the extra free periods might not be the tremendous problem they are now. The students would, at least, be dispersed and with a little imagination and incentive, the student could also have alternative productive experiences that he normally would not have had. A lounge offers a place to get together with your friends, a library the opportunity to browse, an empty classroom the opportunity for quiet study or group activities.

Usually, schools that open up on this very modest basis soon begin to expand even further. Instead of making space available for students simply to do what they want, the schools start offering additional experiences during free time. In Brookline and Winchester High Schools in Massachusetts, during free periods, upgraded noncredit mini-courses are provided on a wide variety of topics reflecting the skills, talents, and interests of students and teachers. For example, Winchester offers over 30 such mini-courses, meeting once a week and ranging from S.A.T. College Board Reviews to "Experimental Fiction" to "Basic Photography" (the latter taught by a student). In both schools, teachers responded in large numbers to the request for volunteers to offer these courses. Not only do they themselves like the experiences, but anything is better than study hall duty. No additional compensation is involved since it is part of the school day and attendance is voluntary.

At Lawrence High in Falmouth, Massachusetts, it was decided to use the auditorium—often the most under-utilized school space because of its size—to offer a variety of programs to interested students. Included among the programs are films (some with a specific educational purpose, some for entertainment), speakers, panel discussions, and folk singing. Students are encouraged not only to participate in these programs, but also to make recommendations and to assist in planning. This, of course, is a very different approach from using the auditorium as a study hall, or for the showing of a film that no one had any choice in selecting other than the audiovisual coordinator or the assistant to the principal. Besides, attendance is voluntary; no one is made to do anything, but a student in his free period must be accounted for somewhere—in the auditorium, a new course, or the library.

Many high schools, such as Lawrence in Falmouth, Massachusetts, Winchester, also in Massachusetts, and Jones High School in Beeville, Texas, find that they can increase their student intake by about 25 percent by using the free access method. In addition to the space saving, it is found that facilities are utilized more effectively—library, auditorium, cafeteria, and student-activity rooms, as well as classrooms. As to expenses, not only is money saved by full utilization of space and facilities, but there is nothing implicit in an open-campus program to entail expenses over and above those incurred normally. On the other hand, spending a modest amount of additional money could enchance its effectiveness.

For instance, at Lawrence High School, a teacher was assigned full-time to develop and supervise the school's auditorium program, and two paraprofessionals were hired; one to supervise the cafeteria/lounge, the other to supervise the school grounds. School authorities felt that they could well afford to take these steps in view of the savings in teacher man-hours resulting from elimination of most corridor, cafeteria, and lavatory duties.

As attractive as students find the use of free space, the availability of mini-courses and the freedom to select and even teach them, if the number of students in the school continues to grow, a saturation point may be reached. Then one finds that a lot of time is spent seeking additional student centers and checking to see if they are there. Because of this, the schools usually move into a much freer situation wherein students may leave the school altogether during free periods or at lunchtime, a true "stretching" of the school walls. Of course, any student may choose to remain in school. By giving students the option to leave during free periods, the pressures of numbers and of administration are relieved. Moreover, the additional freedom of movement granted to students often reduces the tensions generated by the longer school day. In fact, it makes the longer day workable. A note of caution, however. It is no use letting students out of school if there is no place for them to go and no means of transporting them. Simply allowing students to congregate around the school creates a distraction for those inside.

Many open-campus schools are located within walking distance of town centers. There should be some kinds of public facilities—restaurants, shops, libraries, etc.—not very far away. During cold or inclement weather, students will concentrate in the school unless there are other alternatives close by. Schools considering open-campus plans should take this into consideration. For example, during "free time" students who live near the school might return home or sometimes even assist either the family business or small shopkeepers who need part-time help. Those who live long distances away could be assigned to local governmental or community agencies that also need part-time assistants. Whatever the student does during his free time, the problem of students milling around without purpose is relieved and, at the same time, pressure is taken off the community to build an annex to the school to accommodate the extra students.

Jones High School in Beeville, Texas, which is an agricultural and ranching community of 15,000 in Southern Texas, has teaching spaces with a capacity—measured in traditional terms—of 970 students. Yet the school enrolls over 1,200 as a result of an extended day schedule combined with an open-campus plan, which allows students to leave the school during their free periods. This represents a 24 percent addition to capacity.

Up to this point, the "openness" of the school program is fairly loose. The student may or may not go to a mini-course; he may go home or work in the immediate locality in his free periods. However, many schools are beginning to offer their students programed alternative experiences outside of the school buildings instead of just "letting them out." The student still spends the largest part of the day, week, and semester at the home base school. Basic skills and state-required courses are taught during those periods. The remainder of the time, the student is programed into other environments.

This "split" approach offers a change in conventional schooling and a break in the continuity of educational experiences. A semester or year-long period for organized and supervised experience outside of the school makes a lot of sense. It need not come at the same time for every student, but at some time for all.

There are very real advantages to the student in spending part of his day in the outside world. First, it gives him an opportunity to confront the real world, not a simulated one that he might have in the classroom; then, by being put on his own instead of being continuously supervised by a teacher, he may well learn how to assume responsibility for his own actions as well as responsibility to the community in which he works.

The San Mateo Union High School District in California launched a school/community service program in September 1970 following a summer trial period. The program grew out of a concern over the education of nonacademically oriented students although all students are eligible to participate. In particular, school authorities were anxious to provide these students with learning experiences that would enhance their sense of self-worth and would encourage the growth of self-responsibility.

The program has students work as volunteer aides in elementary schools, hospitals, community agencies, the local American Red Cross, etc. Students undergo in-service training while on the job, and receive school credit for their work. Although the program is still in its infancy, over 1,250 students from 7 high schools have been placed in volunteer jobs. They work from 5 to 10 hours a week during and after regular school hours and on weekends, depending on the individual circumstances. The demand of students for these positions, and the interest on the part of the hiring agencies are subject only to limitations of scheduling and transportation.

Although at this time the full complement of teachers is retained by the school, it is possible, as the program progresses and becomes regulated, that fewer teachers will be necessary. After all, 10 hours a week is one-third of a student's time, and if this is spent in out-of-school activities, fewer teachers should be needed.

A program similar to San Mateo's is in effect at Winchester High School, Winchester, Massachusetts, where about 300 students have responded to requests for volunteers from local agencies. Participants work with retarded children, help out in hospitals, join in a Big Brother–Big Sister program, and act as tutors and aides in Winchester's elementary schools. The work is carried out both during and after regular school hours, and although the program is voluntary, students are credited toward graduation with having met certain requirements on the out-of-school jobs.

A different kind of approach to out-of-school learning is one exemplified by Lowell High School in San Francisco. Lowell is an academic, college preparatory high school whose social science curriculum is structured to take advantage of the resources the city has to offer in the social, political, and economic spheres.

In one of Lowell High's social science programs, about two classes (60 students), each semester, study local government, politics, and society by doing field work in the community. Students conduct interviews, take polls, write letters requesting appointments or information, attend meetings, and perform research. The aim is to analyze actual problems and to recommend workable solutions.

Lowell High also has a similar social science program in which individuals can enroll in a research project of 2 or 3 weeks' duration. Students set their own objectives but work within broad guidelines set forth by the faculty. Community resources and people are exploited for research on such topics as "Water Pollution in San Francisco Bay," "Police and the Community," and "Consumer Buying." At the conclusion of the project, students demonstrate their understanding of the subjects they have explored through a written examination or an oral presentation. These alternatives to school curriculum experiences are thoroughly legitimatized through accreditation. These are not the social service, Peace Corps types of program of old; they are as much a part of the student curriculum as the English 4 needed to satisfy state requirements.

Brookline High School, Brookline, Massachusetts, offers four programs to juniors and seniors, which involve educational experiences outside the school. One is a series of special seminars, each running a full 13 week semester, offered in most instances by unpaid, volunteer, nonschool personnel who are qualified professionals in their own fields. For example, one is given by a trained psychologist who offers a course in Psychology and Mental Health. The course meetings take place in his home in the evening, with field trips on certain afternoons.

Another is a series of career experiences, which offer students opportunities to act as teacher aides in various Brookline schools, as legislative aides to local state legislators, and as aides in one or more of the departments of the town government.

They also allow for enrollment for high school credit at local colleges, with course charges paid by the student; and a program of independent study has been organized, in cooperation with and monitored by a member of the faculty, which releases the student from a particular class for a specified period. Now, about 150 students at Brookline High are participating in these programs, with each student spending about 6 hours a week outside the school.

You will notice that whereas some schools have a limited open-campus approach, others have gone much further and have their students out of school up to 30 percent of the time. In the Lexington High School in Lexington, Massachusetts, there are about 170 students enrolled in a program called Education Without Walls or "EWOW." Although the name implies that there is no such thing as a school and that education takes place totally on the outside, this is only partially true.

The program was started in the 1969–70 school year and

is limited to juniors and seniors. The students represent a cross section of the school population. Some are college bound, some are not. The purpose of EWOW is to expand the scope of learning experiences available to students by offering credit for a variety of out-of-school activities chosen by the students themselves. Students are encouraged to define their individual educational needs and then to use the resources of both the school and the community in satisfying those needs.

Students are consulted with regard to the content matter of their school studies. The only courses which they are required to take—by state law—are English, United States history, and physical education. Otherwise, they may select either the more familiar standard high school subjects or courses featuring the interdisciplinary approach favored in the EWOW program (current offerings include "Creative Expression," "Environmental Awareness," and "Decision Making"). Occasionally, the morning schedule of classes is interrupted for special events, such as guest lectures, films, or discussion group presentations, which all EWOW students attend.

Generally, EWOW students spend their morning from 8 to 12 AM in school, their afternoons out in the community. Out-of-school activities include employment (students work as teacher aides in Lexington's elementary schools, as garage mechanics, retail store clerks, etc.) or nonpaying projects (such as producing films or making guitars). The 170 EWOW students average about 20 hours per week in school instead of the customary 27½ hours.

In Falmouth, Massachusetts, an experiment called the "Falmouth Out-of-School Program," which involves sixth graders, was begun this year. The program was planned jointly by teachers and interested community members and has several aims: to enable children to enjoy the benefits of learning resources outside the school; to broaden the school curriculum; and to enlist community talent, interest, and support to supplement the teaching efforts of the school's professional staff.

The originators of the program took an inventory of the area's cultural and social resources and the talents and skills of over 100 community members who volunteered to participate. From this process came out-of-school courses in such subjects as American Indians, instrumental music, hospital activities, seamanship, and a host of others.

At the moment, only one sixth grade class of about 30 children is involved in the out-of-school program at any one time (each class spends about one-quarter of its time outside of the school in the course of a school year). The length of a single out-of-school course varies from a few days to 2 weeks.

Outside the school, each class has two teachers: the regular teacher and the volunteer specialist who is skilled or knowledgeable concerning the subject under study. In addition, the class will have two or three other community volunteers accompanying it. With a class of 30, this means one adult to every 6–8 children, an arrangement which permits a good deal of individual attention.

The extent to which this kind of program could be expanded is limited only by the number of voluntary participants who have something to offer in the way of knowledge and/or an active interest and concern for children.

In Cleveland, Ohio, a somewhat different approach has been taken to the open-campus concept through the Cleveland Supplementary Education Center. The center's program is designed particularly for third, fifth, and sixth grade students. Each school day, about 350 elementary grade students, drawn from both public and parochial schools, spend a full day at the converted warehouse. After regular school hours and on Saturdays, students from all grades are offered an enrichment program. Programs are also provided for teachers.

Due to the scope and richness of its offerings, the Cleveland center's operating costs are about $500,000 per year, including the cost of transporting pupils but not including maintenance. Over 80 percent of this amount goes for salaries. The center has a full-time staff of about 70, supplemented by about 30 part-time staff. However, there are about 70,000 pupil visits to the center each year. On this basis, the cost works out to a little more than $7.00 per pupil visit. And this does not take into consideration but includes the visits of teachers and other adults, for whom the center also conducts programs.

A ready-made site for the Supplementary Educational Center was found in a warehouse located in an area scheduled for urban renewal. The warehouse, scheduled for demolition, had been abandoned and was acquired by the city. Its central location was ideal for a citywide resource center. The warehouse was turned over to the school department on a temporary basis, until renewal would actually take place. "Temporary" will turn out to be 6 years by the end of the 1971–72 school year, when the center will move to another site two blocks away. Use of the warehouse during this time has cost the school department nothing in the way of rental fees.

The cost of renovating the warehouse was $300,000. Spread out over the 6 years the center will have been in operation by the end of the 1971–72 school year, this works out to $50,000 per year.

Included among the center's facilities are a planetarium, music listening and practice rooms, a model country store, an auditorium, and a cafeteria. Among the activities which the facilities and equipment of the center make possible—and which could not be reproduced in each neighborhood school—are the study of astronomy, space science, meteorology, urban redevelopment, the presentation of concerts by professional groups, and student production of slides and films.

As you can see, this is an open-campus program that is supplementary to the regular school program. It is "added on." It does not replace but instead enriches and extends. However, if the participating schools in Cleveland were to substitute some of the experiences in the Supplementary Center for some less rewarding experiences in the traditional curriculum, they would then be operating in the arena of alternative experiences in education. Also, if they revised their required courses to reflect the experiences in the Center, this, too, would be moving toward alternative education.

A somewhat similar approach, with similar limitations, is EPOCH (Educational Programming of Cultural Heritage). At EPOCH, elementary school children from Berkeley and other Bay Area school districts learn about the cultural heritage of the various races that make up the people of their communities. EPOCH facilities include a circular demonstration chamber equipped for multimedia presentations, a resource room in which children can operate their own audiovisual equipment, and a mini-museum containing artifacts and displays.

EPOCH serves two successive elementary school classes in the course of a typical day. It has had about 8,000 pupil visits and about 4,000 student teacher visits since its inception. Its operating budget is about $10,000 per month, which is minimal for the number of students it serves. Once again, this is supplementary rather than alternative education. However, let us not, for that reason, sell short either the Cleveland or the EPOCH programs.

They serve children from a circumscribed geographical area of the community, usually one that is larger than a local school's. One of their objectives, therefore, in addition to providing students with new learning experiences not available to them in their home schools, is to enable them to share these experiences with students drawn from different neighborhoods. Also, they have a specific emphasis: performing and visual arts, ecology, science, communications, vocational education. They provide programs and facilities that could not possibly be duplicated in every school.

Open-campus plans, be they narrow or expanded, are becoming more popular every day. They offer a type of alternative learning environment, sometimes limited in scope, but still an alternative to the conventional school and its curriculum. However, as with any innovation, regardless of cost savings, there are those who are supportive, those who look cautiously and put a toe in the water, and those who summarily reject the innovation. Open-campus programs run the gamut of approval from advocates to skeptics. According to Lester W. McCoy, principal of Beeville High School, they would not return to a conventional school program, even if new construction was possible. According to McCoy, "We have found the educational benefits to be so great and the students' attitudes and responsibility to be so much better than on the old system that we would not go back to it." Beeville has been operating an open-campus plan for 8 years.

Holland High School in Holland, Michigan, has also had an open-campus plan in effect for the last 8 years. As Fred S. Bertsch, Jr., principal of Holland High, puts it, "I don't think any of us here would want to go back to the concentration camp."

However, in one school where an open-campus plan has been implemented quite recently, there is less conviction on the part of some of those involved that the climate of the school has improved. Brookline High School in Brookline, Massachusetts, introduced open campus during the 1969–1970 school year. An evaluation report found that although students overwhelmingly believed that the climate of the school had improved, the faculty was split on the issue. Significantly, those teachers who had been at the school for a number of years tended to agree with the students, while those with less time at the school could see no difference. The report also pointed out that a major part of the dissatisfaction of the teachers with the open-campus program stemmed from their not having been participants in the planning process—a fact which should be kept in mind by school systems contemplating new programs.

Parents' reactions run the gamut from acceptance to rejection. At Brookline High School, after an initial period of skepticism and distrust, community reactions were generally favorable. In fact, parents were found to favor the program three to one. At Winchester, Massachusetts, where a survey was made at the end of the first year of the open-campus program, a majority of parents and merchants responded favorably, and the police were particularly supportive. In New York City, three open-campus schools were closed because the parents rebelled. They said that although their children were enjoying the experience, their Regents grades were lower than those of children who attended traditional schools.

Perhaps from these reactions one can draw some tentative generalization. A program is usually as good as its planning process and its mechanisms for change. When programs are planned collaboratively with teachers, students, and parents, all understand the goals and they stand a better chance of success than programs planned by some remote "specialists" who impose them on the students and the staff. Secondly, if an open-campus program proves extremely popular with the students but, at the same time, takes away time from required studies and thereby depresses examination grades, the program should be flexible enough to make immediate adjustments. Very often the adjustments should be made for individuals rather than groups. Not all students need the same amount of time devoted to all subjects.

Off Campus

While many schools are expanding their alternatives to conventional school curricula, some movements are afoot that would extend this concept even further. Within the past 5 years, schools have been and are being created that are almost completely outside the boundaries of school buildings as such. They might have a small installation that could be called a school at which the student spends a minimum of time, usually for the purposes of programing, counseling, and, sometimes, for taking courses required for state certification. But for the most part, the school building concept is subordinated to the much larger concept of using the whole community as a school. This is different from the open-campus plan where, although the student has experiences away from school, he spends the major part of his time in school. In the off-campus plan, the largest part of the student's time is spent outside of the school.

The most notable examples of off-campus schools are Philadelphia's Parkway Program and Chicago's Metro High School. Both of these schools are complete alternatives to traditional education, yet both are products of and function within the public school system. Both programs started within a year of each other: the Parkway in 1969, Chicago Metro in 1970.

The basic principles of these programs are similar. They proceed on the assumptions that education needs the enriching influence of contact with the community, its industry, its cultural institutions, its shops and streets; that students can learn from people with varied skills and interests—lawyers, electricians, artists, newspaper reporters; that a skilled teacher can help a student use the talents of these people to gain a rich and individualized education; and that students become more independent and motivated learners when they join in decisions about how their school will be structured and how their own education will proceed. The programs favor a fairly small learning community of teachers and students as the basic unit to which the student shall relate, and provide for constant evaluative feedback by this community regarding the direction the student's learning shall take. The diverse backgrounds of students provide a resource for education that becomes an integral part of the school program.

In both schools, Chicago Metro and Philadelphia Parkway, although students are encouraged to make up their own schedules, they must include, in addition to outside resource experiences, basic subject classes and tutored sessions, if necessary. Provisions for the length of time spent in class and the number of meetings per week are flexible.

Metro has developed a four-part program consisting of

learning units, individual placements, independent study, and counseling groups. A learning unit at Metro is the basic course offering. It differs from the more traditional school course since it is divided into 9-week sections of intensified learning experiences and one week of evaluation. It covers less than the traditional academic curriculum but emphasizes basic principles and structure and focuses on specific disciplines.

For example, a science student might be enrolled for two 9-week cycles in Film Biology, viewing films about biological sciences, and in Ecology, studying the relationship of living things to their environment in real field experiments. The student might then enroll in two cycles in Animal and Human Behavior to study the behavioral attitudes and life styles of varied species at the Lincoln Park Zoo.

Learning units cover a wide variety of subjects. Some deal with such basic skills as reading. Well over half of them deal with topics that are not usually covered in a traditional high school curriculum. Each student may choose those units he wishes to take, although he must also follow the general area requirements as established by the Board of Education for graduation.

In addition to the learning units, each student has the option of contracting with a sponsoring staff teacher for an *individual placement.* A placement might find a student assisting a veterinarian, working in an advertising agency, staffing a political campaign office, tutoring elementary students, or observing the work of a specialized lawyer. Placements are fitted to the needs and expressed desires of the Metro student body and allow students to delve with some responsibility into areas of interest which may grow simply from curiosity or, perhaps, from occupational goals.

A Metro student may also work on an *independent study project.* By agreeing with a sponsor on a project of mutual interest, the student proceeds to study closely that area of interest. Study areas may range from the operations of the City Council to the mechanics of a gasoline engine.

Finally, each student at Metro is part of a *counseling group.* Each group, averaging 15 students, meets once a week for varied purposes. Record keeping and programing for each student takes place in the counseling groups. The counseling group, however, is both an active and a reflective body, concerning itself with the relationships of the students to the school, to the teaching staff, and to its own members. Thus, if offers a time for students to get to know each other better in group discussions or activities.

Both programs, Metro and Parkway, lean heavily on outside resources. About half of the approximately 100 courses offered by the Parkway Program are given by the nearly 200 institutions within the city of Philadelphia that participate. These include such diverse organizations as the Franklin Institute, General Electric, the Insurance Company of North America, the Drama Guild, and the Urban League. Similarly, Metro enjoys the services of 56 Chicago business, cultural, and community organizations.

By drawing from businesses, cultural institutions, community organizations, and professional associations, both programs have created a diverse curriculum using the skills not only of the staff teachers, but also of participating organizations and cooperating teachers. Film directors, stockbrokers, amateur cooks, astronomers, actors, graduate students, social workers, and many others have contributed in different capacities. Some teach a learning unit; some help a staff member with a learning unit; some offer conference rooms and, occasionally, unused space for classes; some give valued consultation; some sponsor individual student placements.

In the Chicago program, there is a full complement of Chicago high school teachers. The *staff teacher* offers units in areas other than those covered by the units that are taught by cooperating teachers and participating organizations. The staff also acts as the fundamental operational group in the school, setting up the basic curriculum, working with participating organizations, organizing school projects, and running all-school registration and evaluation sessions.

Metro staff is selected by a joint student–staff committee and must be ratified by the principal. The increased all-school autonomy inherent in this process has allowed for a great diversity in the Metro staff.

The Parkway Project also utilizes regular staff teachers. Their role is similar to those at Metro. The difference lies in the numbers. In Chicago, the complement of the professional staff is about the same as in a regular high school. In Philadelphia, it is about half as many. They try to go "outside" the system for the majority of their teachers.

Parkway has a separate home base for each of its several autonomous units (there are no more than 180 students to a unit). Two out of their three home bases are leased—at minimal rents. These are located in office buildings. The third, situated in an unused elementary school, is rent-free.

Metro's home base is located in an office building in the downtown Loop area of Chicago. They lease about 12,000 square feet and pay a monthly rent of $5,200 (this amount includes reimbursement for renovation expenses borne by the landlord). But Metro also enjoys the use of space donated free by the Standard Oil Company and adequate to house 50 to 60 students.

Essentially, the home bases, housing teacher offices and student lockers, serve as a kind of headquarters and meeting place. The cost of a home base varies widely depending upon such local factors as the state of the rental market, the type of location chosen, restrictions imposed by safety regulations, and the generosity of community institutions and individuals.

As for classrooms and other learning spaces, as distinguished from home bases, most of them are provided by the community, at little or no cost to the school system. In this way, Parkway and Metro avoid most of the cost of maintaining expensive school buildings, equipment, and grounds.

What this means in terms of savings in school construction costs can be seen most clearly if we calculate what it would cost to build a 500-student high school to house those currently in the Parkway Program. If we assume a modest space allowance of 120 square feet per student, a hypothetical high school will have a gross square footage of 60,000. At $40 per square foot (and this may well be under the going rate of urban school construction costs in the Northeast), such a school would cost $2.4 million, plus annual interest on the bonds. And the annual interest alone on such a sum might well be equivalent to the annual facilities costs of a Parkway Program.

As for operating costs, as distinguished from construction costs, the evidence indicates that these depend upon the number of professionals who are employed. In Metro, as we said before, it remains about the same as in a conventional school. In Parkway, it is less.

In both schools, students are encouraged to participate in the school's administration, to evaluate its performance, and to make recommendations for change where they think it advisable. At Parkway, course evaluations at the end of a semester work two ways. On the one hand, the teacher and the student jointly put together a written evaluation of the student's performance—that is how the student is graded. On the other hand, the student works out an evaluation of both the course itself and the teacher's performance in teaching it.

Both schools run a little under 500 students, and in both programs students are chosen at random so as to represent a cross section of the city's high school population. The popularity of Parkway and Metro among students in Philadelphia and Chicago is indicated by the enormous excess of applications over available openings. Since its inception, Parkway has had about 15,000 applicants for its 500 places in the fall of 1972, Metro had 3,000 applicants for 200 places.

These two schools are examples of real alternatives to existing high school education, but it should be kept in mind that they serve very few students. To increase the number of students one must have an equally increased commitment from the community to participate. This is not impossible but it must be carefully planned. Both Metro and Parkway planned for a considerable amount of time and used experts to help them. In Chicago, for example, consultants from Urban Research Corporation of Chicago worked on planning and carrying out all phases of the Metro program, including contracts with participating organizations, curriculum planning, staff development, teaching classes, student counseling, development of administrative procedures, and evaluation.

In Philadelphia, three industrial and three cultural groups combined with the professional staff and some students, parents, and representatives of community groups to form the planning teams.

Another and more recent addition to the school without walls concept is being started in the Madison, Wisconsin, Public High School. Seeking to open on a small scale in September 1972, the school conducted a lottery to select 105 students from grades 9–12 from all parts of the city. These students will work with a staff of four regularly employed high school teachers selected from volunteers. Other instructional help will be received from parents who must pledge a minimum of 2 hours per month in school-related activities and from community volunteers.

The governance provides for considerable autonomy on the part of the students, but the inclusion of the Director of High Schools on the town meeting and the steering committee will provide veto power on any violation of Board policy. Various management groups will determine functions such as building allocation, fund raising, etc. Every student must belong to a management group.

The major objectives are growth in interpersonal communications and the development of a sense of community. The educational program requires every student to attend 4 tutorial sessions of 1½ hours duration each week. Here, he or she establishes with the teacher the curricular plans through a written contract. Some courses may be taken in school, others through community experiences, and still others may be completed at home. Credits and courses for graduation will be established in English, math, social studies, science, and physical education. Board of Education requirements will be adhered to for graduation. Objectives of a behavioral type will be set into the contract, and evaluation will be planned and later measured. Assessment of personal and intellectual growth will be made for each student on each contract. No grades will be assigned.

This alternative program is interesting because it will provide the students with the kinds of educational experiences they feel are important to them while still maintaining that degree of accountability necessary to assure measurable achievement. Success will depend on the sound application of the principles of freedom and self-discipline.

Since this program will have the Madison, Wisconsin, High School as a home base, rental will not be a cost factor. The professional teachers are in the same ratio to students as they are in the regular high school; thus no additional cost. Whatever extra monies are spent will be in the general area of transportation and, in some cases, entrance fees and materials not ordinarily found in the general ordering catalogues. These expenses, however, are minimal and, if it is successful, the real "payoff" will come in student involvement and excitement.

The principles of freedom and self-discipline, as exemplified in the Wisconsin program, are the basis for a rather exciting off-campus alternative school in Toronto, Canada. It started as a summer program for high school students who could not get jobs. SEED—Summer of Experience, Exploration and Discovery— took place in the city of Toronto, Canada, and was financed by supplementary funds. The participants, or students, grouped themselves according to their interests and met in an informal way for discussions, field trips, and other activities. Instead of teachers, they acquired advisors, these being facilitator-type people rather than content-oriented teachers.

When the students of SEED submitted their brief to the Toronto Board of Education, they conceived of their school as an experiment in education. They believed it would provide knowledge of things previously inaccessible to them in their regular secondary schools, and in a way which they believed facilitated learning. Knowing that the Toronto Board was interested in keeping pace with new concepts and reform in education, they had hoped that SEED would serve as a model for future endeavors. These students also believed that SEED would serve as an alternative in education for those students who would otherwise go through school without performing up to their potential or who might otherwise drop out. These students felt that an informal and fairly unstructured learning environment would be most conducive to learning for this type of student.

When the establishment of SEED was approved by the Toronto Board, it was designed to exist as a distinct alternative to the regular secondary school program. However, to ensure that students would not lose a year of their education should they decide not to continue in SEED, the Board felt that the students should be required to take some courses such as languages, sciences, and mathematics from qualified teachers in order to be able to receive credits for secondary school graduation diplomas and university entrance requirements.

One of the aims of SEED is to offer the student a wide variety of studies in which he can participate. Therefore, if a number of SEED students should develop an interest which is not currently taught, they would attempt to contact someone in the community eager to teach this particular "interest" course. The students, along with their advisor and the "teacher," would design a course curriculum around the specific interest. Sometimes the course would take place in school, or, if appropriate, in the home office or agency of the "teacher."

Since SEED offers the student a chance to participate in planning his own education, a high level of maturity is necessary. The students at SEED learn that since they are given the opportunity to guide their own learning, they must hold themselves responsible for whatever they obtain from the program. A student who, while maintaining that he has an interest in a specific area of knowledge, takes no responsibility for seeking out and obtaining this knowledge, is not highly regarded by the other SEED students. SEED offers the student an alternative in education—an opportunity to pursue whatever field of interest he wishes to learn about—but he must be highly motivated to take on his professed interest and follow it through. He must be willing to hold himself *accountable* for his decisions and take the consequences of his own actions.

Many SEED students live by the concepts of cooperation and sharing. SEED is not a competitive program where students are extrinsically motivated to excel for grades, but a program in which each student is intrinsically motivated to learn for himself and to cooperate with others in attaining his goals. The students at SEED do not feel that they are fighting the existing educational system or isolating themselves from the system, but rather that they are working within the present school system, and their school is providing an alternative model of education.

It is anticipated that if the SEED program is continued in future years, the special interest courses now taught by those outside the school may be organized so that they meet the approval of the Ontario Department of Education as courses for secondary school credit. The program, which started with outside funding, is an example of how "seed money" can be effective. The summer program was subsidized, but the fall program is now a regular part of the city of Toronto public school budget. The cost is $1,200 a student, about the same cost as the regular high school per pupil allocation. Money-wise, there is no saving, but its true value will be, as in all alternative programs, in its power to capture students who would have been lost if they had followed the traditional program.

As much as we may think that the off-campus programs in

Philadelphia, Chicago, Madison, and Toronto are revolutionary in nature, one far more extreme is on the drawing boards in Hartford, Connecticut. Called the "Everywhere" School, it is sponsored by the South Arsenal Neighborhood Development Corporation (SAND), a community group operating in a low-income black and Puerto Rican section of downtown Hartford.

Since 1967, SAND has been negotiating with local anti-poverty agencies, the school system, state and local civic groups to inaugurate a novel community development and educational plan. South Arsenal was an area originally scheduled to be demolished, but its residents decided they did not wish their area to be leveled and rebuilt as a high-income housing project or commercial development. The residents wished to remain where they were and renew their community through better housing and better schools.

After a considerable amount of community planning and negotiation with the various agencies involved, SAND developed a new and somewhat radical approach to their educational facilities. Elementary school space was to be dispersed in small units called multi-instructional areas (MIA). Some of these will be newly built sites; other will be renovated facilities. Each MIA will enroll 150 children and be located throughout the community. The school would be "everywhere." Children would be studying out in the immediate neighborhood, in the city, or even in the suburbs. At any one time during a school day, an MIA will house, roughly, 100 children. The other 50 will be out learning in what SAND calls "environmental extensions" in other parts of the city and the suburbs. Two environmental extensions are already in operation as part of the school's experimental MIA. Twenty-five children each day now go to school on a rotating basis at a private school in the suburbs. Twenty-five more spend a day at the local art museum further downtown. SAND is exploring the development of other environmental extensions in such places as a nearby private college, another suburban private academy, and at an insurance company located in a suburb.

In addition to the children who leave South Arsenal each entire day, children from each MIA will be using some common facilities created for the dispersed school—a gymnasium and swimming pool, an arts center, a theater, and an information resource center or library. Each piece of the school will form a central part of a "neighborhood commons," the basic unit for the community as a whole. The commons will include housing for 20 to 50 families plus school and community services. There is also an area for retail stores.

The planners of SAND will be using the bulk-purchase, off-the-shelf, approach to systems building, both in the housing and the school space, as described in Chapter One. Largely by these methods and by open planning, they are predicting that their space for new schools will come in at no more than $25 per square foot compared to an average of $35 per square foot which is the present cost in the area for conventional construction and conventional school designs. They actually believe their costs will be closer to $20 per square foot, but they are playing it safe.

One of SAND's experimental MIAs is located in a warehouse. This is a good example of the economies of "found" space. The use of a 5,000-square-foot section of the warehouse has been made available to SAND by the University of Connecticut, which leases it and operates a 4-H Club in another section of the building. SAND spent about $20,000 on fixing up its space (or about $4 per square foot), including fire-proofing, carpeting, new lighting, etc., but this low cost was possible because a great deal of the labor and materials were donated by neighborhood people and interested outsiders. SAND hopes to acquire the warehouse as part of the urban renewal package and modernize it into the school's arts center.

They are also planning several joint partnership installations, some with housing developments, others with public and private agencies. For example, they are planning a central kitchen for the school, jointly occupying space with housing devoted to the elderly. The kitchen would supply food services to the MIAs and also provide cafeteria services for the elderly in its building.

There is also a possibility that the Hartford Public Library will decide to build a branch in the South Arsenal development. If the library officials make such a decision, the result will be a joint partnership structure with the school's information resource center, thus creating a facility useful to the entire SAND community. It could also be more economical than two separate buildings.

In addition, SAND plans that all of the Everywhere School's facilities—the gym, theater, information resources center, etc.—will be available to the adult community in the evenings and on weekends. The MIAs will be used for adult education (especially bilingual education). The planners of SAND believe that this will eliminate the need for a community center which would have cost a minimum of $1 million.

SAND and its Everywhere School is an excellent example of attempting to gain multiple economies by employing many of the suggestions made in the section on space. They are doing this by combining building systems, by using "open" space, by finding partners, by establishing a home base school, and, possibly, by becoming involved in several joint occupancies. If the SAND plan materializes as its planners expect it to, the Everywhere School will represent a major change in the way we think about schools and schoolhouses. It will also represent a remarkable breakthrough in schoolhouse economy.

As exciting as some of these off-campus programs are, caution should be exercised before embarking on any of them. For example, there can be legal complications. Planners must check state regulations as to the number of hours a student is "compelled" to stay in school each day. In Massachusetts, the state Board of Education readily agreed to waive the requirement for a 5½-hour day, to be spent within school buildings. Instead, the Board agreed that the time a student spends *outside* the school may be counted toward meeting the requirement. However, in order to ensure that educational standards are maintained, the Board requires that school systems submit to the State Department of Education detailed descriptions of the off-campus programs which they propose to implement.

Another legal issue which particularly concerns school teachers and administrators is that of liability for injuries incurred by students while outside of the school on an open-campus program. This issue cannot be laid to rest definitively by the conclusions reached in one community or another. Each community will have to satisfy itself through local interpretation of pertinent state laws.

There are also human adjustment problems involved in alternative experiences. Students and staff often have difficulty in making the transition from traditional patterns of education.

For example, some students have particular difficulty in taking the responsibility that comes with freedom; not all students can cope with a learning process that imposes on them a heavy obligation for self-direction and self-responsibility. Teachers, too, find it difficult to assume the multiple demands of their role. Teaching, counseling, curriculum development, making outside contacts, are all very demanding tasks.

The success of off-campus schools depends to a great degree on the extent and quality of the planning. In sending students into the community during the school day, it is essential that representatives of the public—parents, school abutters, local merchants, public library staff, and police—participate in the planning process. This is particularly important because experience has shown that there will be a considerable segment of the community that will be skeptical of off-campus programs unless they understand their objectives and are taken into the planning.

The question of cost becomes an important one in planning an off-campus school. Off-campus schools can cost less than open-campus or conventional schools. First, by placing students in spaces other than schools, school buildings do not have to be provided. Secondly, "teachers" in hospitals, factories, agencies of all kinds usually either donate their time or earn less than professional educators. Thirdly, materials, equipment, the technologies of learning are usually provided by the host institution, mainly because they are part of their own operating equipment.

All of this, as attractive as it may sound, can be misleading. Some off-campus schools have been very short-lived because they thought this "giving" atmosphere would last forever. People who donate their time usually lose interest after a while and move on to some other kind of "charity." After the first blush of social consciousness, most agencies and industries want to get paid for their services. Having helped education and students prove their point that the outside world can offer more exciting and meaningful experiences than the schools, or at least help enrich the school experience, they feel that their part of the experiment is completed. If the schools want to continue, the agencies and outside organizations feel that part of the existing school budget should be allotted to them to help pay their maintenance and staff. This attitude usually comes as a shock to public educators since allocating public funds to private organizations, or even to other public agencies, has never been a practice. It takes a whole new way of thinking about how one cuts the education pie. It is this unwillingness to share the education dollar on the part of those who control public funds that can defeat off-campus schools. Many are willing to embrace the concept of the community as school provided they do not have to pay for it.

Perhaps the only way that off-campus programs will work is by state legislation defining how the educational dollar can be spent. If a "school building" is any place a student learns, then a whole variety of agencies can qualify for capital budget allocations. If teachers are defined as all who can facilitate learning, then it should not matter whether they are doctors in hospitals or lathers in factories, so long as they can work with students. Experiences that take place outside of school buildings will be legitimatized and institutionalized only if they receive part of the public monies spent for education.

NEW STRUCTURES

Many of the schools described in this section are born of the specific unmet need of a particular school system, a community, a group of parents, or even a group of youngsters. For most youngsters the accepted type of public school education will be sufficient. For others, it is not. There are youngsters who chafe in the regular educational mold, just as there are teachers who are convinced that there are other and better ways to make learning come alive. Their concept of alternative schools rejects as inadequate such modifications as open-campus or off-campus schools. They seek a totally new kind of school—literally, an alternative method of education.

In almost all instances, these "other ways" schools are reacting to the trend of bigness. Usually, they are small, do-it-yourself, noninstitutional-type learning environments, sometimes housed in existing school buildings but more often housed in anything from storefronts to geodesic domes, churches, or any other space made available to them. Some of these schools are subject to the governance of the school system, while many others operate completely outside of the public school network. The movement started as a number of independent schools run by groups of parents for the purpose of asserting their own distinct and individualistic concepts of education.

John Holt,[3] in discussing why many alternative schools do not want to work within the system, says that the school that flies the flag is, in the long run, *accountable to that flag* and to the power and to the values which it represents. That is the basic contention of all ventures which aspire to a radical alternative "within the system." They claim that by staying on the outside they have been able to create exciting, viable ways of learning, partly because of the people they attract to work in their schools and partly because of the mobility this type of teaching affords. Public school officials are beginning to regard these "other ways" schools not just as competitors, but as possible alternatives that public education can live with and that may help to solve some of the problems stemming from discontent with a system many consider too rigid. In this way, the independent "private" alternative schools have had some impact on public education.

One excellent example of such schools is an experiment being conducted at Berkeley, California. A number of independent alternative schools were already in existence in Berkeley—all hunting for money in order to survive. Since they were not generally averse to joining the "system," Federal funds were granted to bring them into a network of alternative schools that would eventually be supported by local tax funds.

The city of Berkeley has approximately 15,000 students in its public schools, and in 1973 expects to place 5,318—one-third of its population—in a series of such experimental alternative schools. These schools are to cost no more per student than for his counterpart in the regular schools. The ethnic backgrounds of those who will be attending these alternatives are about 40 percent white; 40 percent black; the remainder Chicano, Spanish surname, Chinese, Japanese—very much like the full district.

By 1973, Berkeley will be offering 22 specific alternatives to the regular Berkeley school program. And all of these are required to maintain, with a 10–15 percent margin, the same

[3]Jonathan Kozol, *Free Schools*, p. 15, Houghton Mifflin Co., Boston, 1972.

ethnic mix as the full school district. It is conceivable, therefore, that an option might fail before it began if it could not draw sufficient interest from blacks, whites, Chicanos, and Orientals. Thus, while the Casa de La Raza and the Black House each have an obvious focus, each must attract an ethnic mix of both students and teachers.

Berkeley's experimental alternative schools program has three goals: the elimination of *institutional* racism; the right of parents (and children) in conjunction with school authorities to have alternatives as to school, teaching style, and program; and the delivering of basic skills to those students previously falling below the norm. These concepts were developed when Herbert Kohl was invited to come to Berkeley. He listened to youths and what they thought their real needs were. He did not listen to adults who thought they knew what they were. From these interviews and meetings, he created a concept of school that was in a way a rebuilding station for youths no longer believing in the integrity of the institutions created by adults whose words did not match their deeds.

The goals of the Berkeley alternative schools, as developed by the students for students are: to be able to state their own vocational, social, and personal needs; to know how to get the experiences needed to meet those needs; to know how to cope with social and intellectual frustrations; to know how to teach themselves or how to take advantage of the knowledge and experience provided by the community they choose to live in; to master reading, writing, and math and some basic social skills; to be more aware of and be able to deal with racial and sexual attitudes.

It would be impossible to describe all of the 22 Berkeley alternative schools, but some are particularly unique. For example, the Other Ways Basic Skills and Survival School is one in which the students plan their own programs and initiate their own classes. Small classes with personalized learning are conducted in such subjects as wilderness, urban, psychological, financial, social, and political survival. The community is used as an extended classroom, utilizing shops, craft centers, local colleges, apprenticeships in business and industry, with students as teachers of each other to help in mastery of reading and other skills. The Other Ways site has been developed as a learning facility and social center. Students are exposed to a large variety of adults not usually encountered in their home or school setting.

The development of the 1972–1973 program was to be under the leadership of Robert Wilson. At a recent conference on alternative education, he described its direction:˙

> Other Ways is an educational project designed to give its students the skills they will need to function in an increasingly complex world. The curriculum, then, will necessarily stress scientific, social, and literary skills. The courses will provide students with those skills they will need if they wish to go on to college, and if not, with enough information to get a job and to develop in whatever areas they may later choose. It is assumed that if they read well and have a background of scientific knowledge, they can instruct themselves in innumerable areas.
>
> There will be 100 students this year and 12 teachers so that classes can be small and flexible enough to relate to students' individual needs. Students will also be involved in the school on a teaching level. Under the guidance of individual teachers, students will instruct people younger than themselves in basic reading and writing skills. As a result, our students will be equipped with the ability to communicate the knowledge they are learning and will be helping younger people to develop basic educational skills.

Another kind of high school alternative is the Performing Arts minischool, a school within a school. It grew out of the concern by educators in the Performing Arts department of the Berkeley High School that the main campus was too big and impersonal and that some kids are lost without more one-to-one contact. A number of instructors in the drama and music unit worked on the original plans. It started with an enrollment of some 200 students and teachers who themselves wanted something different and opted for this alternative.

Its first home was the corridor and upstairs area of the Community Theater, but it has now moved into its own quarters. A teacher tenet is respect for youngsters and recognition of the talents, skills, and insights they have to give each other. Students with experience teach classes. Parents share their knowledge with the students. There were so many demands for space in the school that, rather than expand the population and lose the intimacy with which it was originally concerned, a second school was opened. Again, the alternative was created by prodding from students, parents, and teachers.

Other alternatives at Berkeley include a school for 80 students called Odyssey, in which each student builds his own educational program. It may vary from a free-form day to a very tailored academic experience. One of the main concepts of Odyssey is community involvement. Each student is required to participate in a community service project once a week. These include work with hospitals, child care centers, tutoring, ecology. In some ways, this is similar to the Other Ways School, except for the fact that the focus of this school is on community service.

One of the most interesting of the Berkeley experiments in alternative schools is the Jefferson Three-Part Model for approximately 665 students. A single school, kindergarten through third grade, decided to create three schools within itself, each one a distinct alternative to the others. When parents register their children in the school, they have three options. One is the Multi-Cultural Bilingual model in which the main effort is to create an environment where culturally diverse parents, staff, and children can learn to understand, appreciate, and respond to mutual needs. Another is the Individualized and Personalized Learning model (IPL), which provides a psychological environment and self-instructional materials. Based on the premise that students learn differently, this model provides varied materials and kinds of support. The third option is the traditional model, a teacher-directed program with emphasis on skills and subject matter. The primary source of learning is the teacher's knowledge of her subject and her ability to present it in creative and challenging ways.

The Jefferson program is based on the belief that teachers, parents, and students will be more committed and involved when they have a choice as to the mode of education most nearly accommodating their own life styles and expectations.

The first step in selecting the alternative was to call in parents and describe the three choices. This took place in the spring of 1970. Many parents felt divided between the multi-cultural and the individualized options. Those who wanted the traditional option seemed secure in their choice. Jefferson staff

spent the summer of 1971 refining the three choices as they reflected the reactions of the parents. When school opened in the
fall, there was a matching of students to approaches. More parents opted for the individualized school model than did teachers.
The solution was for some teachers to move transitionally from
the traditional to the individualized. When school closed in June
1972 for the summer break, parents once again registered their
preference for the kind of instructional program they wanted for
their child. Principal Mary Giorgi reported that when school re-
opened in the fall, all but a handful of parents got their choice.

This is a particularly interesting model since it does not
force parents, if they want an alternative, to find it in some more
distant school. Many schools are beginning to look seriously
at the possibilities of creating alternatives within a neighborhood school. It is convenient; it does not force staff to leave a
school or even a community because he or she wants to teach in
a different environment; and it builds on the neighborhood and
the community spirit rather than dissipating it.

In the fall of 1972, five new alternative schools opened
in Berkeley. The John Muir Child Development Center for 400
students from kindergarten through third grade is year-round
for those parents who want it. Classrooms are self-contained,
with the teacher assuming the major responsibility for the instructional program for each child in the class. The alternative
is based on the "open classroom" concept.

Volunteer participation from parents, adults from the
community, older students, and student teachers is actively
solicited, since the emphasis is on utilizing adults as assistants
and tapping the resources of their individual competencies.

The Franklin Multicultural School accommodates about
300 students in grades 4 through 6. This alternative comprises
three subschools and a supplementary program specially designed for those students characterized as high potential but
who have been getting low grades. University of California
tutors will be used as support for the high potential but low-
achieving pupils. The tutors will work with the children in the
alternative on a regular one-to-one basis. The three subschools
will offer La Raza classes, Asian studies classes, and multicultural studies.

The purpose of the La Raza classes is to develop proficiency in conversational and written Spanish and English and to improve school attendance by Spanish-speaking students. The Asian classes are designed to improve self-image through awareness of past history and contributions and appreciation of the uniqueness of the different minority groups, of the multicultural classes to increase understanding of the nature and worth of all cultures, to find new ways of working together toward common goals, and to help each child learn by himself.

Another alternative is "On Target," a school for 140 students in grades 10 through 12. This school provides instruction in science, math, business, industrial arts, and prenursing subjects. These experiences will serve as preparation for careers in business and industry related to science and technology. Features of this alternative include use of a Career Center, visits with representatives from many companies, field trips to institutions with many of the occupations relevant to this school, and extended time for class work and some "on-the-job" experience.

The alternative experimental schools at Berkeley have many common elements. First, each is developed around a theme or focus, one created by students, teachers, and parents; enrollment is strictly voluntary for both students and teachers; each utilizes as many available resources as possible from anywhere around; each is flexible and usually takes time in the summer to readjust its curriculum and reorder its organization; each has a strong emphasis on learning, specifically, basic skills; and, most important, each has an identity. It is this last point that separates it from an open- or off-campus school. Most of the Berkeley schools are on campus. Although they have a certain degree of openness and flexibility, each is primarily a self-contained school with its own goals and objectives. It does not require that four majors be taken within the school in order to leave the school the rest of the time. It builds the "majors" into a whole educational experience. There is no division between what is required and what is optional. It is all in one. It is a true alternative, not a modification or an accommodation as one might describe an open- or off-campus school. It has other advantages. Since in Berkeley the alternative schools enroll one-third of the school population, they are a recognized and important part of the system. They cannot be easily ignored or "snuffed out." Secondly, they are fully paid for, with the exception of some Federal and foundation funds (start-up money), by the public school systems, and, as we said before, carry the same per pupil cost as for all students. This immediately gives them legitimacy and some degree of security. Both of these factors are extremely important to the survival of alternative schools.

An approach somewhat similar to that of incorporating the alternatives into the public school system is being taken by the Ann Arbor, Michigan, school system. The Pioneer High School was created as an alternative school in 1967, and has now given birth to Pioneer II. The difference between the two is that the new school is far "freer" in concept than its parent school, although it, too, is funded by and responsible to the Board of Education. Time had proven that freedom was not analogous with change and, therefore, the school system was ready for a more independent approach.

"We're discussing what our main goals are for the school," explained a girl in the Pioneer II project, "and exactly what classes will be offered." "I guess you would call what we're doing a kind of orientation week," another student interjected. In this particular group, the "rap session" had set forth several main goals for Pioneer II students, such as "finishing high school, creating a real learning environment, really getting to know people. . . ." One student leaned forward as if to emphasize his feelings to the group: "At Pioneer II we're trying to learn more and accomplish more work. The important thing to me is that we can work at our own speed instead of the level of an entire class." "There is no limit to the number of classes we can take," he said. It was also explained that as long as enough students were interested in a subject, a class would be formed. "For once I have a real interest in school, in learning, and in the people around me," said another enthusiastic Pioneer II student.

Pioneer II, according to school officials, will be geared to provide a structure in which students can learn from each other, where the environment in which the students are encouraged to learn is greatly expanded, and where a learning-centered education will allow the individual to work according to his own abilities. Students attending the school will receive full academic credit, and the curriculum generally will be determined by the student body through these various discussion groups.

Pioneer II started in October of 1971 with 100 applicants chosen on a voluntary and random basis from the parent school, the Pioneer High School. It is staffed partly by teachers from the parent school and in part by community residence people. Once again, the cost is no more than the regular per capita cost for all students. This is another example of a total alternative "another way" school within the public school system.

Perhaps the "alternative" that has created the largest stir in this country within the past two years is the British Infant School—an experiment in open education. It started in Leicestershire, England, and captured the imagination of British educators and Americans as well. Much has been written by the proponents of open education. Few, however, realize that it is an alternative; most view it as a methodology or another way of teaching. This may be true; it also qualifies as an alternative since it offers a completely new approach to schooling and learning. To add to its advantages, it needs no new kind of space or, for that matter, new kinds of materials. The teachers may very well be the same teachers if they are willing to accept a learning environment that is different from the one they are used to. Because of the fact that it does not dislocate either schools or teachers, it has the potential of being one of the most powerful alternative education modes that exist today.

"British Infant School," "Leicestershire Method," "Integrated Day," "The Open Classroom"—these names are heard increasingly among theorists and practitioners of early childhood education. The terms all refer to a new approach to teaching that discards the familiar elementary classroom setup and the traditional, stylized roles of teacher and pupil, for a far freer, highly individualized, child-centered learning experience that might possibly hold the key to a radical reformation of primary education, if not for all education. It has spread widely throughout the British school system since World War II, and in the past 5 years has been introduced in a variety of American schools, ranging from rural Vermont and North Dakota to inner city classrooms in Philadelphia, Washington, Boston, and New York.

The informal type schools are distinguished by the degree to which they have become "de-institutionalized." Children move relatively freely about such schools, in classrooms and corridors alive with color and things of all sorts. Old chairs, rugs and carpets, ovens and animals, all give a warm, human, nonschool (in the traditional sense) atmosphere to the building.

Teachers here seem to accept a fuller, broader interpretation of the idea of "individualization." Children are seen as unique or different in terms of their total growth patterns as human beings, rather than in a narrow, skill-development sense. Teachers in informal schools place far more value on detailed observation of a child's work over a long period of time as a primary evaluative source than they do on more formal testing procedures.

Teachers and headmasters or principals play a far more active role in making day-to-day curricular decisions of all kinds than do their counterparts in more formal schools. If, in fact, teachers are more attuned to children and their needs and interests in such schools, citywide or districtwide "programs" or curricula make little sense and the *individual teacher* becomes a dynamic curriculum agent.

Teachers in such schools seem to accept fully the notion that children's learning proceeds from the concrete to the abstract, and that *premature* abstraction is one of the great weaknesses of the traditional school. Thus the emphasis on concrete materials, and encounters with real people and places whenever possible.[4]

Although many schools have instituted open education in some classes, mostly where teachers, parents, and children were accepting of the concept, few schools devoted themselves *totally* to open education. One that did, however, is the St. Paul Open School, a research, demonstration project of the St. Paul Public School System, serving children from the primary grades through high school. It is based on the theory that children learn in different ways, at different times, from things around them that interest them and from each other—and that children learn fastest when pursuing their own interests.

The innate urge to explore, so evident in an infant, is self-perpetuating if the child receives pleasure and satisfaction from such activities. In conventional schools, exploratory activity is restricted to certain times and places, and is permitted only in limited ways for all children at a specified pace. When this happens, the proponents of open education feel that curiosity is reduced, creativity and spontaneity are not fostered, and natural drives to learn in school are reduced.

⁴Vincent R. Rogers, "Open Schools," *Educational Leadership*, February 1972, pp. 401–402.

In the St. Paul school, the timetable for learning comes from the children's readiness, rather than an artificially established age. The school's task is to provide an environment in which the skills for effective living are important and needed, a personally supportive, nurturing, and safe climate, and exciting, stimulating activities for the mind to explore and speculate upon.

The school began with certain assumptions as to what were to be included in its design. For example, there were to be major resource areas, each of the resource areas or "theaters of learning" providing a kaleidoscopic variety of learning experiences. One example is the shop area, where students are at work on projects of their choosing, in wood, metal, plastics, electronics, printing, duplicating, motors, welding, crafts, etc. Students may be building bookcases, polishing stones, fiberglassing a canoe, or designing a school intercom. Each of the resource areas contains dozens of activity areas and the possibility of thousands of projects to be pursued independently or with others.

The music/drama/dance areas provide oral and instrumental music for individuals, ensembles, large groups; and in such areas as opera, symphony, popular, jazz, etc. Listening areas for music and dramatic readings are available. Tape recorders, video tape recorders, stereo, Moog synthesizers, and musical instruments are essential. Classic, modern, and folk dance develop free or creative movement that helps students gain coordination, grace, beauty, posture, and rhythm—not to mention vocabulary, expressiveness, and artistic appreciation. Drama, formal or extemporaneous, enhances self-discipline, creativity, and understanding of self and others.

Most areas incorporate skills-teaching. Unlike the conventional method of teaching skills as "tasks," often in a vacuum, the St. Paul learning areas incorporate skills in their content. For example, the student who is building a train in the shop reads directions, plans, designs, orders materials, measures and calculates, engineers and researches for reduced friction and wind resistence, decorates the body, writes for race entry blanks, and evaluates the project. Building a train involves math, reading, physics, art, and working with others.

Teachers seek to integrate learnings from many areas into projects and activities. Such efforts build vocabulary and aid concept-development so that the student continually expands learning and relates material in other areas. Learning fractions is not an isolated math activity into which the math teacher tries to breathe life, but useful knowledge in such areas as shop, home economics, and photography. Accelerated learning in many areas related to building a chug is the result of integrated learning practices.

Each resource area contains a small library of books, magazines, films, etc. The student is encouraged to look things up, explore, delve into a topic, follow how-to-do-it materials and conduct research. The major resource areas provide an incredible array of learning activities: repairing a clock, upholstering, silk screening, mastering trigonometry, organizing a political party, interning on a job or in a community agency, planning and preparing a television script, electronic cooking, writing school publications, researching the development of air transportation, conducting traffic surveys, experimenting with the effects of light on plants, discussing Shakespeare—in short, the kind of activities most schools want but somehow are not sufficiently geared for as a regular diet.

Not only are "interesting" learning areas available to students, but students have a role in selecting their own courses and activities. They even devise their own daily schedule. The student becomes an active agent in designing his own education. The school's design exploits the student's tendency to concentrate on tasks of interest, tasks he assigns himself. There are no required courses. Instead, the student's natural curiosity and drive for mastery lead to a considerable range of exploratory activities and self-initiated learning pursuits. Compared to the usual school where young students are walked in lines, seated within the grasp of the teacher, and controlled in all dimensions, even very young students in the Open School rapidly learn to find their way about a complex building, go to lunch, devise and follow a schedule independently. This is surprising to visitors accustomed to more structured school procedures.

The teacher's role also changes from information giver and prodder to that of a facilitator arranging learning experiences, clearing obstacles and barriers to learning, suggesting possibilities, helping students with personal goals and purposes, and being a friendly guide. Each teacher in a sense becomes a director and planner of a learning empire in which the student's interests are stimulated and catered to.

Many kinds of people in the Open School enterprise teach and help young people grow and develop. Parents assist as volunteers. People with expertise teach or prepare materials under the direction of certified personnel. Paid aides provide a variety of services from clerical to teaching. The teacher's specific knowledge and skill with students becomes extended many-fold through the use of resource people. One of the best categories of resource people are the students themselves. One teaches leatherwork, another has an extensive stamp collection, another is skilled and patient at helping young children read, another organizes a paper airplane club along the lines of the *Scientific American* contest, another knows German, and so forth. When students teach, they not only learn their subject more thoroughly themselves, but they also learn presentation and the organization of information, some psychology of learning, how to be more articulate, and personal effectiveness. They learn these things in one of the most efficient ways—by doing, by experience.

Since learning occurs in many places, trips are planned to take advantage of courses, activities, people, and events in the community. Students work as interns, volunteers, and employees. Field trips make the community a part of a larger classroom. For too long schools have built high walls and have turned inward, away from life. The Open School is involved in the world and all of life.

All students do not develop skills or interests at the same age or rate. Organizing students into single-age groups or fixed groupings decreases opportunities for satisfying the various personal growth patterns. Many schools are moving toward nongraded approaches. Activities in the Open School are based on interest and what the student can actually do rather than on age restrictions. Students learn much from one another and are in many instances natural teachers. The immediate presence of older students provides leadership models for younger students to study. For the older child, responsibility and leadership opportunities enhance feelings of importance and defuse the teenage antiestablishment subculture.

The student population at the Open School has been carefully planned to reflect the cultural diversity of the city. In a way, it resembles a miniature democratic society. The Open School's problems are examined by all affected and decisions reached through careful study, discussion, and negotiation.

The likelihood of acceptance and commitment to decisions is enhanced when one has helped share their outcome. Staff meetings are open to participation by students and parents. An Advisory Council of staff, parents, students, and citizens-at-large studies problem areas and suggests policy.

The St. Paul Open School originally opened with a budget that was 25 percent higher per student than if he were in the regular public school system. However, as the idea caught on, more people came to volunteer their services, more students began to take on teaching tasks. Others were able to learn more on their own without teachers assigned to them. The whole school started to take on an air of "we can do it ourselves." The results were startling. As more students entered, they could be absorbed without increasing the staff; hours were staggered so that extra space was not needed. The school now runs at the same cost as all of the other traditional schools, but expects that in the very near future it will drop below that cost.

Another type of total open school is the Jefferson County Elementary School in Lakewood, Colorado. At the recommendation of a group of parents who expressed great interest in creating a different kind of school within the district, two "Open-Living Schools" were created and are now operating.

Predicated on a set of concepts similar to the St. Paul School and other schools that have "opened education," the program is highly individual and very personal. It seeks to meet the affective needs as well as the cognitive needs of the child. These affective needs are identified as: self-esteem, self-confidence, self-initiative, self-reliance, self-discipline, self-knowledge, self-evaluation, and self-respect.

The learning environment has, as the name implies, an open-living atmosphere of rich and varied experiences in which the teacher is the challenger, guide, and observer of the learning process. The atmosphere and program are marked by their humanistic thrust. The schools are free to create a curriculum not bound by the content, emphasis, or measuring devices which characterize the conventional curriculum. This franchise is under review because of the necessity of applying accountability principles under state law.

The schools have an enrollment policy which permits the registration of any student from any home in the district who, with parent approval and support, chooses this alternative to programs offered in other district schools.

The schools are staffed with professional educators and volunteer help who have applied or volunteered for available positions after having shown themselves to be informed and enthusiastic about this approach to serving the growth needs of youngsters.

The schools are operated at two different sites—one in a rural mountain area and one in a more populous suburban area. The total enrollment of the two schools is 275.

The schools operate on the same per pupil cost ($585) as any other elementary school. The cost of bus transportation is a responsibility of the parents. There are 12 teachers plus the co-leaders who spend half their time as teachers. There are also lay assistants. The whole staff, including volunteers, is responsible to children—therefore, when visiting the school, it is difficult to distinguish the "teachers" from all the others working with the children.

Open education is not really new. Most good teachers have treated each child, as much as possible, as an individual and have tried to create educational experiences that interested him. Perhaps it is only now, however, that we are so conscious of the need to extend those experiences which tend to be more humanizing. Our dedication to educating the masses has always carried with it the tendency to overlook the individual. But today Americans are becoming uncomfortable about the quality of life in America. The proliferation of environmental hazards, the increasing mechanization of our lives and the resulting loss of meaningful human contact, have made us more receptive to educational ideas that emphasize a simpler, more concerned type of education.

However, noble as these goals may be, we have not yet proven that open education is the means of achieving them. We have little, if any, research that tells us that open education is going to recapture the human touch. There is much enthusiasm and some promise in this approach but as with all panaceas, and especially with the American attitude of "if it's a change, it must be good," one must be very careful about their wholesale adoption. I bring this up particularly with reference to the British Infant School or the Open School. Somehow, the trip across the ocean brought with it a certain amount of glamor. The disciples who imported the method are far more fervent and dogmatic than its creators. The open school as an alternative has many advantages, but only for some children, primarily those who are creative, imaginative, and individualistic. For those who need structure and discipline, it is a dismal failure. To say that this is the only way to educate would be doing a great disservice to large numbers of children and to the whole concept of the open school as an alternative. It is, indeed, an alternative, but only one in a series of options. Not to recognize this would be unfortunate.

A completely different kind of alternative education is the commune-type school. Communes, as such, are being created across the world. They are cropping up in the rural and desert regions of the southwest and for many are a way-station in and out of the hippie counterculture. Like gypsy colonies, they may produce a fascinating culture, or they may come to nothing. However, there are certain commune-concept schools that, while not new, are just recently receiving some attention.

Communes like the Amish and Mennonite religious groups are raising new problems for educational authorities engaged in the pros and cons of forced school attendance. There are ideological communes that have been devoted to political ideologies. There are those that are devoted to cultivating the land, such as the agricultural communes in Israel. But these are not the commune-type schools we are talking about. Even though many of the religious, ideological, and agricultural communes are heavily oriented to education, it is not their prime mission. There are, however, commune-concept environments that are springing up throughout the country wherein education is the prime objective. They aim to create a promising blend of cognitive, affective, and skill development, combining the best in formal teaching, apprenticeship, and free exploration of a complex environment. Many of these take the form of residential or semi-residential schools.

A type of semiresidential school based on the commune concept is being designed by the System Development Corporation in Santa Monica, California.[5] It is not yet in operation. Its planners call it an experimental school for the urban poor.

[5] *An Experimental School for the Urban Poor: Preliminary Design Formulation.* Santa Monica, California: System Development Corporation, January 1970.

Its designers are for the most part noneducators. In brief, the design of the school is to serve severely disadvantaged people; to include those traditionally enrolled in grades K–12 on one campus; to maximize community inputs into the learning enterprise; to utilize an ombudsman for grievance purposes; to remain open 15 hours per day; to give each student an individual room that is his for study or otherwise; to secure new types of professionals with freshly defined responsibilities; and to employ and pay every enrolled student as a member of the school work force.

Efforts will be made to combine cognitive development with work skills. Since the student age range is about 5 through 18, the work assignments for which youngsters will be paid will be differentiated. The school is expected to coexist with conventional public schools and, if successful, to be imitated on a larger scale.

Probably the most exciting feature of the proposal is its work-ethic. Molding an entire school around *internal* jobs is difficult. It is a bold notion and deserves a trial. Every student will have an opportunity to hold a job alongside his academic program. Some portion of each day, the student will work. The jobs will be varied in type, skills required, hours worked, and wages received; within broad limits, all jobs will be open to all students, with placement a function of proficiency, maturity, past performance, and job availability. In brief, there will be a work culture as nearly optimal as possible and still reflecting the patterns that exist in the larger society. The work will be significant, the money will be real, the opportunities will be visible, and the prerequisites will be realistically related to academic progress.

Since the payment feature is unusual and might be misunderstood, three points of clarification need to be made. First, students will not be paid for "going to school"—i.e., for the business of progressing academically. They will be paid for work at school; the prime prerequisite for getting one of the jobs will be that they are going to school. In practice, this distinction must not be confused; the two are separate, though importantly related, activities.

Second, this will not be "make-work" for which the students get paid. It will be, in fact, the business of operating the school. School is a micro-community; it mirrors most of the functions of society at large—transportation, food, building and maintenance, supply, clerical work, administration, training, equipment repair, purchasing, not to mention child care and teaching. These are jobs that must be done if the school is to operate; they are normally assigned to hired (classified) employees; in this case the employees will be students.

Third, the emphasis is on the principle of employment, not on its value as vocational training. If, for example, an academically talented student wants to work in equipment repair, he can; it is the fact of his employment that is of primary importance. If at the same time he will be learning a skill that will benefit him in later life, all the better; but he need not be making a career decision when he applies for "work at school."[6]

In a way, the school is based on the commune concept. You "work the land" in order to survive. You share services, benefits, and responsibilities. Although the school will not be as self sufficient as the Amish, or Mennonite, or Israeli, it is a move in that direction. To the best of my knowledge, this has not been done before—as a school—in this country. It certainly has promise and an attractive philosophy. But, of course, it remains untested.

Another type of modified commune concept is being planned by the Columbus, Ohio, Board of Education. It is presently referred to as the "Family Development Center," and its objective is to create a powerful educational environment where adults and children can learn together; where public welfare, health, and educational resources can be concentrated efficiently; where employment skills, household skills, and artistic temperaments can be developed simultaneously; and where instruction can be supplied by families in which each member has teaching responsibilities.

The learners in the center would be families. Selected families of all races would be invited to move into housing facilities selected for that purpose. In Columbus a soon-to-be-abandoned military base would be the site. The families chosen should be representative of the broader society, but among them would be some with unemployed parents with low-educational levels and children who have learning problems.

Families where the parents were unemployed would be

_____
[6] *Ibid,* pp. 7–8.

among those chosen for learning. Extensive efforts would be addressed to bringing the adults to the point of employability. During the early period of the family's enrollment at the center, family support would be on the basis of welfare payments. As soon as employable skills could be developed for adults, part-time employment would be sought. From this point forward, the adults would work and learn simultaneously. Each family's curriculum would be individually planned and fitted into the program of studies created for the center.

The minimal length of learner family tenure would be one year. Some families might need to stay longer than that period of time. Families could enter and leave at various points in the year. The staff of the center would help in locating housing, appropriate educational facilities, and employment for families when they leave.

Faculty members would live there too. The faculty of the center would be made up of professionals from a number of fields. The entire environment would be a learning laboratory. The members of the faculty families would be teachers and learners simultaneously. The curriculum would be rich, informally organized, and designed to meet the specific needs of the students of all ages. The faculty would have at its fingertips the city, its libraries, its museums and art centers, its theaters, its universities, its employment potentials. Instruction would be individualized, with all types of teaching approaches being used.

For some purposes—art, music, physical education, and recreation—adults and children might learn together. For other purposes, classes and seminars would be formed. Classes would not be restricted even then to conventional age ranges. The classrooms could be anywhere—on the site or in downtown areas or in the suburbs—wherever learning purposes could best be served.

Faculty families could be chosen on the basis of diversity of talents as well as willingness to participate in such an exciting venture. Faculty families should have teaching potential in the basic learning skills, the arts, music, homemaking, recreation, physical education, health education, social skills. Formal teaching certification requirements in many cases would need to be abandoned for at least some family members.

The staff of the center would include social workers, medical and psychiatric specialists, and psychologists and their families. The center should also have a well-trained research staff. Social workers could assist with many of the welfare and employment problems; they could also help with family selection and relocation. The physical and medical health specialists would make their contributions in many important ways.

The program of Columbus, Ohio, is probably closest to the religious commune of the Amish and the nationalistic commune of the Israeli. In both, the total family is involved. However, here the purposes are different since the Family Development Center has as its prime objective secular training for normal day-to-day needs.

Another commune concept, started back in 1961 as a counterculture school in Montara, California, is known as the Pacific High School. It is not supported by public funds and draws young people who have not made it in their own culture. They are inclined to be disoriented and confused. Ivan Illich called for de-schooling, for de-conditioning the learner, but at no time does he deny the need for some type of education. In the first chapter we spoke about Illich's proposal of apprenticeship as a way of learning. In Pacific High School, an alternative program has been established very much along these lines. Their emphasis is on the 14- to 18-year olds, and their approach is really quite simple. Young people apply and say what they would like to do. The staff will refer them to any people who can help, or will try to find such people for them. They will also expect the apprentice to look about in his community and use any of his own resources to find such assistance. It is up to the apprentice to get in touch with anyone who is suggested if he thinks that person can help.

After working together for awhile, if either feels that the relationship is not working out, or feels used by the other, or just loses interest or patience with working together, the relationship is ended as honestly, quickly, and easily as possible. If there is confusion, maybe it can be worked out, but it is better to end the relationship than to allow ill will to build up and fester over a period of time. Apprentices should also move on if they find they are not as interested as they thought they were, or if they feel they have learned all they can from a particular teacher.

Primarily, the philosophy is that trading some work for learning from and with someone is a good way of learning *Anything.* A distinction that must be made is that in some fields the apprentice may engage in work on his own once the apprenticeship is over; but in other fields he may still have to go through qualifying or licensing procedures before he is permitted to practice. The point of the apprenticeship in these fields, like medicine or law, is that the apprentice will have acquired a more realistic basis on which to decide whether he wants to go on.

From those enrolled in the high school program, a quarterly report is expected from both student and teacher. For a full year's credit the apprentice would have to be involved in one or more apprenticeships for at least 180 days (9 months). To graduate, he would have to complete the time required by the state either in some other program or in that program.

The school itself had interesting beginnings. It started in the summer, when housing was no problem and people could sleep outdoors. When the rains came, so did the problems. What little money it had it spent on an architect. Plain housing for forty people was a basic necessity. The outcome of the consultation was to build domes. Today, almost 12 years after its inception, 12 domes are in existence. As stated by one of its founders:

The added openness and willingness to experiment with the domes is analogous to what is happening in the rest of the community. We have learned that we get a richer, more educational community when we allow for the widest possible student influence. We have moved from a place where our community meeting was often a rubber stamp and the place was governed by the staff to a situation where the meeting is the actual governing body of the community. The students have as much power as they choose to exercise. We have learned to let more of the education just happen. Before, it seemed as if we were doomed either to being hampered and restricted by a schedule, or to being snowed under by chaos. We have loosened up the schedule and we have found that more productive activity takes place. As we have abandoned linearity in housing we are rapidly abandoning it in education. Rather than rely on regularly scheduled classes, we are endeavoring to create a rich mosaic of educational activities. Formal classes, planned happenings, spontaneous celebrations and disasters, a couple of people working together on what interests them, . . .are the main ingredients of the success of this program.

Evaluation of this counterculture school is difficult, probably mostly because no plan for evaluation was ever envisioned. In speaking to some of the leaders, you learn that many of the youngsters are extremely mobile; they come and go. Of those who have graduated, some have gotten involved in everything from serious academic scholarship to heroin. One wonders how different the results of this kind of education are from almost any other.

Those who direct the counterculture school say:

> *Although our graduates have access to higher education and jobs, it is not our purpose to prepare them for entry into the dominant culture. We are an institution born of, and linked to, the counter culture. Our ideals for everyone in the community are frankly utopian and we are proud of it. Given the state of civilization at this time, the alternative is unthinkable.*

It is difficult to comment on the dollar costs of commune-type schools. Their concept is very different, and it tends to be all-engulfing physically and spiritually. Often it includes payment to parents and faculty families, together with the expense of residential accommodations—a sort of total educational environment. Perhaps the only cost one can consider is whether or not these young people would have been lost to themselves and to society if they had not found a haven in a commune. This, of course, is always debatable, and statistics are almost impossible to collect. I think one just has to be satisfied with the thought that at least for some, the communal experience has had its rewards.

Until this point we have spoken about alternative learning experiences, whether within or outside the public school structure, that are designed for all students, both the academically and the vocationally oriented. However, there is a whole group of alternative schools being formed, some small, some large, whose sole purpose is to provide an education for the youngster who is a disciplinary problem. Call him potential dropout, disruptive student, or just plain misfit. For him, an alternative is not really an expanding experience, such as the commune, the open school, or the counterculture environment. It is neither an off-campus nor open-campus school, since it makes no pretence of melding its operations with the ongoing curriculum or even building a new curriculum within the environment. It is a totally new structure. It adopts a radical approach. It does not modify or adapt; it starts anew.

The most recent alternative program of this type is in the metropolitan Denver area for undermotivated potential high school dropouts. It is the Cherry Creek High School "I" Project. There are two locations. One is a cottage-type school 4½ miles from the Cherry Creek High School campus which accommodates 50 eleventh and twelfth graders. Another is a campus for ninth and tenth graders. Thirty students are in this program. Each school is a self-contained unit, and in many ways does not resemble a school. One is more apt to find students sitting on the floor studying than in the chairs provided. Both at the cottage and in the campus program a soft drink machine, rock music, and close teacher–student relationships are the scene. A typical day is not typical. It is open to change or flexibility of scheduling, to more kids taking part in an hour's discussion about society' problems or the novel they are reading than a regular course of study in social studies or the English novel.

Yet the mastery of skills plays an important part in their education. It is felt by many who direct schools for potential or realized dropouts that what they need are entry skills into society; that they do not reject their culture as do those in the communes or the counterculture environments, but that they simply do not have the skills to make them acceptable and able to function in the prevailing culture. Therefore, the "I" Project programs are made of laboratory-type courses in basic skills centered around a diagnosis, prescription, assessment framework. Pretests and post-tests are used to evaluate the student's proficiencies at the end of each 9-week period. The idea is to accept the student where he is functioning, help him to relate or realize his weaknesses and do something about them. At the same time, mini-courses, that is, short-term 6- or 9-week classes based on student interest, are devised to motivate students to build on their strengths and remediate their weaknesses. Skills and interests are intertwined.

The students in the program, upon referral, were termed undermotivated students. Yet to see a group of them tackle the problem of setting up their own company to sell art objects they themselves had made would surprise any educator or businessman who had viewed their attitudes prior to entrance into the program. The kids are typical long-haired teenagers seeking answers to life. "Here they learn to feel good about themselves, to take responsibility for some of their own education, to expect to succeed rather than to fail. They learn to make decisions and prepare to take jobs to live in today's world. We try to create an environment responsive to their individual needs," states Carlos Cuaron, Team Leader.

The cottage program has a team of three teachers and two interns from the University of Denver. The eleventh and twelfth grade students at the cottage spend the morning in academic pursuits and the afternoon in jobs or related work activities. Students are given credit for consistant work and retention of jobs.

Because of the young age of the students in the 9th- and 10th-grade campus program, jobs are not as easy to find. Students are integrated into other classes on the campus when they show desire or are capable of handling them. Prevocational concepts are introduced such as how to get a job; how to keep the job; and learning about the world of work. The focus here is on the student. They learn about themselves, learn how to understand and relate to others, and learn to understand how they affect other people.

Lyle Johnson, Director of the program, feels that this is a successful approach to take with high school students who are about to drop out of school. "Previously," Johnson pointed out, "everything was predetermined for us as to what we should learn. But students today are not goal oriented; they're role oriented. They are less concerned with 'making it' in the business world than in selecting a life style that is meaningful. The trend is for the teacher to become a facilitator of learning, to become a counselor teaching how to find out about things rather than just giving out information. He will arrange the environment to meet these needs. It's a return to the Socratic method, learning through a process of dialogue rather than just telling."

Once again, as we find with almost all alternative programs, they either cost the same or less than the regular per pupil cost to a school system. Project "I" falls into the category of costing less. Although there are new personnel employed, they are not all professional teachers; thus the lower cost. People from the community and industry help out in the world of work activities. Students take on more responsibilities. And yet, the final measure is to look at what it is accomplishing for young-sters who would normally be considered social rejects.

In the Molalla, Oregon, school district, most of the children are economically deprived. In fact, they have the highest concen-tration of welfare families in the state of Oregon, most of them having recently come from rural areas and not having adjusted to urban living. Of the 3,000 students in the system, about 600 cannot fit into the traditional model of school. The school sys-tem is currently developing a series of alternatives to try to keep these youngsters in school. A unit may have as few as 30 young-sters whose only "obligation" is to take one course—modern problems—a requirement set by state law. Other than that, each youngster, with the guidance of his sponsoring teacher, develops his own schedule. Students may spend the day either within the school or the community. But during the course of the school year, each student must have the following experi-ences: work, service, teaching, and exchange.

Another alternative is provided for youngsters who gen-erally can get by with the regular high school program but have problems in a particular subject. Instead of flunking him, the program permits him to receive credit for this subject by his tutoring students at the grade schools in the same subject. This allows him to review what he has missed, to learn at the same time that he is teaching. In this way he can "catch up." One hundred sixty students participate in this program.

Another alternative is to release 24 boys from each regular school day for one-half day to actually construct an $18,000 home. A teacher will be their sponsor, and the youngsters will receive credit in math, English, and construction. Many other youngsters will be involved indirectly in such aspects as book-keeping, design, landscaping, etc.

I have described only a few of the alternatives offered the dropout in Molalla. The key to the success of this program is its variety. New "alternatives" are springing up all the time as some close down. They make it very hard for a student to drop out. If he drops out of one alternative, there is another waiting for him to drop into. And all of this costs no more than the educa-tion of the other students. It is only a matter of utilizing space, resources, and people in another way.

An interesting alternative junior high school for 125 students has been established by the Office of Delinquency Prevention of Louisville in cooperation with the public schools. It is being supported by the Kentucky Crime Commission, the Kentucky Department of Economic Security, and the Kentucky Department of Child Welfare. The purpose of the school is to provide an alternative to institutionalization of those youths under 16 years of age who are required by law to go to school, but are beyond the control of the school. These would include: institutional returnees, students normally taken to court on charges of being "beyond control of school," habitual truants for whom all normal procedures have proven ineffective, referrals from court of students charged with other than school-related delinquencies. Additional purposes are to provide individualized or small-group instruction for those youths, in academic areas, geared to their individual achievement levels (emphasis on reading and math), to provide individual and group counseling for those serious behavioral problem youngsters, to provide a warm climate of acceptance and understanding for those youths who have traditionally been rejected by school and society, to provide, wherever feasible, an orientation to the world of work.

Three "schools" have been established away from regular school buildings, with each staffed for a potential enrollment of 75 students. Each school is staffed with three certified teachers, four paraprofessionals, a counselor, a home–school coordinator, and a clerk. Over-all supervision consists of a director, a clinical psychologist, and a supervisor of counselors and social workers. Initial enrollment consisted of approximately 20 per location, and additional students are enrolled as they are identified by their behavior and as the staff is able to absorb more of these "high-risk" individuals into the culture of the school.

Another Louisville, Kentucky, project, also cosponsored by the Office of Delinquency Prevention and the public school system, is a pilot project for 120 students in the inner-city high school with the highest dropout rate (annually almost 30 percent). The purpose is to determine if many of these dropouts can be held in school by designing individualized programs geared to the individual achievement level. The project is based on the hypothesis that many of these students drop out because they have been advanced in classes to levels where they cannot hope to succeed, and that many are compelled to take jobs where the hours are not compatible with school hours. It is further based on the philosophy that it is better to give a student credit for a year's advancement from where he is than to say "do this prescribed grade level work or get out."

In a portable classroom adjacent to the high school, a learning lab has been equipped with programed learning materials. Two shifts are operated, one during regular school hours and the other from 3 PM to 10 PM. Each shift has a certified teacher who works out contracts with students and evaluates their achievement, and a paraprofessional who assists with the programed materials. Credit is given for meeting the contract, and the number of days in attendance or hours worked per day are not mandatory. Students are enrolled in the program at the time they have their dropout interview with the assistant principal. In some cases where the student is having trouble in only one or two academic areas, he is permitted to remain in regular school and may take the troublesome subjects in the contract school.

The cost of these two schools runs higher than the cost of keeping a student in a regular high school. But these students are not for the regular high schools; the only "schools" they could go to are state institutions for incorrigibles. The dollar cost is higher in state institutions because most of them are residential. Hence the "savings" in these two programs far outdo the dollar savings. If these young adults can be salvaged and can live in society and earn their keep, the cost is minimal. However, it is hard to get taxpayers to think this way. Payment for prevention programs when there are so many others to pay for is hard to accept, despite the fact that the dropout without a skill and without a job very soon becomes a costly problem for the community.

Another approach to alternative schools for the dropouts or the potential dropouts are area schools. They offer "special" education, usually in vocational and technical areas and serve many schools and communities in the area. Their objective is manpower training; they use personnel from industry as teachers, and present a real alternative to general education in the high schools.

A prime purpose of initiating a vocational area school or

for affiliating with an established one is to meet the needs of noncollege-bound students and, at the same time, to help satisfy the manpower needs of local business and industry. Youths entering the labor market without an academic degree seem to fare better if they have had vocational training. Business and industry readily affirm the value of vocational education.

An example of a vocational area school is the Metropolitan Youth Center in Denver, Colorado. It is a joint effort of the Jefferson County Public Schools and the Denver Public Schools. The school, which opened in 1964, is actually four schools in one—three centers in Denver and one in Jefferson County. The school is designed principally for potential dropouts who, in a way, have been talked into getting a high school diploma. Guidance counselors, teachers, and parents sometimes are able to convince the "about to be" dropout to try one more form of education before making that almost irrevocable decision.

The Metropolitan Youth Center is an alternative to the conventional high school. The school offers a wide range of vocational courses on a completely individualized, tutorial basis. Students enter at any time of the year and graduate at any time. The school is open 12 months of the year, 5 days a week, from 1 to 7 PM. Night classes are held on Tuesdays and Thursdays from 6 to 10 PM.

The three centers in Denver and the one in Jefferson County serve up to 2,000 students a year. The cost per student is about the same as for the regular high school student, although the services are far more intensive. This is accomplished because of the cooperation of local business and industry. They lend personnel and equipment to the Metropolitan Youth Center because the students enrolled there may very well become their employees. A well-trained employee, they feel, is well worth this contribution.

Another such single-focus school is Project "12" in Tulsa, Oklahoma, a unique alternative area high school for dropout students. The project began in August 1970 under funding by the Youth Opportunity Service of the Office of Economic Opportunity. Students come from all areas of the county, and ordinarily are enrolled in the project simply on the basis of available space. Preference is sometimes given to individuals who can demonstrate an unusual immediate need to be in school. These include students who are referred to the project by a community agency or court official.

"Diverse" describes the student body, whose only common denominator is the failure to "make it" in the traditional high school setting. During its initial year, the project has worked with approximately 170 students, some 125 of whom graduated or planned to satisfy graduation requirements by the end of the year.

Curriculum is similar to that offered in traditional high schools. It does, however, have some distinctions. The most significant of these is its heavy emphasis on "practical" needs such as family planning, career exploration, income management, and the improvement of self-image.

Instruction is more innovative and individualized than usual. Community consultants and "field" learning situations are included to insure an over-all flexible approach toward teaching and learning. Project "12"'s per student cost, substantially lower than the district's, is estimated at $450 per student.

The structure within Project "12" is totally nongraded, with students, ages 14–26, working together in small groups or individually with contractual assignments. Approximately 200 dropouts are anticipated as students of Project "12" each year.

Area schools generally are more economical because they concentrate on a particular cluster of skills and provide a grouping of people and equipment to transmit the skill to the student. It is far less expensive to have everything in one installation than to have each school duplicate costly machinery and equipment. Another cost-saving feature of area schools derives from the fact that, because they emphasize learning by doing—handling, examining, constructing—open, flexible, loft-type areas, with few permanent partitions, are more desirable than numerous "fixed" spaces. Thus, the relative simplicity of area center design means that the time needed for both design and construction will be significantly less than the time needed for a typical school. And time means money, especially in view of the high and rapid inflation in current construction costs.

But more important than the dollar cost factor is the "cosmetic" factor. Students want alternatives, other ways of doing things. They prefer other environments and other teachers, with backgrounds that are different from those in the schools. Area schools not only provide the kind of education that is difficult to offer in an ordinary high school, but they provide an excitement for learning that youngsters often miss in the run-of-the-mill school.

Most of the schools described so far are under the aegis of the public school systems and, in that way, have an "uncertain" security. If they are not too much of a threat to the establishment, if they remove the dissidents from the classroom, and if they have community support, they stand a good chance of being retained in the budget. However, there are those schools that do not want to be accountable to the standards of the establishment, that want complete control over their ideology and the manner in which it is translated into education. They are known as "free schools"—beholden to no one but their group of directors. This movement of independent schools differs from the traditional concept of independent or private schools inasmuch as it usually consists of small, intimate environments generally overseen by the parents or other members of the community. The curriculum, who does the teaching, the ideology, are all under the control of the parents and the community. Most of all, though, they seek to challenge the establishment, its values, its people, its goals. This is where it differs radically from the conventional private school which, in most instances, prepares its students to fit into the established society.

Free schools are cropping up all over the country. A group of angry, dedicated, or enthusiastic parents decides to open its own school. They find space, usually inexpensive, such as a parent's apartment or an abandoned store, and then proceed to solicit students and teachers. Usually, both are fairly easy to get. Parents of children who do poorly in school are anxious for an alternative if the regular school does not provide one. Many teachers are tired of the regimentation and inflexibility of many of the public schools. They, too, are searching for an alternative. The "free school" may offer just this to parents, students, teachers alike. However, with their independence come problems much the same as with large city experiments such as the Philadelphia Parkway School and Chicago's Metro. Public contributions start to diminish, the landlord after a year or so wants to rent his store, the apartment owner wants the use of his apartment throughout the day, teachers begin to look for more permanent work where there is some upward mobility and security. All in all, the lack of money makes "free schools" precarious and usually temporary enterprises.

In addition to budgetary stresses, free schools lack a community of colleagues from whom to learn and from whom to gather some educational standing. Because of the many such problems inherent in "free school" movements, a group got together in 1969 in Milwaukee to form the Federation of Independent Community Schools. It is one of the many such confederations that are forming throughout the country.

These independent or free schools in Milwaukee are not supported by the tax structure. Their funds come from tuition, some small foundation support, city agencies that cooperate with the educational system, and volunteer services of parents and students. Most of the parents are black, Spanish, and poor, and disenchanted with what public education has done for their children. They get "strength" from each other through the Federation and help each other out financially when necessary.

The Federation was designed, with technical assistance from Marquette University and the University of Wisconsin in Milwaukee, to insure two conditions that were very important to the founding parents: that each community school remain completely independent in all areas of the decision-making process so that each school would respond in its own way to the cultural and educational needs of the community in which it functions, and that all independent schools in Milwaukee (meeting the designated screening criteria) would work together to discuss mutual problems and coordinate common services and resources. The Federation is currently composed of 7 independent community schools serving approximately 2,000 children. Each school is dissociated from the public school in its neighborhood and from the other members of the Federation.

One can see immediately that this process can be a salvation to independent schools. Not only do they have a community of schools from which to learn and at times even to borrow, but they can start sharing services and resources. Just as with public education, this can be an enormous savings in money and talent.

As the independent community schools in Milwaukee continue to restructure their learning environments, they progressively demonstrate that certain aspects of the restructuring process are common to the seven schools, although they may be uniquely expressed in each individual school–community program. For example, the schools have identified four major components of change in the development of their alternative approach to urban education: conception of community, approach to decision-making responsibility, approaches to staffing, and approaches to curriculum development.

The interpretation of "community" has been expanded to encompass broader areas of involvement and responsibility. Each independent community school is a community involving cooperative efforts and responsibilities mutually assumed by youth, adults, and school staff. The conception conforms with the special relationship urged by Professor Preston Wilcox, an early exponent of community control. There should be "a community building which is used as a school—not a 'school' which is also used by the community. The school must become a focal point for community planning; not just an educational center in the narrow sense." Implementing this conception means bringing resources into a central coordinating focus instead of reaching out to fragmented programs that have not been specifically designed to meet the needs of a particular school and community. In each of the independent community schools, programs are being developed to insure the most effective utilization of resources from the total community of metropolitan Milwaukee—and from national sources as well. The responsibility for identifying needs and pulling in needed resources rests with each community.

The structure of the individual school reflects a redistribution of decision-making responsibilities and controls, with specific powers assigned to a Community School Board. The composition of each board varies, but each school is an autonomous corporation controlled by the people of the neighborhood through annual open elections. The precise number of elected representatives on the Board of Directors varies from school to school but all have a majority of people elected *from* and *by* the community. School staff administrators and/or teachers are also represented.

A major change planned in the functioning of each school is the involvement of community residents in all classroom instructional experiences as well as in community activities. This provides a completely new approach to staffing. Each school has a group of parent volunteers and at least two "Community Trainees." The "Community Trainees" are an initial step in a New Careers Training Program designed to help a larger group of parents from each school develop the know-how and skills for making effective use of the decision-making responsibilities and powers they have assumed. The Career Ladder for the New Career Training Program was planned to prepare "Community Teachers" and "Community Resource Specialists" in a university-accredited, but parent-planned, series of workshops and on-the-job training experiences. The training program is open to all interested residents from each school. In addition to upgrading their own skills in preparing for new careers in community schools, the trainees expect to serve as action agents in mobilizing other residents and bringing them into closer working relationships with their respective schools.

Another approach in staffing is the direct participation of students in working with other students as tutors, guides, and instructors for small groups, and as teachers' aides.

Those who support the "free school" movement feel that whatever educational reform may mean to the various individuals and groups in our society, decisions about educational programs must include those who are most directly involved or no major changes will occur. Needed changes can take place—but only when residents exercise greater influence and assume complete responsibility for their institutions.

The cooperative efforts exhibited by parents whose children attend the seven community schools demonstrate that the urban poor are deeply interested in the future of their children and care enough to go to the extremes of taking over a failing school system and restructuring it to provide long-term high quality educational experiences for their communities.

Boniface Community School, housed in a relatively modern building, is in a community that has had a long history of leadership, involvement, and notoriety in the Civil Rights movement of the 60's. Perhaps the excitement of that period is being expressed in the present decision of the parents and faculty to move toward the "freeing up" of the over-all school program. The school is being reorganized into multi-age units, from the primary grades through the middle grades. Special programs for the junior high age group range from opportunities to tutor each other and younger students, to practice in test-taking skills. Middle and upper grades have a wide range of free-choice activities in the afternoons. Strong emphasis is being placed on black history, self-expression, and creativity in art, dance, music, and communication skills. Renewed emphasis is being placed on individualizing all instruction. Boniface Community School has a total enrollment of 215 students, 98 percent black and 2 percent white.

There are 86 families in Boniface Community School. The parent body elects the community board, which is the key decision-making body for the school. Approximately one-quarter of the parents attend meetings. The parents meet with the staff once a month and there are four officers who represent and meet with them in these meetings. The school board, elected by the parent body, is made up of 15 members including community, staff, and parents. The board makes decisions on the hiring and firing of personnel, plans curriculum, and assists in financing. The staff includes 17 full-time teachers and 10 part-time, in addition to 7 paid aides.

Francis Community School, another "free school" that is part of the Federation, is located in a rapidly deteriorating area of the inner city, and has had a long history of responding to the changing needs of shifting populations and fluctuating economic and physical conditions of the community. The student population of Francis Community School represents a unique challenge to the parents and the faculty. Forty-six percent of the students have been transferred from the Milwaukee Public Schools. A cooperative program has been developed with the State Mental Health Committee in recognition of the school's success in working with public school "disrupters."

Francis operates with approximately 165 students; 95 percent black and 5 percent white. The curriculum is geared to meet the needs of all students. The lower primary grades are multi-age, with intensive individualized programs for all levels in math, social studies, language arts, gym, music, and dancing.

Since they were aware that there were many inner city youth who were roaming the streets as a result of suspension or exclusion from public and private schools, the staff of Francis Community School developed an Educational Rehabilitation

Program. One of the basic assumptions of the program is that the student with educational problems is in a state of constant personal conflict and stress when placed in a regular structured classroom. The staff uses a variety of activities that encourage the student's interaction with his peers so that he will feel his own importance as a person. Much counseling, of course, is on a one-to-one basis.

Parent participation in Francis Community School has always been an important element. Aside from participating in the Adult Education Program which the school offers, the parent body, which steers the community board, is the decision-making body for the school. The school board is made up of ten members elected in open election and representing the parent body, school staff, and community. The board is responsible for the hiring and firing of personnel, the planning of the curriculum, and assisting in the financial activities of the school.

In addition to 16 staff members, Francis receives the services of a nurse, doctor, psychologist, and guidance counselor once a week, and a reading specialist 5 days every 2 weeks under the auspices of the Title I program. Francis Community School has also had a parent-elected director since the 1969–70 school year.

At Harambee, another school in the Federation, students, parents, and teachers "pull together" towards establishing a community education center for the young people. The school mixes 200 students (90 lower-level students, grades 1–4; 76 upper level students, grades 6–8; 34 day care and kindergarten) in an ungraded, multi-age system which emphasizes individualized instruction. To meet this learning goal, the staff is extensive: 17 master teachers, 7 coteachers, a student counselor as well as a school psychologist, one speech therapist, and 30 university volunteers. School enrollment is 82 percent black, 11 percent white, 6 percent Puerto Rican, and one percent other.

The United Nations flag and the "growing" design painted in bright colors on the doors of the school express the activism of Harambee. The guiding concept of the school is "Harambee," Swahili for "let's pull together." A Parent Board, Student Council, monthly community newspaper, the Harambee *Shopper*, and twice-weekly "Community awareness mods" are expressions of the school's spirit.

School means more than books. "Community Awareness mods" for the upper-level students meet two nights a week at the school. The "mods" center on talks by a student or teacher. The purpose of the mods is to foster a "unity level—anything so that students and teachers have a level relationship," one Student Council member explained. This concept of "unity level" is integral to the workings of the student group. The Council may give reports at the mods, but the Student Council doesn't want to make *decisions* for the student body, only suggestions," the Council member emphasized.

At Harambee, children move ahead according to ability and individual development rather than rigidly according to age. They may begin at the age of three and make a continuous progression through the departmentalized multi-age, nongraded program.

Harambee parents are involved in every aspect of the community effort, from responsibility for the cleanliness and maintenance of the buildings, to assisting in the classrooms, to fund raising, to cooking, to positions of policy-making on the Board of Directors.

Michael Community School, located in an area of active urban renewal, is the largest of the community schools with a population of 335 students. The school population reflects diverse ethnic backgrounds: 5 percent American Indian, 10 percent Spanish-speaking, 42 percent white, 43 percent black.

For instructional purposes, the student body is divided into Primary, Intermediate, and Upper—multi-age groupings. In an effort to better meet the needs of the individual students, a Reading Center and a Math Center have been established for individual and small group work. In addition, each student has a daily elective period during which he may select a class from such diverse interest areas as health, knitting, dance, guitar, wrestling, and cooking. These elective courses can vary according to the needs and interests of the students and the availability of instructors drawn from the teaching staff, community members, and other interested persons.

Extracurricular activities such as dancing, sports, and photography are offered for the older students, with the school building being open 2 nights a week for their use. In addition, the Student Council, composed of duly elected student members, provides opportunities for the students to take an active role in deciding what should be provided for the total school population.

Being a "community" school, Michael's also offers activities for other residents of the community. The Spanish Center offers adult education programs in high school equivalency and English for the Spanish-speaking. Driver Education is also available.

In an effort to assist in the development of concerned future teachers, Michael's provides classroom space for two university education classes. The students in these classes are given opportunities to do service work throughout the school. These student volunteers work with small groups or individual students in many areas as needed by the school.

The School Board, composed of nine members, has six members elected from among the parents and three members elected from the community-at-large.

Bruce-Guadalupe Community School, located on the south side of the inner city, has a majority of Spanish-speaking families. The steady development of this constituency is evidenced in Federation meetings, in school planning and in their recent decision to hire a parent-selected administrator.

Bruce-Guadalupe Community School has instituted a unique system of instant translation to enable Spanish-speaking and English-speaking parents to "converse" together at parent meetings. Priority is being placed on achievement of fluency in both Spanish and English for youth and adults of the community. Preliminary plans are being developed for a Latin American (Bilingual) Cultural Resource Center for developing and utilizing instructional materials that accurately reflect community pride in their heritage. The Center could also serve as a cultural exchange resource for the mutual benefit of the Spanish-speaking community and the Black community (on the north side of the inner city). The residents of the neighborhood, through open school board elections, play a dominant role in deciding school policy.

Bruce-Guadalupe Community School has continued to meet the needs of the diverse ethnic groups that come to it. Of the total enrollment of 140, 44 percent is Mexican American, 24 percent Puerto Rican, 22 percent white, and 10 percent Indian. The school has been particularly successful in designing an individualized curriculum which meets the needs of the large number of Spanish-speaking students. The first three grades are entirely bilingual and the upper levels are divided in multilevel, multi-aged groupings. Special attention is given to improving basic educational skills such as mathematics and reading with additional classes in Spanish and English as a second language. Extracurricular activities include a newly organized basketball team.

Working in close cooperation with Bruce-Guadalupe Community School, the Spanish Center has been able to provide Adult Education classes for members of the community. The Spanish Center also rents several classrooms from the school for other activities.

None of these schools sounds as if it will revolutionalize education. They all challenge the usual way of doing things but the dent they make is not drastic. Indeed, all they really want is to be left alone "to do their particular thing." They can tolerate staff changes and even at times a high mobility among students, but their most serious problem is the hand-to-mouth financial situation.

It is no longer uncommon for public school administrators, board members, and teachers to spend time in free schools trying to pick up ideas that can be incorporated into their programs. Free schools, just like "new structures" schools, are serving as a laboratory for trying out new ways of doing things. Why may we not accept them for just that—pilot operations, and allow them at least minimal public funds with which to subsist? Of course, they would be the first to turn down such funds if there were "allegiance" strings attached. On the other hand, should not public education be secure enough to dispense with that condition? These schools may be few in number, but the free school movement is with us and public education might do well to accept it.

Bibliography

(Limited to books, monographs, and periodicals published from 1970 to the present)

CHAPTER I

Books and Monographs

Accountability and Performance Contracting, ERIC Clearinghouse on Educational Management, University of Oregon, Eugene.

Bruner, Jerome S.: *The Relevance of Education,* Norton, 1971.

Coons, John E., William H. Clune III, Stephen D. Sugarman: *Private Wealth and Public Education,* Harvard University Press, Cambridge, 1970.

Education Vouchers: A Preliminary Report on Financing Education by Payment to Parents, Center for the Study of Public Policy, Cambridge, March 1970.

Future Directions for School Financing, N. E. A. Finance Project, Gainesville, Florida, 1971.

Goodlad, John I., M. Frances Klein and Associates: *Behind the Classroom Door,* Charles A. Jones Publishing Co., Worthington, Ohio, 1970.

Guide to Alternatives for Financing School Buildings, Educational Facilities Laboratory, Inc., New York, 1972.

Guthrie, James W., George B. Kleindorfer, Henry M. Levin, and Robert T. Stout: *Schools and Inequality,* The MIT Press, Cambridge, 1971.

Herndon, James: *How to Survive in Your Native Land,* Simon & Schuster, 1971.

Hill, Thomas W., Cornelius P. Quinn, and Bruce D. Wood: *Collective Bargaining Guide for School Administrators*, The Darnell Corporation, Chicago, 1971.

Illich, Ivan: *De-Schooling Society*, Harper & Row, 1971.

Johns, Roe L., Irving J. Goffman, Dern Alexander, and Dewey H. Stollar, eds., *Economic Factors Affecting the Financing of Education*, National Educational Finance Project, Volume 3, Gainesville, Florida, 1970.

Katz, Michael B., ed.: *School Reform: Past and Present*, Little, Brown and Co., Boston, 1971.

Lessinger, Leon M.: *Every Child a Winner: Accountability in Education*, Science Research Associates College Division, Palo Alto, Calif., 1971.

Listokin, David: *Funding Education: Problems, Patterns, Solutions*, Rutgers University, New Brunswick, N.J., 1972.

Repo, Satu: *This Book Is About Schools*, Pantheon Books, New York, 1971.

Skinner, B. F.: *Beyond Freedom and Dignity*, Alfred A. Knopf, New York, 1971.

The Schools and the Environment, IDEA, Dayton, Ohio, 1972,–1973.

Toffler, Alvin: *Future Shock*, Random House, New York, 1970.

Periodicals

Berke, Joel S.: "The Current Crisis in School Finance," *Phi Delta Kappan*, September 1971, p. 2.

Blascke, Charles: "Performance Contracting," *Nation's Schools*, March 1972, pp. 37–41.

Carr, Ray A., and Gerald C. Hayward: "Education by Chit: An Examination of Voucher Proposals," *Education and Urban Society* 2, February 1970, pp. 179–191.

Carter, John W., Jr., Stephen L. Phillips, Edward Clarke: "The State Role in Financing Public Education," *Planning and Changing: A Journal for School Administrators*, January 1972, p. 188.

"Eleventh Annual Cost of Building Index," *School Management*, September 1972, p. 19.

Furno, Orlando, and Paul Cuneo: "Cost of Building Index 1970–1971," *School Management*, January 1971, p. 10.

Heller, Robert W.: "Educational Vouchers: Problems—Issues," *Educational Leadership*, February 1972, p. 424.

Hentoff, Margot and Nat: "The Schools We Want: A Family Dialogue," *Saturday Review*, September 19, 1970.

Hoyle, John R., and Eldon L. Wiley: "What Are the People Telling Us?" *Phi Delta Kappan*, September 1971, p. 49.

Illich, Ivan: "Why We Must Abolish Schooling," *New York Review of Books*, July 2, 1970, p. 9.

Johns, R. L.: "The Coming Revolution in School Finance," *Phi Delta Kappan*, September 1972, p. 18.

Lessinger, Leon M.: "Accountability in Public Education," *Today's Education*, May 1970, pp. 52–53.

Lutz, Frank W.: "A Case for the Blackboard Economy," *Phi Delta Kappan*, January 1971, p. 290.

Olson, Martin N.: "APPS—A National Network for Better Schools," *Phi Delta Kappan*, October 1971, pp. 89–93.

Peck, John E.: "Future Developments in School Finance," *School Management*, August 1972, p. 11.

Riles, Wilson: "California and the Serrano Decision," *Planning and Changing*, January 1972, p. 169.

"School Law 71—What Happened and Why," *Nation's Schools*, March 1972, p. 11.

Schrag, Francis: "The Right to Educate," *School Review*, Vol. 79, No. 3, May 1971, p. 359.

Seltzer, R. W.: "Public Education: Is Its Demise Near?" *Clearing House*, September 1971, p. 6.

Stake, Robert E.: "Testing Hazards in Performance Contracting," *Phi Delta Kappan*, January 1971, p. 83.

Stein, Annie: "Strategies for Failure," *Harvard Educational Review*, May 1971, p. 186.

"The Fourth Annual Gallup Poll of Public Attitudes toward Education," *Phi Delta Kappan*, September 1972, p. 33.

"The Magnitude of the American Establishment, 1971–72," *Saturday Review*, December 18, 1971, p. 68.

Webb, Harold V.: "A Realignment of Educational Finances," *Education Digest*, March 1972, p. 1.

CHAPTER II

Books and Monographs

Alexander, William M., J. Galen Saylor, and Emmett L. Williams: *The High School: Today and Tomorrow*, Holt, Rinehart and Winston, New York, 1971.

Alioto, Robert F., and J. A. Jungherr: *Operational PPBS for Education: A Practical Approach to Effective Decision-Making,* Harper and Row, New York, 1970.

Andrew, Gary, and Ronald Moir: *Information-Decision Systems in Education* F. E. Peacock Pub., Itasca, Illinois, 1970.

Bishop, Lloyd K.: *Individualizing Educational Systems: The Elementary and Secondary School,* Harper & Row, New York, 1971.

Bolton, Dale L., ed.: *The Use of Simulation in Educational Administration,* Charles E. Merrill, Columbus, Ohio, 1971.

Bremer, John, and Michael von Moschzisker: *The School without Walls: Philadelphia's Parkway Program,* Holt, Rinehart, and Winston, New York, 1971.

Brickman, William W., ed.: *Automation, Education, and Human Values,* Peter Smith, Magnolia, Massachusetts, 1971.

Centralized Purchasing and Warehousing Feasibility Study, Rockland County School Districts, Peat, Marwick, Mitchell, and Co., New York, 1969.

Clinchy, Evans: *Joint Occupancy: Profile of Significant Schools,* Educational Facilities Laboratory, New York, June 1970.

Cook, Desmond L.: *Educational Project Management,* Charles E. Merrill, Columbus, Ohio, 1971.

Education Explorer—A New Look to New Learning Spaces (Monograph), 3104 16th Avenue South, Minneapolis, Minnesota.

Eisele, James E.: *Computer-Assisted Planning of Curriculum and Instruction: How to Use Computer-Based Resource Units to Individualize Instruction,* Educational Technology Publications, Englewood Cliffs, N.J., 1971.

Ely, Donald P., ed.: *Audiovisual Resources for Teaching Instructional Technology: An Annotated List of Materials,* Syracuse University, Center for Instructional Communications, 1971.

Fuller, R. B.: *Operating Manual for Spaceship Earth,* Simon & Schuster, New York, 1970.

Gartner, Alan, Mary Kohler, and Frank Riessman: *Children Teach Children,* Harper & Row, 1971.

Gordon, George N.: *Classroom Television: New Frontiers in ITV,* Hastings, New York, 1970.

Gordon, Roger L., ed.: *An Evaluative Look at the Standards for School Media Programs,* Report of the 1970 Northeast Regional Audio-Visual Leadership Conference, Hershey, Pennsylvania, January 1970; Philadelphia, Temple University, 1970.

Griffin, C. W., Jr.: *Systems—An Approach to School Construction,* Educational Facilities Laboratory, February 1971.

Guide to Significant Schools in the New York City Area, School and Architecture Committee, New York Chapter, The American Institute of Architects, New York, 1971.

Hansen, John, and Arthur Hearn: *The Middle School Program,* Rand McNally, Chicago, 1971.

Heath, Douglas H.: *Humanizing Schools: New Directions, New Decisions,* Hayden Book Company, New York, 1971.

High-Rise and Mixed-Use Study, The Metropolitan Toronto School Board Study of Educational Facilities, Toronto, Canada, April 1970, Draft.

Johnson, M. Clemens: *Educational Uses of the Computer: An Introduction,* Rand McNally, Chicago, 1971.

Kohn, Sherwood: *Profiles of Significant Schools: Three High Schools Revisited—Andrews, McPherson, and Nova,* Educational Facilities Laboratory, 1970.

Margolin, Joseph B., and Marion R. Misch, eds.: *Computers in the Classroom,* Spartan Books, 1970.

Meier, James: *Leasing of School Property,* Unpublished paper for Professor Reutter, Teachers College, New York, January 1970.

Meredith, J. C.: *An Introduction and Guide to the Preparation of Computer-Assisted Instruction Materials,* Educational Technology Publications, Englewood Cliffs, N.J.

Miller, Richard I.: *Selecting New Aids to Teaching,* Association for Supervision and Curriculum Development, Washington, D.C.

Mini-Pac: Differentiated Staffing, The Educational and Cultural Center, Syracuse, 1971.

Myers, Donald A.: *Decision Making in Curriculum and Instruction,* IDEA, Dayton, Ohio, 1970–1971.

Novotney, Jerrold M.: *The Principal and the Challenge of Change,* IDEA, Dayton, Ohio, 1970–1971.

Open-Space Schools, American Association of School Administrators, Washington, D.C.

Report of the Massachusetts Business Task Force for School Management, The Massachusetts Advisory Council on Education, September 1970.

School: More Space/Less Money, Educational Facilities Laboratory, November 1971.

Seiler, K., III: *Introduction to Systems Cost-Effectiveness*, John Wiley & Sons, New York, 1969.

Silberman, Charles E.: *Crisis in the Classroom*, Random House, New York, 1970.

Technology and the Management of Instruction, Association for Educational Communications and Technology, Monograph 4, Washington, D.C., 1970.

Television in Instruction: What Is Possible, National Association of Educational Broadcasters, Washington, D.C., 1970.

The Computer in Education, IDEA, Dayton, Ohio, 1972–1973.

The Flexibly Scheduled School of 1980, IDEA, Dayton, Ohio, 1970–1971.

The Open-Plan School. IDEA, Dayton, Ohio, 1970–1971.

The Year-Round School, Linnet Books, Hamden, Connecticut.

Thomas, J. Alan: *The Productive School, A System Analysis Approach to Educational Administration*, John Wiley & Sons, New York, 1971.

Umans, Shelley: *The Management of Education*, Doubleday & Co., New York, 1970.

Wedemeyer, Charles A. (Chairman): *The Open School—Supplement to Final Report of the Governor's Commission on Education*, State of Wisconsin, January 1971.

Periodicals

Anderson, Robert: "Four Quarters Make a School Year," *School Management*, June 1972, p. 7.

"An Open Plan Encourages an Open Program," Open Plan 2, *School Management*, August 1971, p. 29.

"A Systems Approach to the Educational Facility," *Training in Business and Industry*, September 1971, p. 38.

Bakers and Peters: "School Maintenance and Operations" *The Interstate*, Danville, Illinois.

Barnard, Charles E.: "Counseling By Computer," *Think*, 1971.

Bogul, E. G.: "Disposable Organizations," *Phi Delta Kappan*, October 1971, pp. 94–96.

Boutwell, Clinton: "Differentiated Staffing as a Component of a Systematic Change Process," *Educational Technology*, August 1972, p. 20.

Caivelti, Gordon, and Bruce Howell: "Help for the Man in the Middle," *School Management*, March 1971, pp. 22–23.

Caldwell, Bruce A.: "Differentiated Staffing: Who Is Labor and Who Is Management?" *Educational Technology*, Volume X, No. 12, December 1970, pp. 59–60.

Canfield, John Taylor: "Dear Machine: Don't Call Us, We'll Call You," *Educational Technology*, June 1971, p. 23.

Cohodes, Aaron: "Systems-Built Schools Grow in England and the U.S.," *Nation's Schools*, September 1971, p. 14.

Coleman, James E.: "Toward Open Schools," *The Public Interest*, Fall 1967.

English, Fenwick: "The Differentiated Staff," *Educational Technology*, February 1970, p. 24.

Ernst, Leonard: "The Year-Round School," *Nation's Schools*, November 1971, p. 51.

Eurich, Alvin, Harold B. Gores, and Ole Sand: "High School 1980," *The Bulletin—NASSP*, May 1971, p. 42.

Flanagan, John C.: "The Plan System as an Application of Educational Technology," *Educational Technology*, September 1972.

Fletcher, J. D., and P. Suppes: "CAI in RDG Grades 4–6," *Educational Technology*, August 1972, p. 45.

Gunn, Hartford W., Jr.: "New Techniques for Public Communication," *Technology Review*, July–August 1971, pp. 24–29.

Jerman, M., J. P. Martin, and A. Sobers: "A CAI Program for the Home," *Educational Technology*, Volume XI, No. 12, December 1971, p. 49.

Keefe, I. W.: "Differentiated Staffing," *The Bulletin—NAASP*, May 1971, p. 112.

"Make-Do Site Makes an Unusual School," *School Management*, July 1971, p. 15.

Mead, Margaret: "Are Any School Administrators Listening?" *Nation's Schools*, June 1971, p. 41.

Mukler, Walter A., Jr.: "New Roles Can Facilitate Change," *Educational Leadership*, March 1972, p. 515.

"No Doubt about What They Had in Mind," Open Plan 3, *School Management*, August 1971, p. 32.

Pasnick, Marion: "Factory Building to Modern School in Six Months," *School Management*, July 1971, p. 12.

Prasch, John: "New Roles for Educators," *Educational Leadership*, March 1972, p. 499.

"Prospecting for Space," *Nation's Schools*, April 1971, p. 17.

"Report on Facilities in New Schools and Additions," *School Management*, September 1972, p. 56.

Rooney, E., L. Gill, and F. J. Gill: "An Educational Telephone Network," *Educational Technology*, December 1971, p. 37.

Shaw, Duane C.: "Use of the Computer in Educational Management," *Educational Technology*, Volume 12, No. 2, February 1972, p. 39.

"The District Budget on a Computer," *School Management*, December 1971, p. 16.

Tonigan, Richard: "Who Should Plan Your Major Maintenance Projects?" *School Management*, September 1971, p. 41.

"When the Walls Come Tumbling Down," Open Plan 1, *School Management*, August 1971, p. 28.

"Year-Round School: Coming, Coming, Here!" *School Management*, August 1971, p. 36

CHAPTER III

Books and Monographs

Affleck, Tim, and Allen Graubard: *Free The Children . . . The New Schools Movement in America*, Pantheon, 1972.

Berg, Ivar, and Sherry Gorelick: *Education and Jobs: The Great Training Robbery*, Praeger Publishing Co., New York, 1970.

Bhaerman, Steve, and Joel Denker: *No Particular Place to Go: The Making of a Free School*, Simon & Schuster, New York, 1972.

Brown, Larry, and the Task Force on Children Out of School: *The Way We Go to School*, Beacon Press, Boston, 1971.

Clark, Kenneth: *Alternative Public School Systems*, Equal Educational Opportunities, Harvard University Press, Cambridge, 1969.

Glasser, William: *Schools without Failure*, Harper & Row, New York, 1969.

Gross, Ronald, and Beatrice Gross, eds.: *Radical School Reform*, Simon & Schuster, New York, 1969.

Gross, Ronald, and Paul Osterman, eds.: *High School*, Simon & Schuster, New York, 1971.

Hack, Walter G., et al.: *Educational Futurism 1985*, McCutchan Publishing Corp., Berkeley, 1971.

Herndon, James: *How to Survive in Your Native Land*, Simon & Schuster, New York, 1971.

Holt, John: *What Do I Do Monday?* Dutton, New York, 1970.

Kohl, Herbert, R., and Victor Hernandez Cruz, eds.: *Stuff.* World, New York, 1970.

————: *The Open Classroom,* Vintage Books, New York, 1969.

Manning, Duane: *Toward a Humantistic Curriculum,* Harper & Row, New York, 1971.

Postman, Neil, and Charles Weingartner: *The Soft Revolution: A Student Handbook for Turning Schools Around,* Delacorte Press, 1971.

Purdom, Daniel M.: *Exploring the Nongraded School,* IDEA, Dayton, Ohio, 1970–1971.

Reimer, Everett: *School Is Dead: Alternatives in Education,* Doubleday, New York, 1971.

Rich, John Martin: *Humanistic Foundations of Education,* Jones Publishing Co., Worthington, Ohio, 1971.

Rogers, Vincent: *Teaching in the British Primary School,* Collier-Macmillan Canada Limited, Toronto, 1970.

Saylor, J. Galen, and Josua L. Smith, eds.: *Removing Barriers to Humaneness in the High School,* Association for Supervision and Curriculum Development.

Schoonmaker, Alan N.: *A Student's Survival Manual: Or How to Get an Education despite It All,* Harper & Row, 1971.

Student Activism and the Relevancy of Schooling, IDEA, Dayton, Ohio, 1970–1971.

Terry, Mark: *Teaching for Survival,* Ballantine Books, New York, 1971.

Torrance, E. Paul, and R. E. Meyers: *Creative Thinking and Learning,* Dodd, Mead & Company, New York, 1970.

Periodicals

Divoky, Diane: "Berkeley's Experimental Schools," *Saturday Review,* October 1972, p. 44.

Evans, Richard I.: "The Freedom School Movement: Freedom to Learn Badly?" *Educational Technology,* Volume XII, No. 1, January 1972, pp. 40–41.

Green, Maxine: "The Avant Garde in the Classroom," *Record,* September 1969, p. 120.

Gross, Ronald: "From Innovation to Alternative," *Phi Delta Kappan,* September 1971, p. 22.

Harris, Beecher H.: "Schools without Subjects," *Educational Leadership*, February 1972, p. 420.

"Help Me! My Students Are Dying," *Nation's Schools*, February 1972, p. 53.

Illich, Ivan: "Schooling: The Ritual of Progress," *The New York Review of Books*, December 3, 1970, pp. 20–26.

————: "The Alternative to Schooling," *Saturday Review*, June 19, 1971.

Kohl, Herbert: "Growing Pains—Mini Schools," *The Grade Teacher*, January 1971, p. 8.

Moxley, Roy A., Jr.: "Freedom in a Free School," *Educational Technology*, Volume XII, #1, January 1972, pp. 42–43.

Schrag, Peter: "End of the Impossible Dream," *Saturday Review*, September 19, 1970, p. 68.

The Bulletin of the National Association of Secondary School Principals, October 1970, Edition on "Small Schools, Also, Innovative."

Alternative Schools

In Operation as of This Printing

CALIFORNIA
Experimental Schools
Berkeley Unified School District
Office of Project Planning and Development
1414 Walnut Street
Berkeley, California

Apprenticeship Service Program
Pacific High School
Los Gatos, California

COLORADO
Cherry Creek Senior High School
Metropolitan Denver, Colorado

KENTUCKY
The Brown School
Louisville Public Schools

Central High Contract School (Pilot Project)
Louisville, Kentucky

Junior High Alternative Schools
Louisville, Kentucky

Teenage Parents' Program (TAP)
Louisville, Kentucky

Alternative Educational Programs
Paducah Public Schools
Paducah, Kentucky

MASSACHUSETTS
Cambridge Pilot High School
Cambridge, Massachusetts

The Highland Park Free School
42 Hawthorne Street
Roxbury, Massachusetts 02119

MICHIGAN
Ann Arbor Public Schools
Ann Arbor, Michigan

Center for Advanced Independent Studies
Grand Rapids, Michigan

Center for Alternative High School Studies
Grand Rapids, Michigan

Centers for Secondary School Studies
Grand Rapids, Michigan

Park School
Grand Rapids, Michigan

MINNESOTA
Marshall University High School
Minneapolis, Minnesota

Learning Centers Program
Park Square Court
400 Sibley Street
St. Paul, Minnesota 55101

St. Paul Public Schools
Independent School District No. 625

The Career Study Center
St. Paul, Minnesota

NEW YORK
Freedom School Program
Hempstead High School
Hempstead, New York

OKLAHOMA
Project "12"—School for Dropouts
Tulsa, Oklahoma 74120

SOUTH DAKOTA
Shannon County Dropout Prevention Program
Pine Ridge, South Dakota

Index

About the Author

Shelley Umans is the Director of the New York City Board of Education's Regional Center for Planning and Management. She has been a member of the staff of Teachers College, Columbia University, and a consultant to school systems throughout the country on innovative approaches to school management, educational technology, alternative forms of education, and the planning of new communities. She is the author of *New Trends in Reading Instruction, Designs for Reading Programs*, coauthor of *Teaching the Disadvantaged* and author of the *Management of Education*.